WHEN WILL AYUMU MAKE HIS MOVE?

2

SOICHIRO YAMAMOTO

EDITORIAL ASSISTANCE:
MADOKA KITAO / NEKOMADO

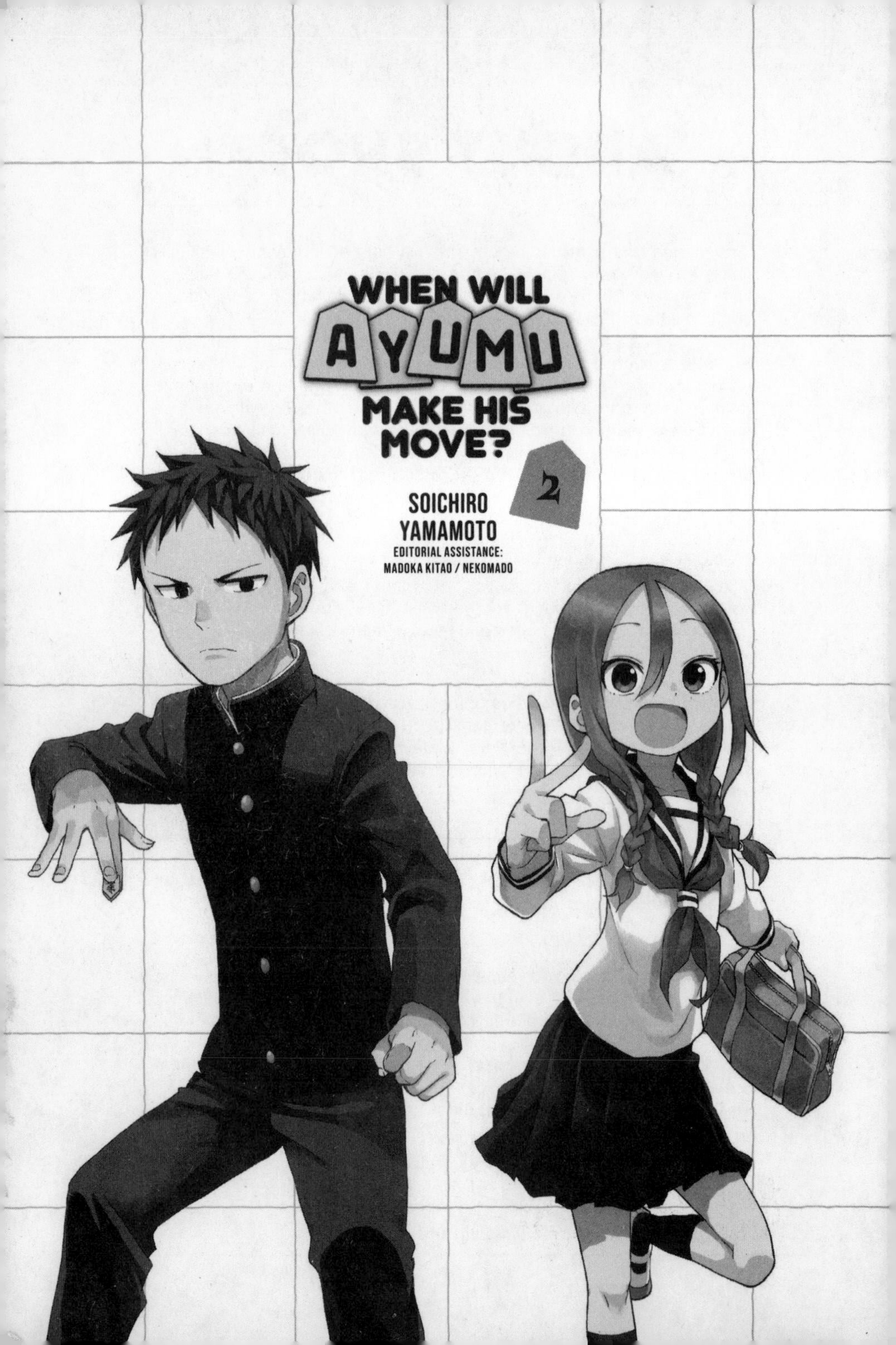

ABOUT SHOGI

This manga is a nearly-rom-com set in a high school shogi club. This game isn't well known outside Japan, but if you're familiar with chess, it's easy to grasp! Check out this explainer before reading, or jump right in and come back if you want to learn more!

Shogi is a two-player board game in the same family as chess. It's ancestor arrived in Japan over a thousand years ago and evolved into roughly its current form around the sixteenth century. Two players face off across a board with nine ranks (rows) and nine files (columns). Each player has a small army of pieces that start on their side of the board, and players can move one of these pieces per turn. The goal, like in chess, is to "checkmate" the other player's king piece by putting it into a situation where it cannot avoid being captured.

The two players are called *sente* and *gote* ("moves first" and "moves next"). These are sometimes called "black" and "white" in English; however, all pieces in shogi are the same color. They are differentiated by orientation, with the pointed end facing the opposing player.

PIECES AND MOVES
There are many different types of pieces, each with its own set of legal moves. Some of these will be familiar to chess players: For example, pawns move one square forward, while bishops move any number of squares diagonally. See the following pages for a detailed list of pieces and their moves.

When a piece legally moves into a square already occupied by an enemy piece, the enemy piece is "captured"—meaning that it is removed from the board and held "in hand" by the capturing player. (Pieces cannot move into squares occupied by friendly pieces.)

DROPPING
One big difference between shogi and chess is that, instead of moving a piece, players can use their turn to place a piece they have in hand back on the board under their control. This is called "dropping" a piece.

A piece can be dropped almost anywhere on the board, although there are some restrictions. A player can never have two unpromoted pawns on the same file, and a piece cannot be dropped onto a square from which it has no legal move.

PROMOTION

If a piece reaches the three ranks at the far end of the board (the "enemy camp"), it can be "promoted." The piece is flipped over to reveal its other side, and gains a new set of moves. For example, a promoted pawn becomes a *tokin*, which moves like a gold general. (Note that kings and gold generals cannot be promoted.)

Promotion is not compulsory unless the piece would have no legal move otherwise. If a piece is left unpromoted, it can be promoted at the end of any subsequent move that begins within the enemy camp.

CHECK AND CHECKMATE

Moving a piece into a position that would let the enemy king be captured on the next move is called an *ote* ("king move"). This corresponds to "check" in chess. The "checked" player must protect their king, either by moving it, capturing the checking piece, or placing (or dropping) another piece in between the two. If the checked player has no way to save the king, they lose the game. This corresponds to "checkmate" in chess. As in chess, it is also against the rules for a player to make a move that puts their own king in check.

CASTLES

A key concept in shogi strategy is the castle (in Japanese, *kakoi*, "enclosure"). A castle is a formation of pieces that protects your king. Over the centuries, shogi players have come up with many types of castles, and also ways to undermine and attack them.

Note that building a castle involves arranging pieces using standard legal moves. This makes it different from the special move of "castling" in chess, although the objective (protect the king) is similar.

SHOGI PIECES

 FUHYO

English name: Pawn (P)
Move: One square directly forward
Comments: Unlike in chess, pawns do not capture diagonally

 TOKIN

English name: Tokin (+P)
Move: Replaced by gold general rules
Comments: Most English-speaking players use the Japanese name for this piece instead of "promoted pawn"

 KYOSHA

English name: Lance (L)
Move: Any number of squares directly forward

 NARIKYO

English name: Promoted lance (+L)
Move: Replaced by gold general rules

 KEIMA

English name: Knight (N)
Move: L-shaped "jump" two squares forward and one square to left or right
Comments: Knights can "jump" over pieces that are in their way. Unlike in chess, they cannot jump in any direction.

 NARIKEI

English name: Promoted knight (+N)
Move: Replaced by gold general rules

 GINSHO

English name: Promoted knight (S)
Move: One square in any direction except left, right, or directly back

NARIGIN

English name: Promoted silver (+S)
Move: Replaced by gold general rules

 KINSHO

English name: Gold general (or just "Gold") (G)
Move: One square in any direction except diagonally backward (left or right)
Comments: Gold generals cannot be promoted.

 KAKUGYO

English name: Bishop (B)
Move: Any number of squares diagonally

 RYUMA

English name: Promoted bishop (or "Dragon horse") (+B)
Move: Any number of squares diagonally OR one square in any direction

 HISHA

English name: Rook (R)
Move: Any number of squares forward, back, left, or right

 RYUO

English name: Promoted rook (or "Dragon king") (+R)
Move: Any number of squares forward, back, left, or right, OR one square in any direction

 OSHO

English name: King (K)
Move: One square in any direction
Comments: Kings cannot be promoted. This tile is used by the higher-ranking player, while the lower-ranking player traditionally uses the *gyokusho* tile (below) for their king.

 GYOKUSHO

English name: King (or "Jewel") (K)
Move: One square in any direction
Comments: This tile is used as the king of the lower-ranking player, but the rules are the same as for the *osho* tile.

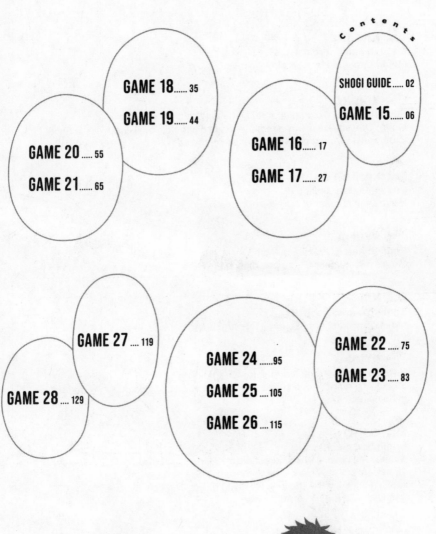

Contents

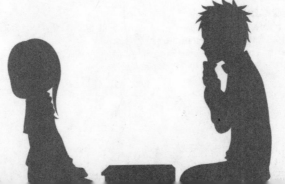

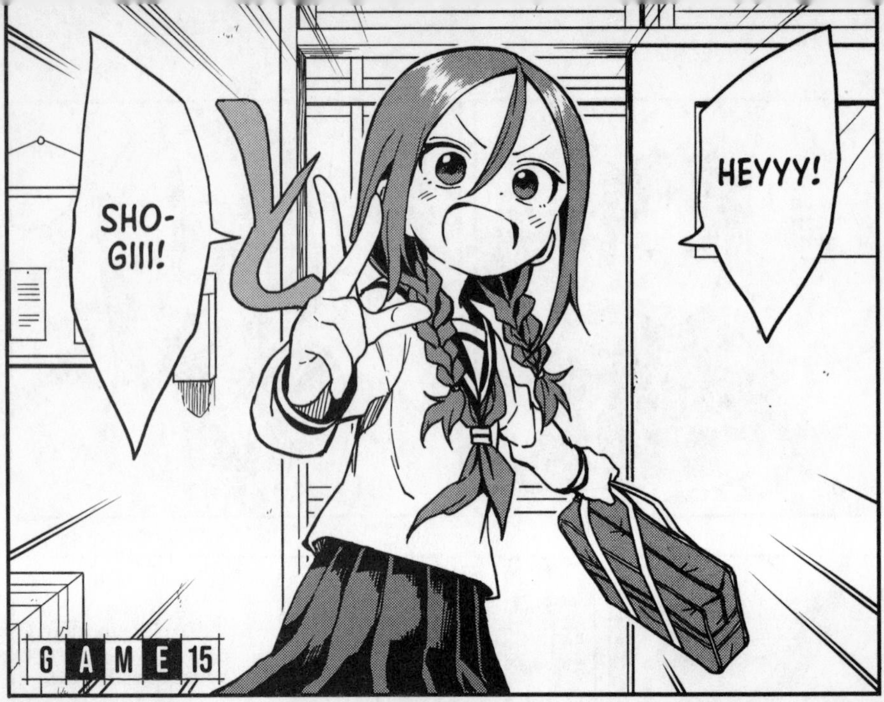
HEYYY!
SHO-GIII!
GAME 15

Label: TO

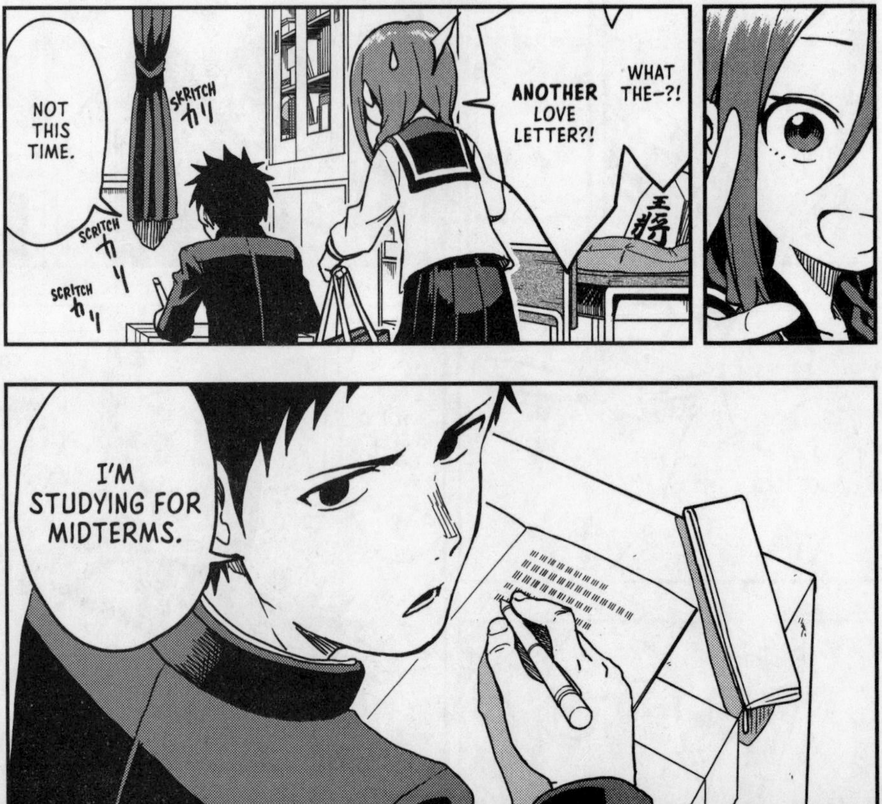
WHAT THE-?!
ANOTHER LOVE LETTER?!
王将
SKRITCH カリ
NOT THIS TIME.
SCRITCH カリ
SCRITCH カリ
I'M STUDYING FOR MIDTERMS.

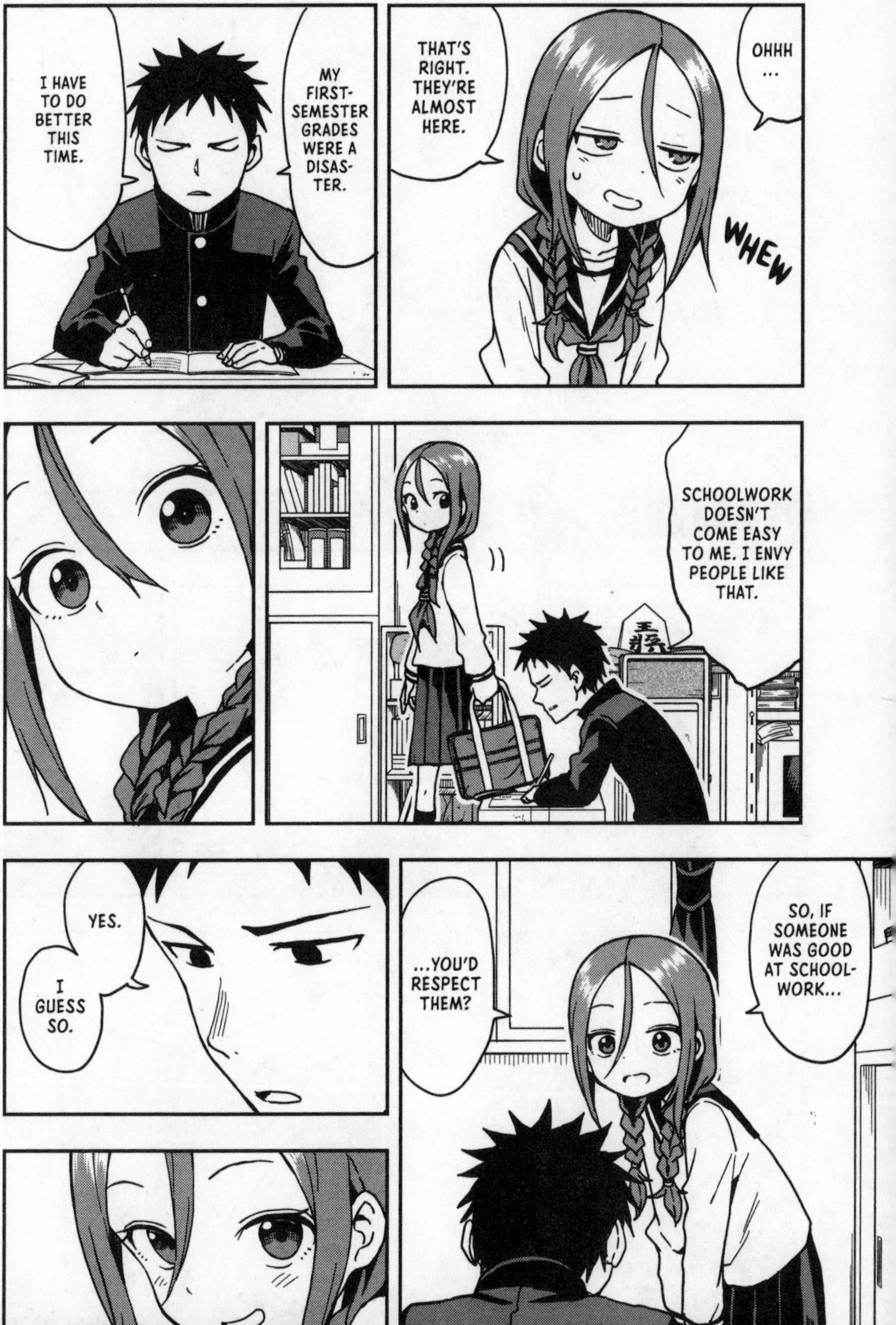
OHHH...
THAT'S RIGHT. THEY'RE ALMOST HERE.
WHEW
MY FIRST-SEMESTER GRADES WERE A DISASTER.
I HAVE TO DO BETTER THIS TIME.
SCHOOLWORK DOESN'T COME EASY TO ME. I ENVY PEOPLE LIKE THAT.
SO, IF SOMEONE WAS GOOD AT SCHOOLWORK...
...YOU'D RESPECT THEM?
YES.
I GUESS SO.

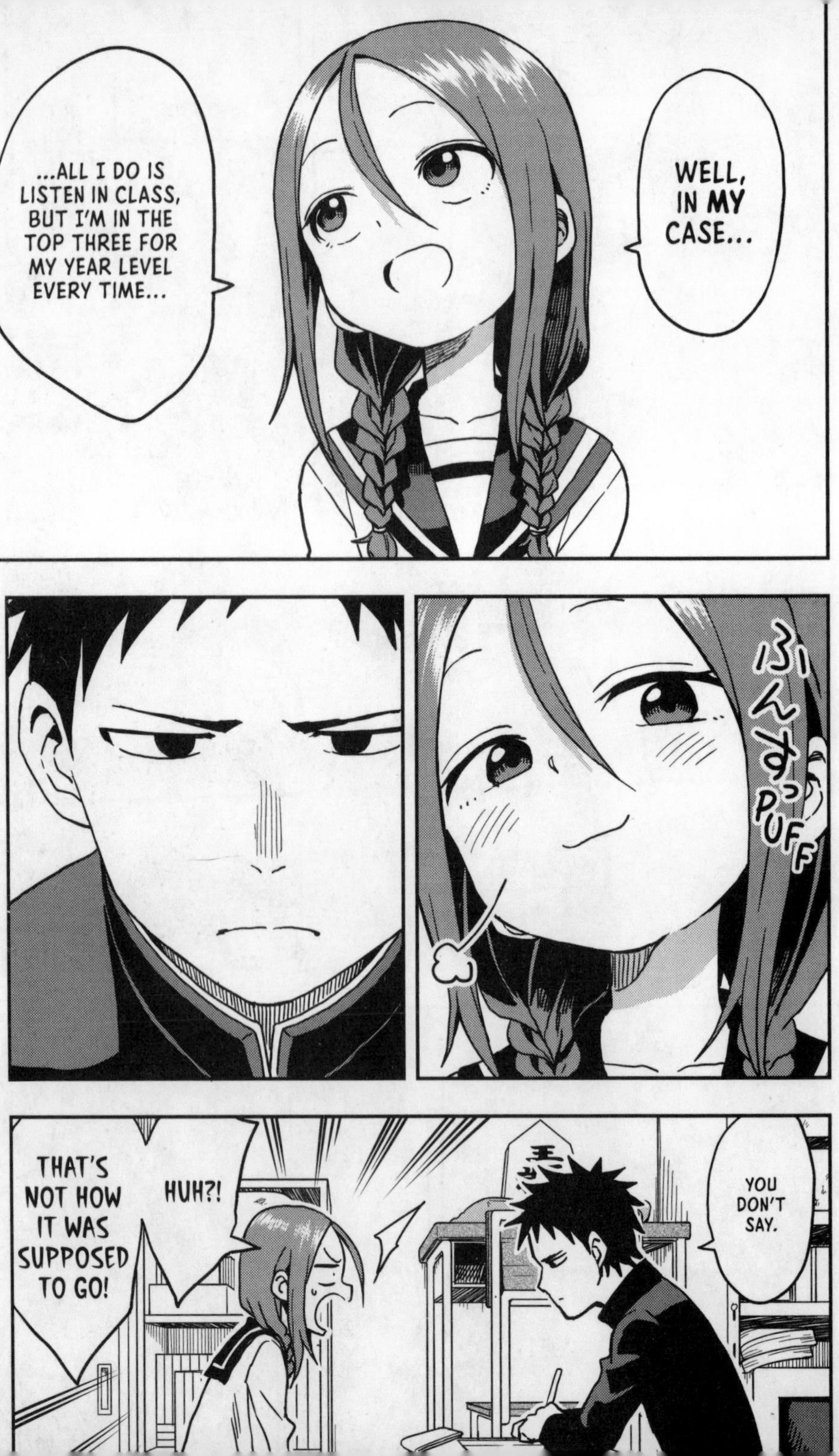
WELL, IN MY CASE...
...ALL I DO IS LISTEN IN CLASS, BUT I'M IN THE TOP THREE FOR MY YEAR LEVEL EVERY TIME...
ふんすっ
PUFF
YOU DON'T SAY.
HUH?!
THAT'S NOT HOW IT WAS SUPPOSED TO GO!

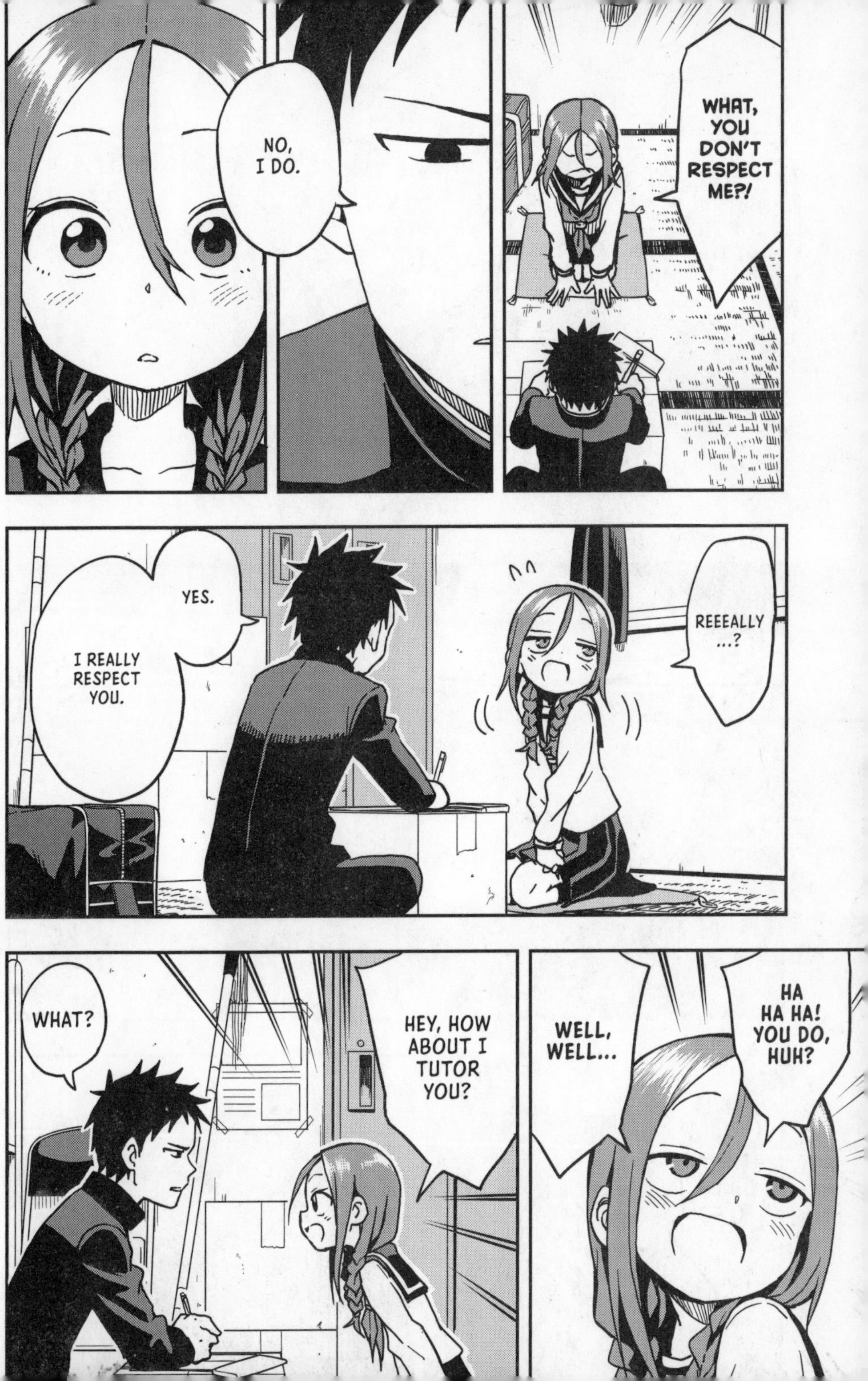
WHAT, YOU DON'T RESPECT ME?!
NO, I DO.
REEEALLY ...?
YES.
I REALLY RESPECT YOU.
HA HA HA! YOU DO, HUH?
WELL, WELL...
HEY, HOW ABOUT I TUTOR YOU?
WHAT?

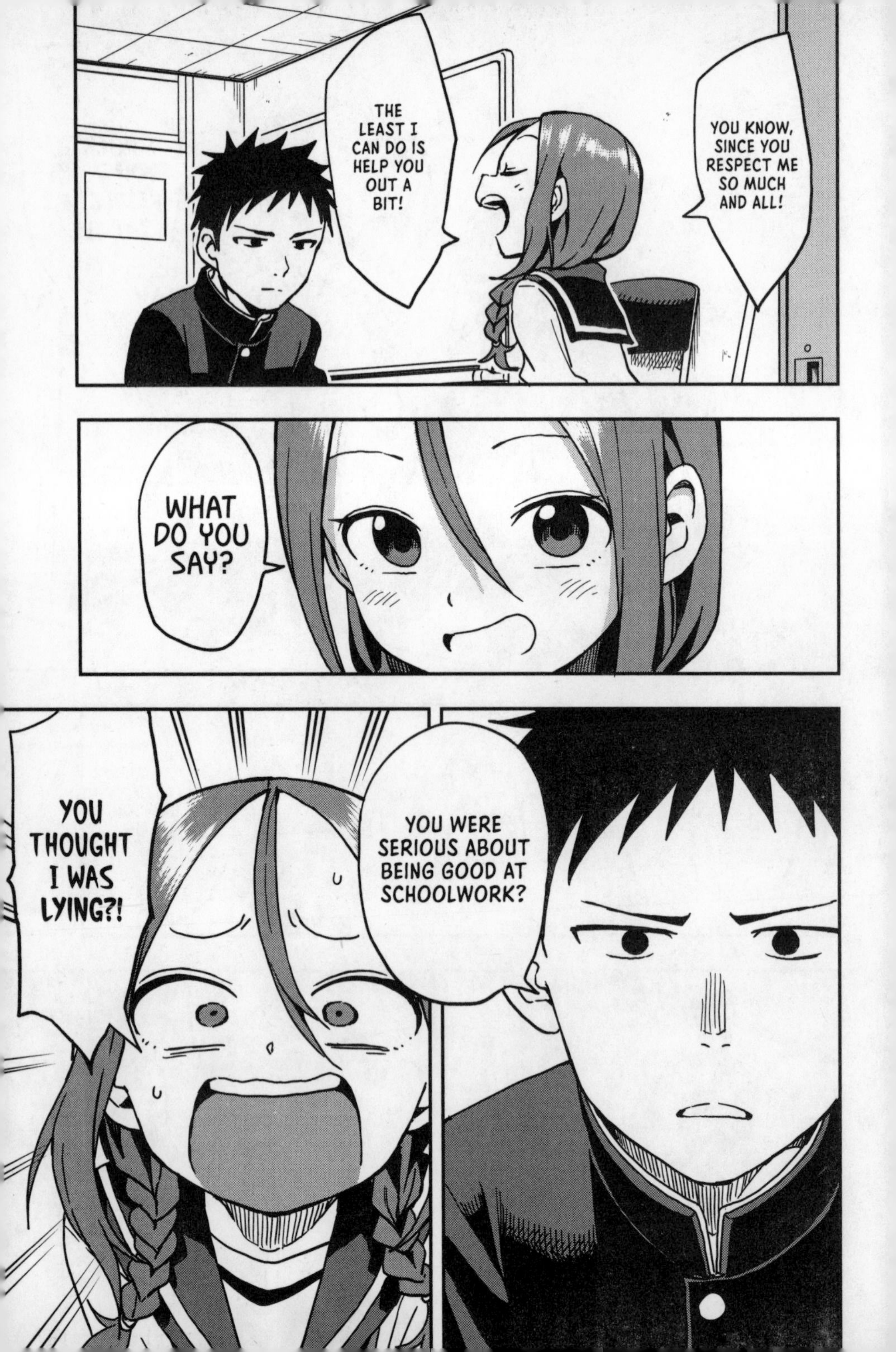
YOU KNOW, SINCE YOU RESPECT ME SO MUCH AND ALL!
THE LEAST I CAN DO IS HELP YOU OUT A BIT!
WHAT DO YOU SAY?
YOU WERE SERIOUS ABOUT BEING GOOD AT SCHOOLWORK?
YOU THOUGHT I WAS LYING?!

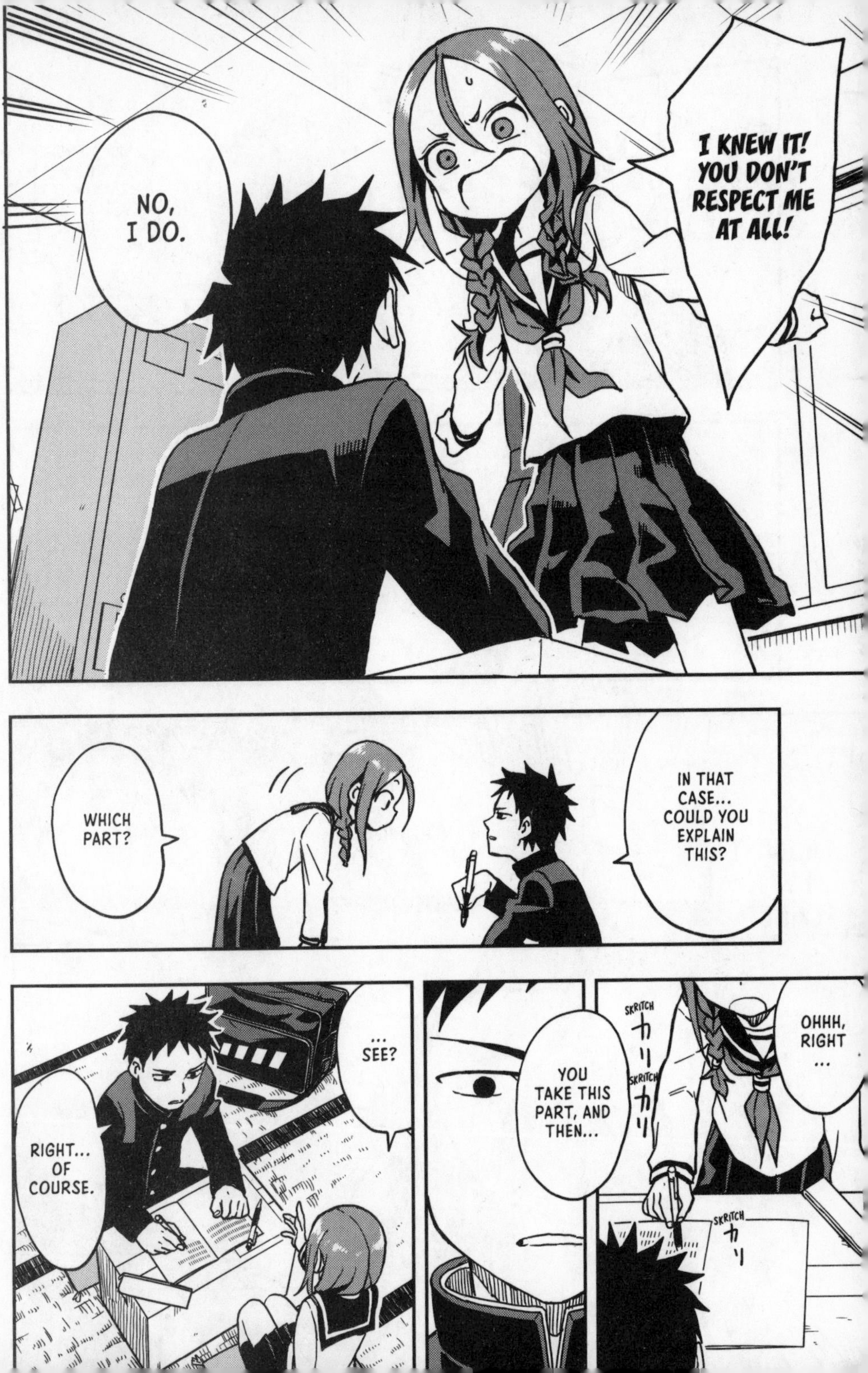
I KNEW IT! YOU DON'T RESPECT ME AT ALL!
NO, I DO.
IN THAT CASE... COULD YOU EXPLAIN THIS?
WHICH PART?
OHHH, RIGHT ...
SKRITCH カリ
SKRITCH カリ
SKRITCH カリ
YOU TAKE THIS PART, AND THEN...
... SEE?
RIGHT... OF COURSE.

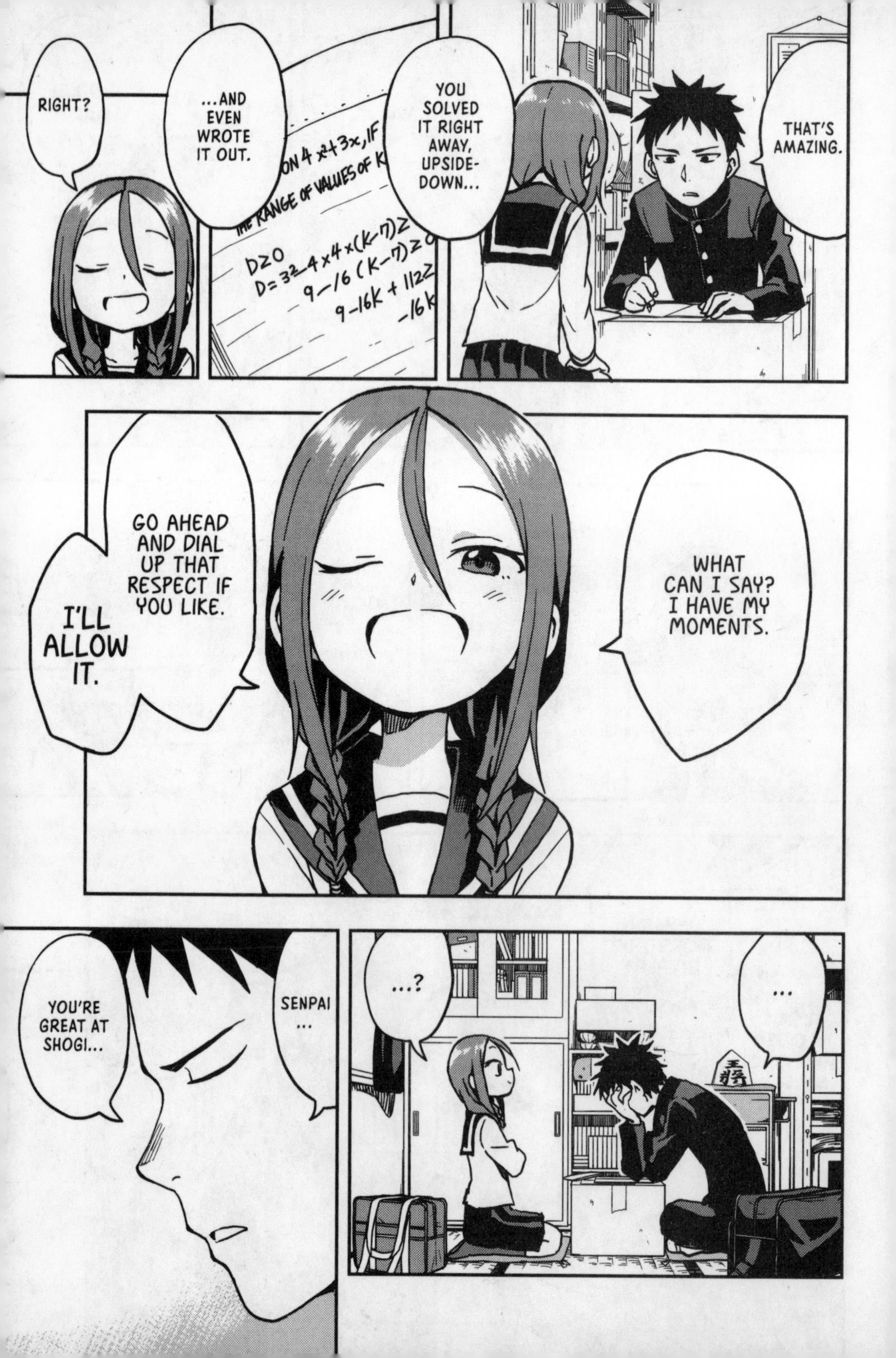
THAT'S AMAZING.
YOU SOLVED IT RIGHT AWAY, UPSIDE-DOWN...
...AND EVEN WROTE IT OUT.
THE RANGE OF VALUES OF K
D≥0
RIGHT?
WHAT CAN I SAY? I HAVE MY MOMENTS.
GO AHEAD AND DIAL UP THAT RESPECT IF YOU LIKE.
I'LL ALLOW IT.
...
...?
SENPAI...
YOU'RE GREAT AT SHOGI...

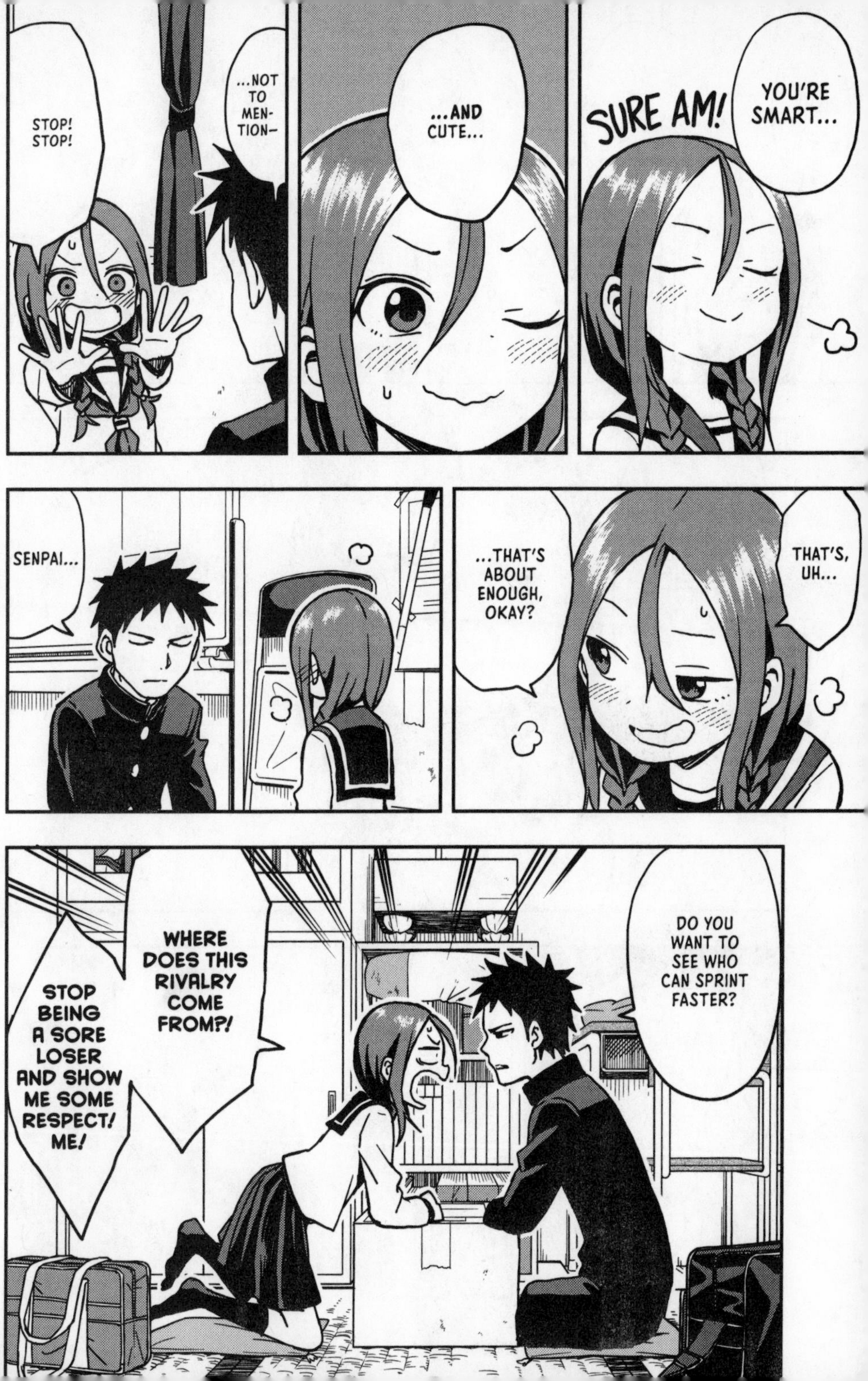
YOU'RE SMART...
SURE AM!
...AND CUTE...
...NOT TO MEN-TION—
STOP! STOP!
THAT'S, UH...
...THAT'S ABOUT ENOUGH, OKAY?
SENPAI...
DO YOU WANT TO SEE WHO CAN SPRINT FASTER?
WHERE DOES THIS RIVALRY COME FROM?!
STOP BEING A SORE LOSER AND SHOW ME SOME RESPECT! ME!

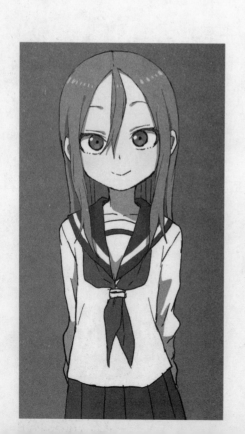

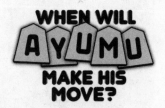

WHEN WILL
AYUMU
MAKE HIS
MOVE?

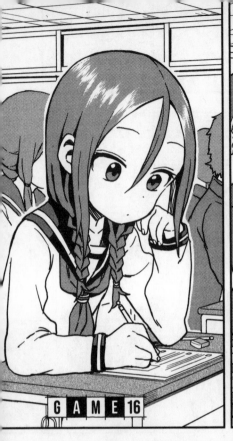

GAME 16

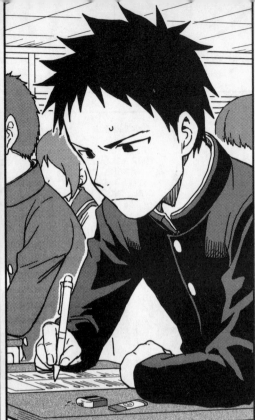

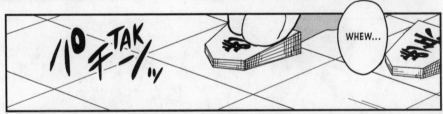

WHEW...

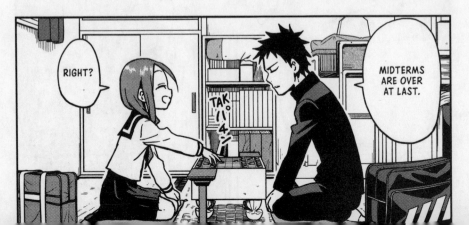

RIGHT?

MIDTERMS ARE OVER AT LAST.

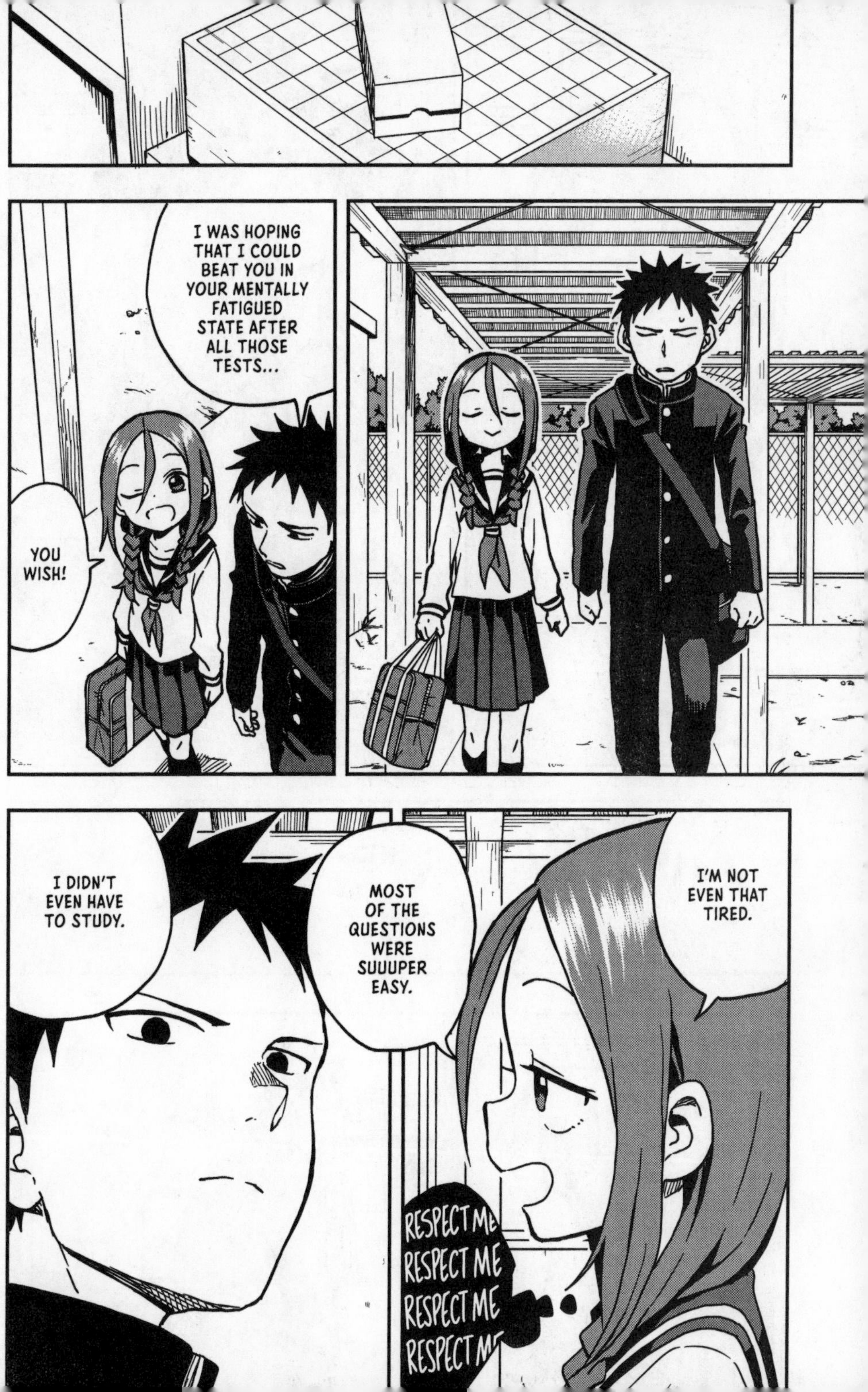
I WAS HOPING THAT I COULD BEAT YOU IN YOUR MENTALLY FATIGUED STATE AFTER ALL THOSE TESTS...
YOU WISH!
I'M NOT EVEN THAT TIRED.
MOST OF THE QUESTIONS WERE SUUUPER EASY.
RESPECT ME
RESPECT ME
RESPECT ME
RESPECT ME
I DIDN'T EVEN HAVE TO STUDY.

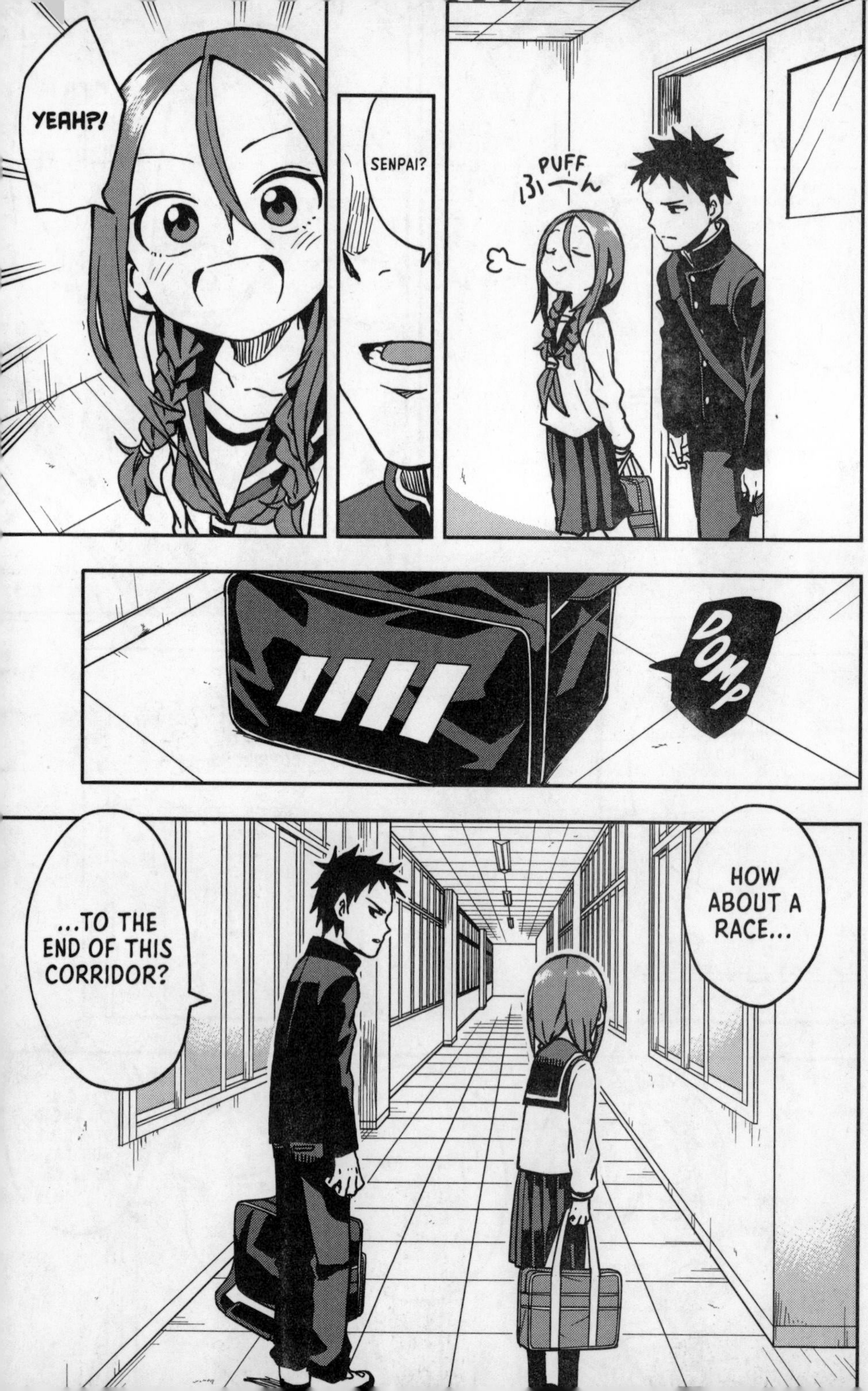

PUFF
ふーん
SENPAI?
YEAH?!
DOMP
HOW ABOUT A RACE...
...TO THE END OF THIS CORRIDOR?

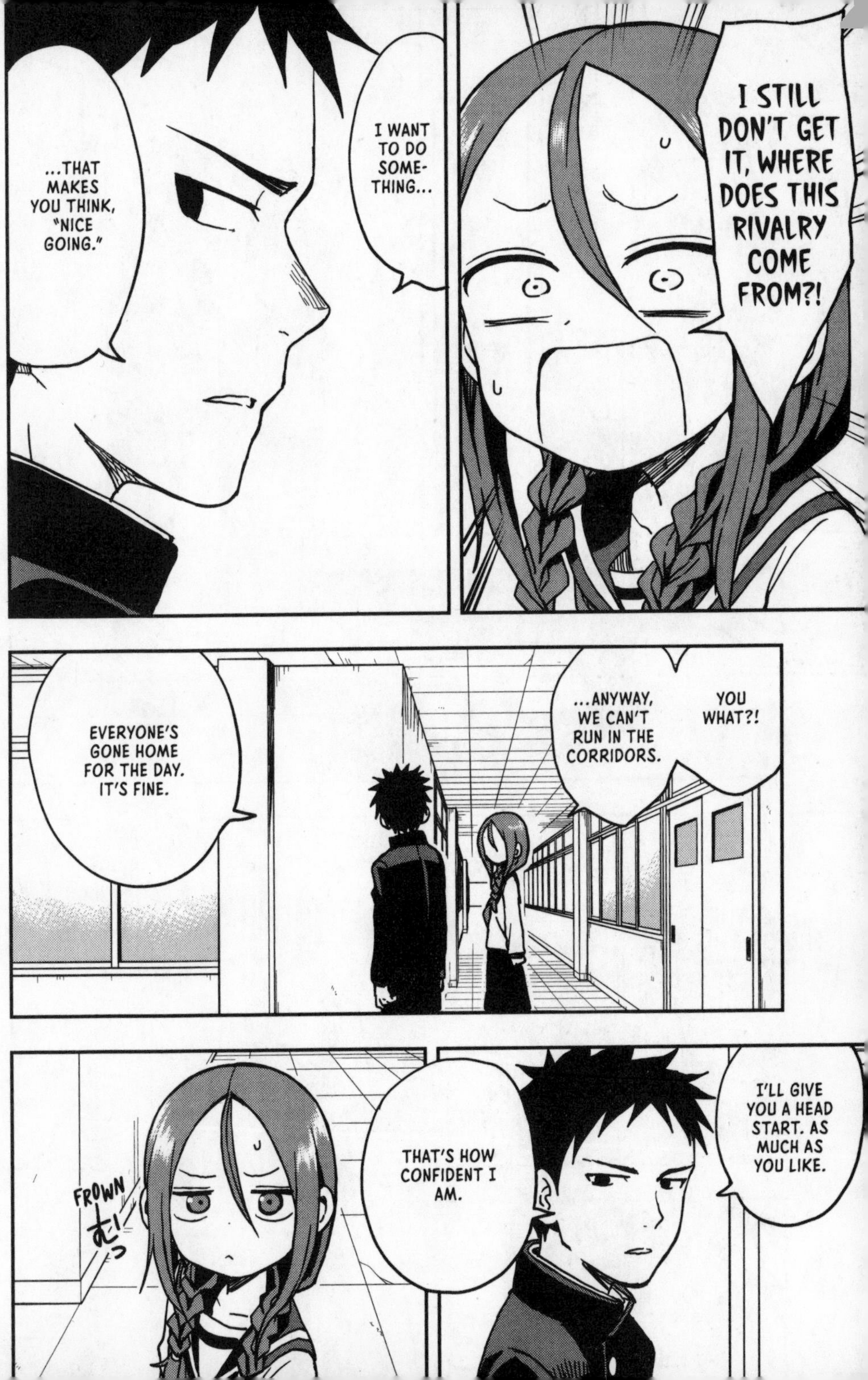
I STILL DON'T GET IT, WHERE DOES THIS RIVALRY COME FROM?!
I WANT TO DO SOME-THING...
...THAT MAKES YOU THINK, "NICE GOING."
YOU WHAT?!
...ANYWAY, WE CAN'T RUN IN THE CORRIDORS.
EVERYONE'S GONE HOME FOR THE DAY. IT'S FINE.
I'LL GIVE YOU A HEAD START. AS MUCH AS YOU LIKE.
THAT'S HOW CONFIDENT I AM.
FROWN
むっ

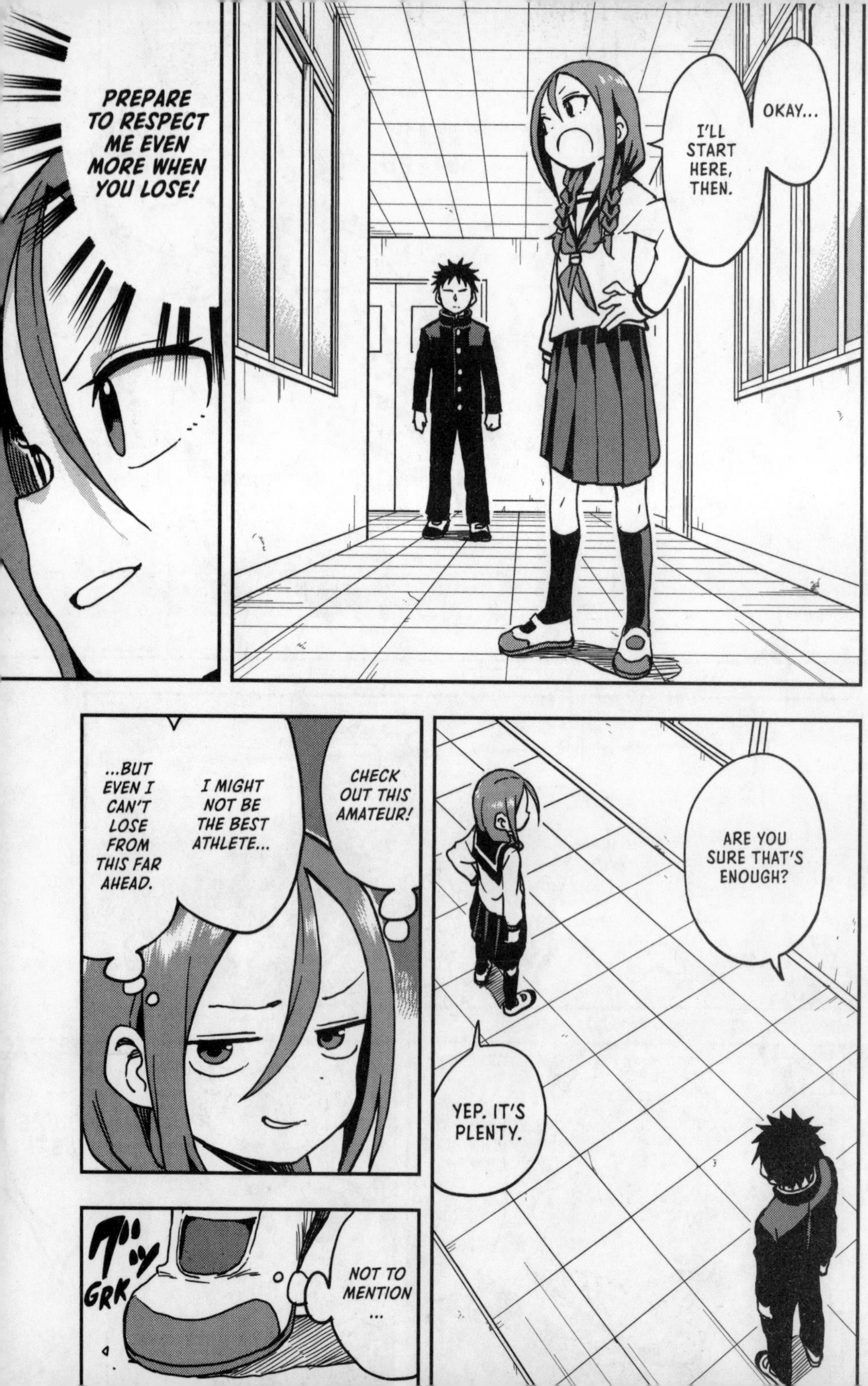
OKAY...
I'LL START HERE, THEN.
PREPARE TO RESPECT ME EVEN MORE WHEN YOU LOSE!
ARE YOU SURE THAT'S ENOUGH?
YEP. IT'S PLENTY.
CHECK OUT THIS AMATEUR!
I MIGHT NOT BE THE BEST ATHLETE...
...BUT EVEN I CAN'T LOSE FROM THIS FAR AHEAD.
NOT TO MENTION ...
GRK

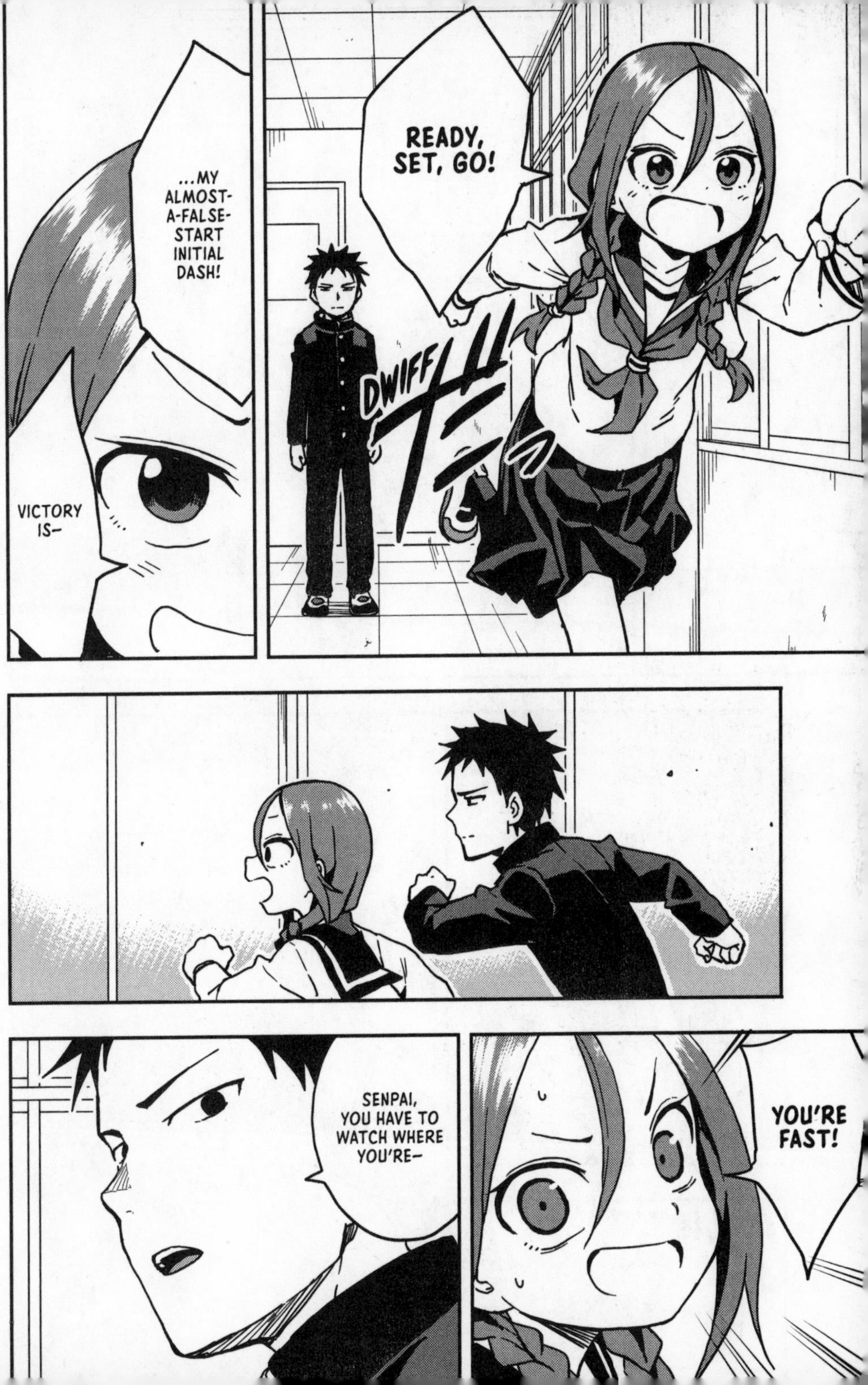
READY, SET, GO!
DWIFF
...MY ALMOST-A-FALSE-START INITIAL DASH!
VICTORY IS–
YOU'RE FAST!
SENPAI, YOU HAVE TO WATCH WHERE YOU'RE–

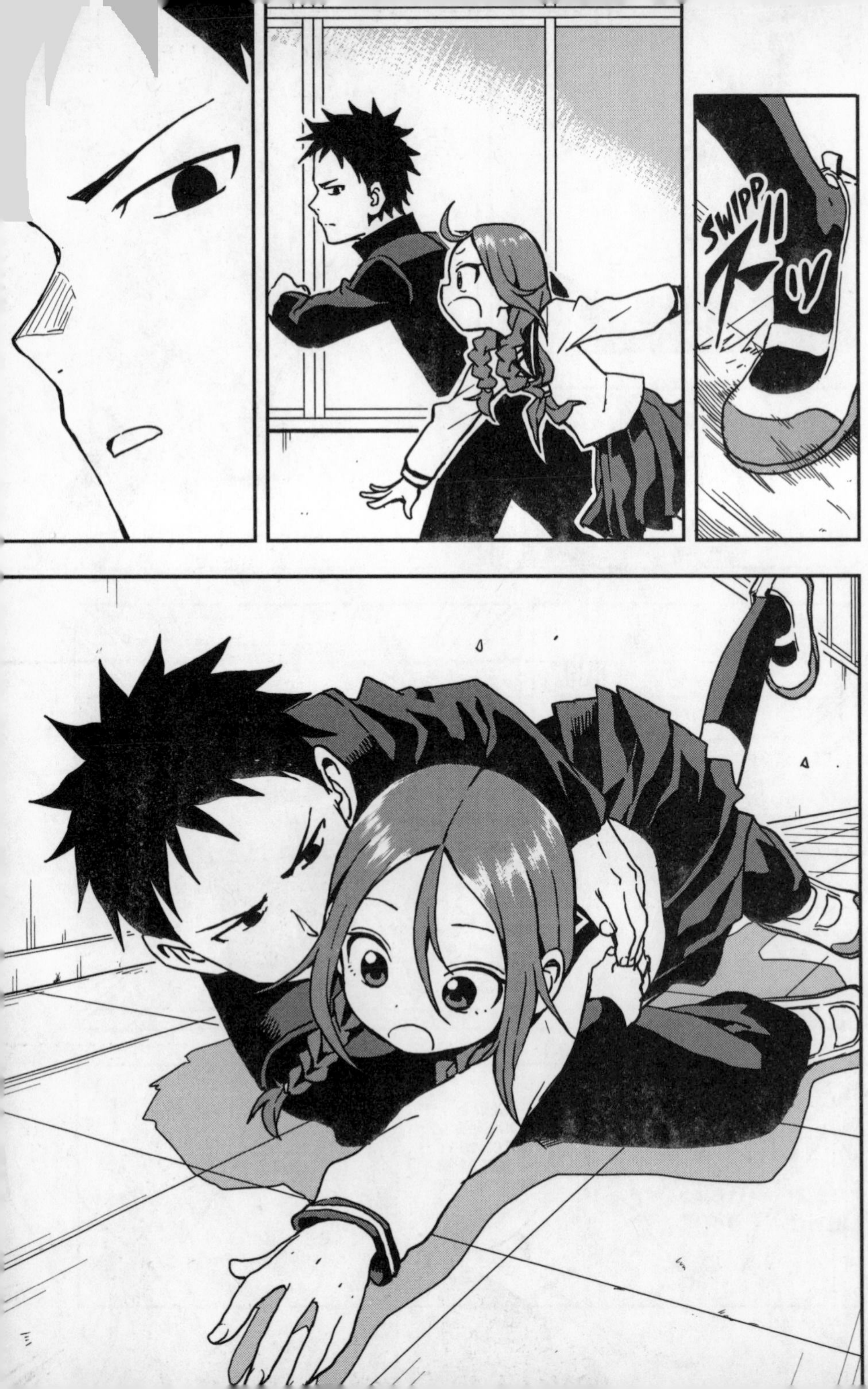
SWIPP

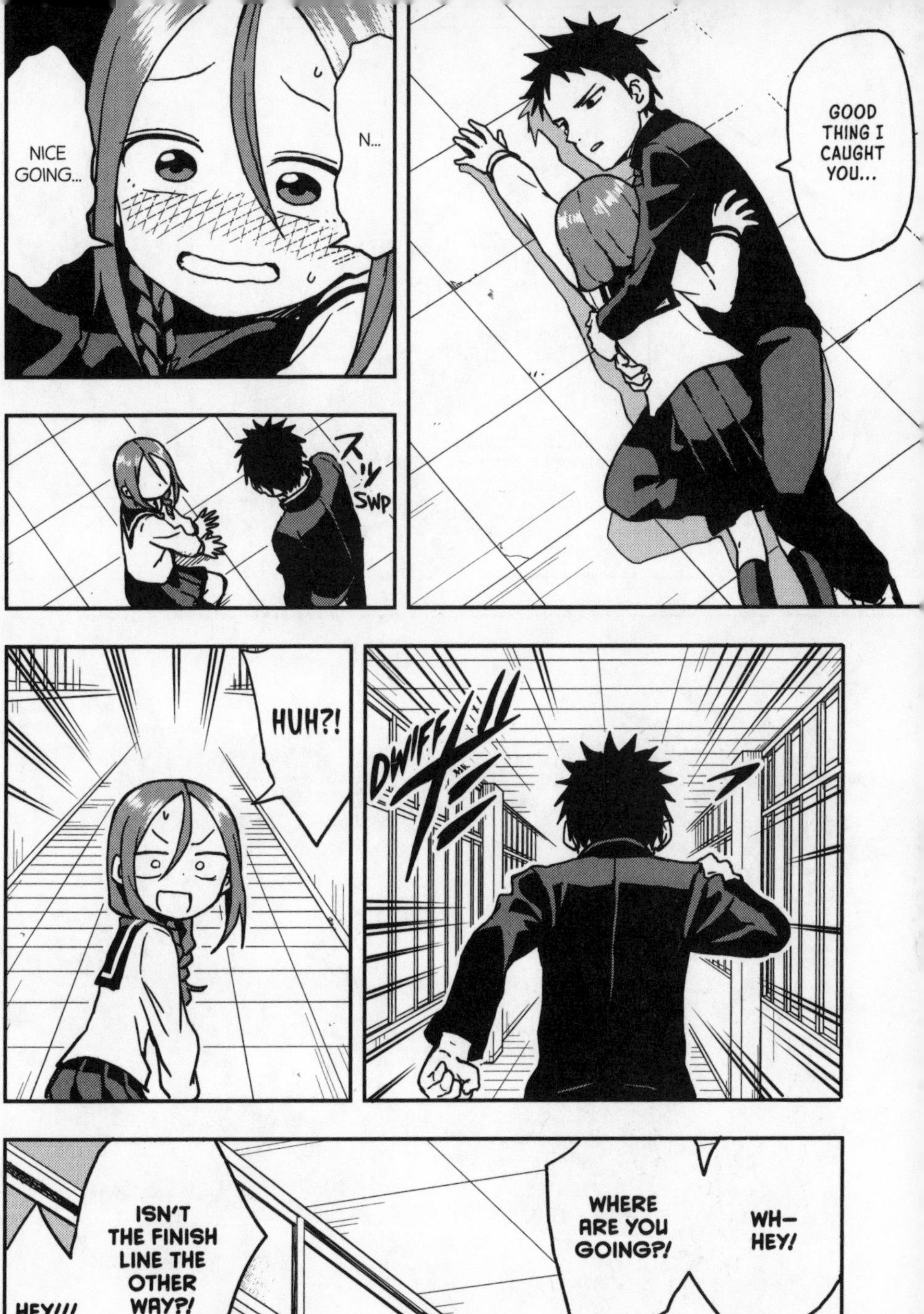
GOOD THING I CAUGHT YOU...
N...
NICE GOING...
スッ
SWP
DWIFF
HUH?!
WH— HEY!
WHERE ARE YOU GOING?!
ISN'T THE FINISH LINE THE OTHER WAY?!
HEY!!!

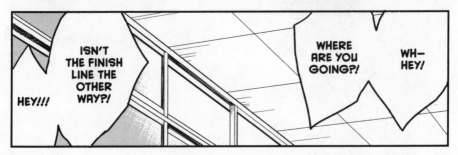

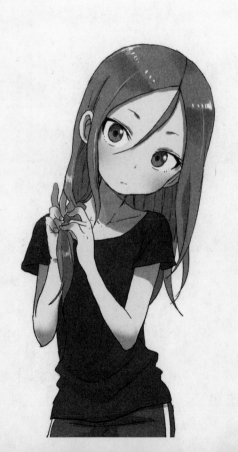

WHEN WILL AYUMU MAKE HIS MOVE?

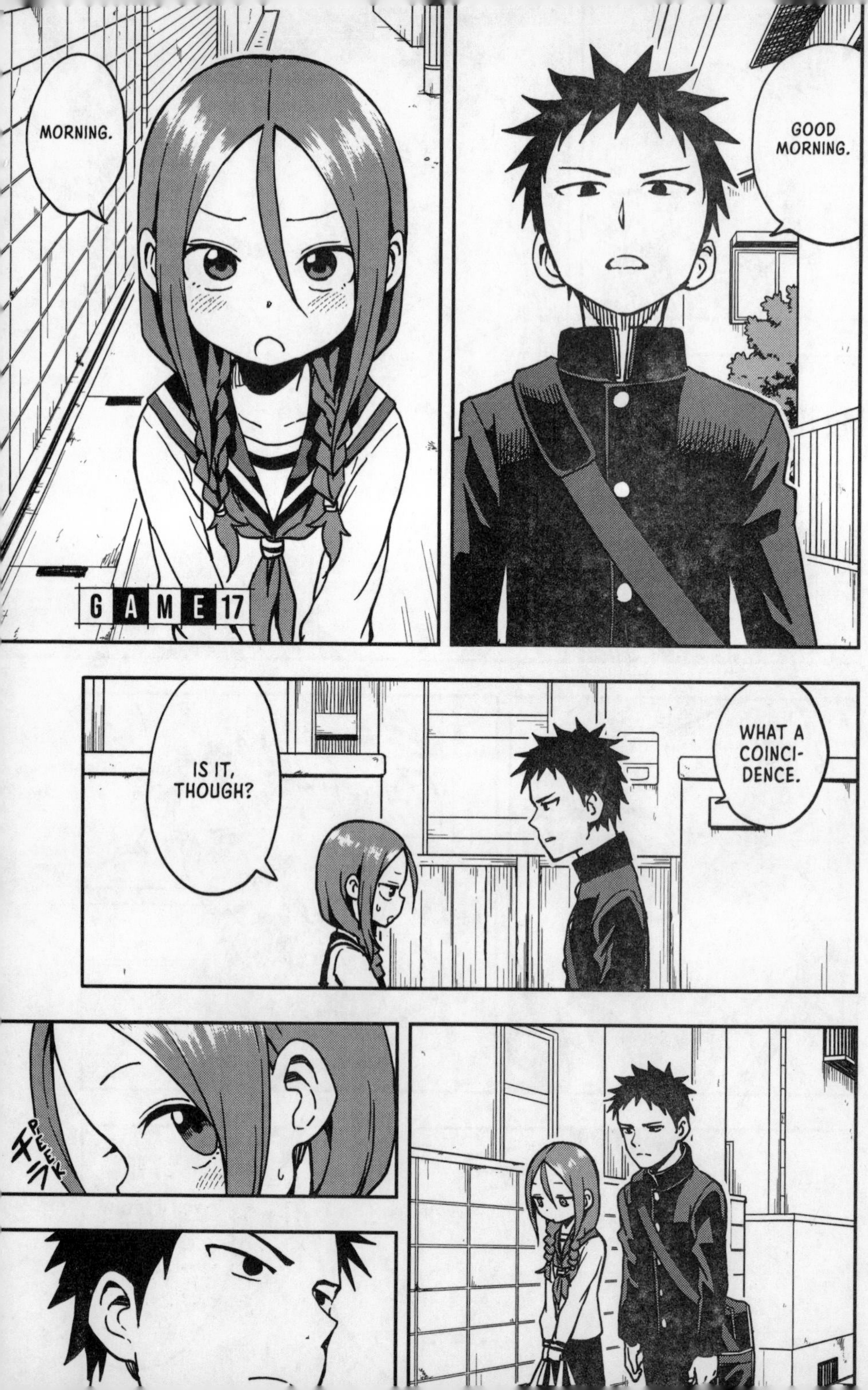
GOOD MORNING.
MORNING.
GAME 17
WHAT A COINCI-DENCE.
IS IT, THOUGH?
PEEK

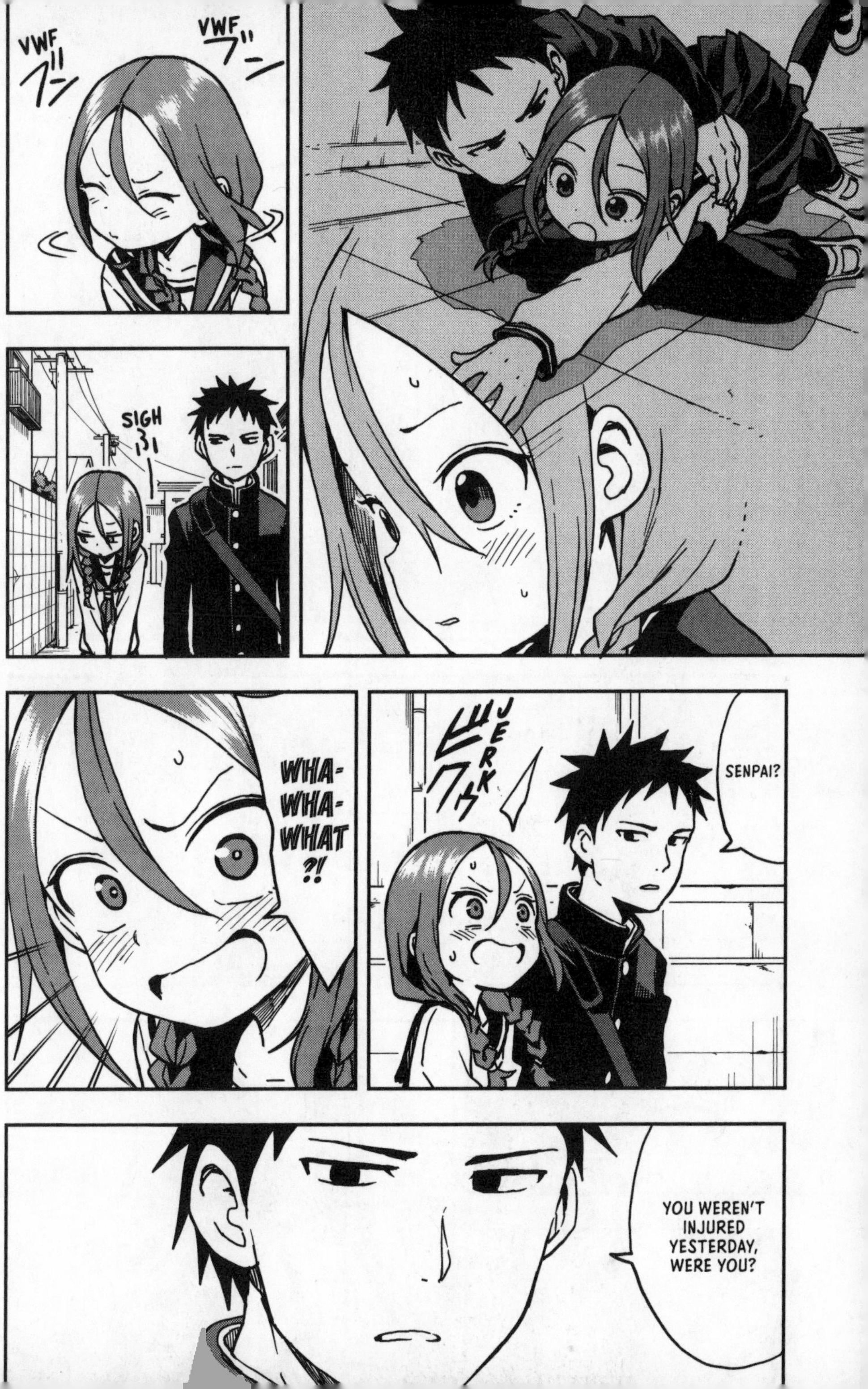
VWF
VWF
SIGH
JERK
SENPAI?
WHA-WHA-WHAT?!
YOU WEREN'T INJURED YESTERDAY, WERE YOU?

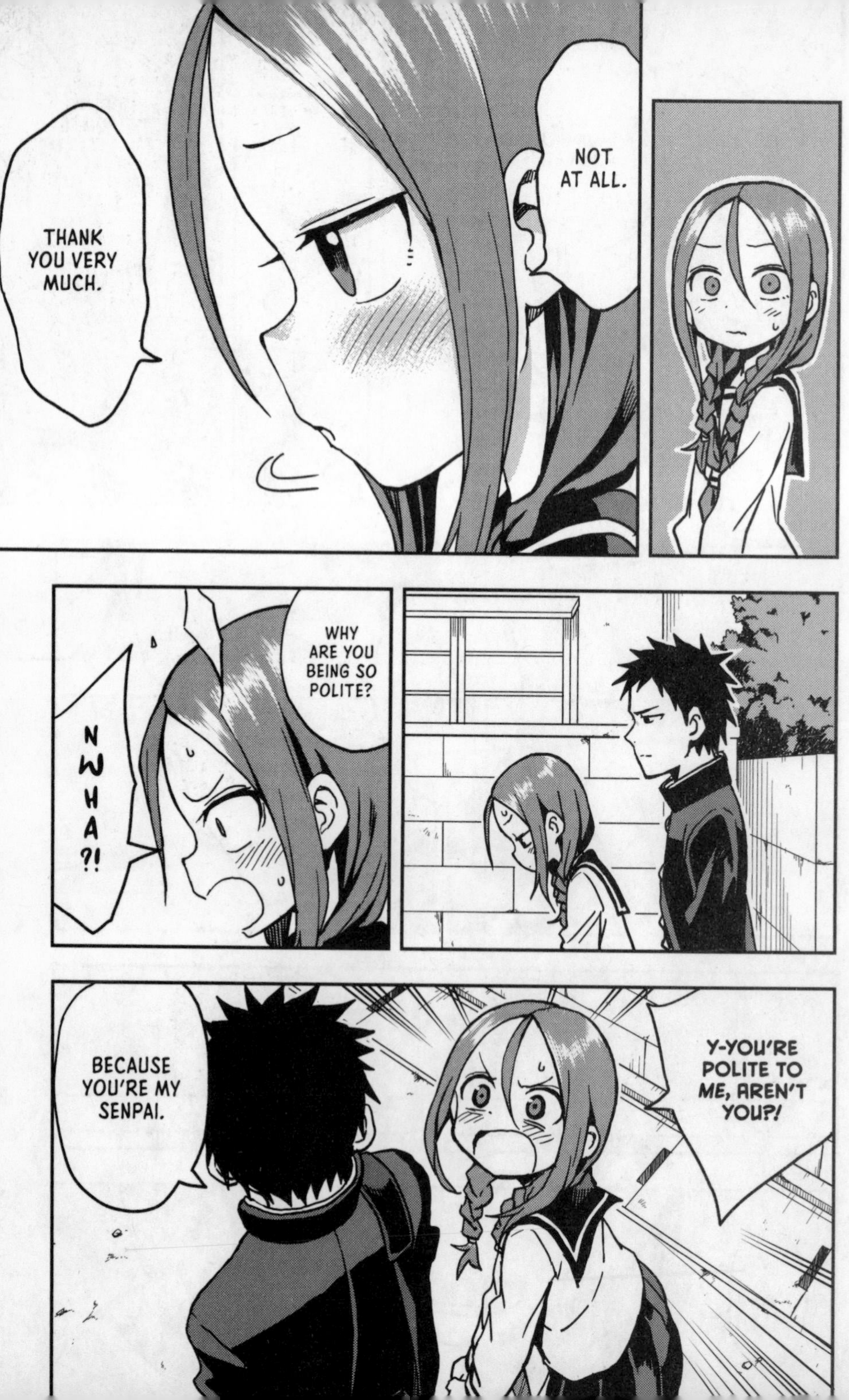
NOT AT ALL.
THANK YOU VERY MUCH.
WHY ARE YOU BEING SO POLITE?
NWHA?!
Y-YOU'RE POLITE TO ME, AREN'T YOU?!
BECAUSE YOU'RE MY SENPAI.

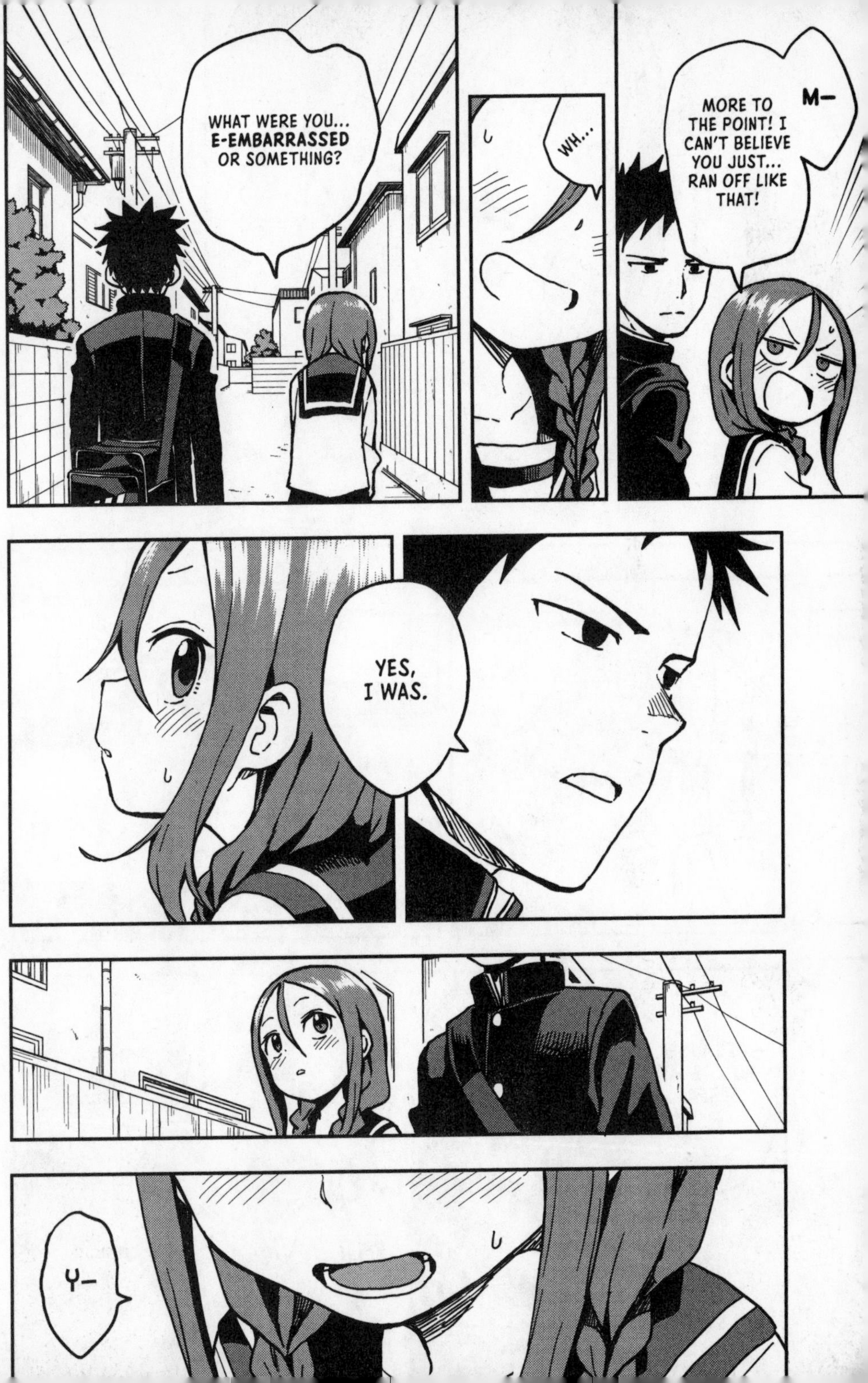
M—
MORE TO THE POINT! I CAN'T BELIEVE YOU JUST... RAN OFF LIKE THAT!
WH...
WHAT WERE YOU... E-EMBARRASSED OR SOMETHING?
YES, I WAS.
Y—

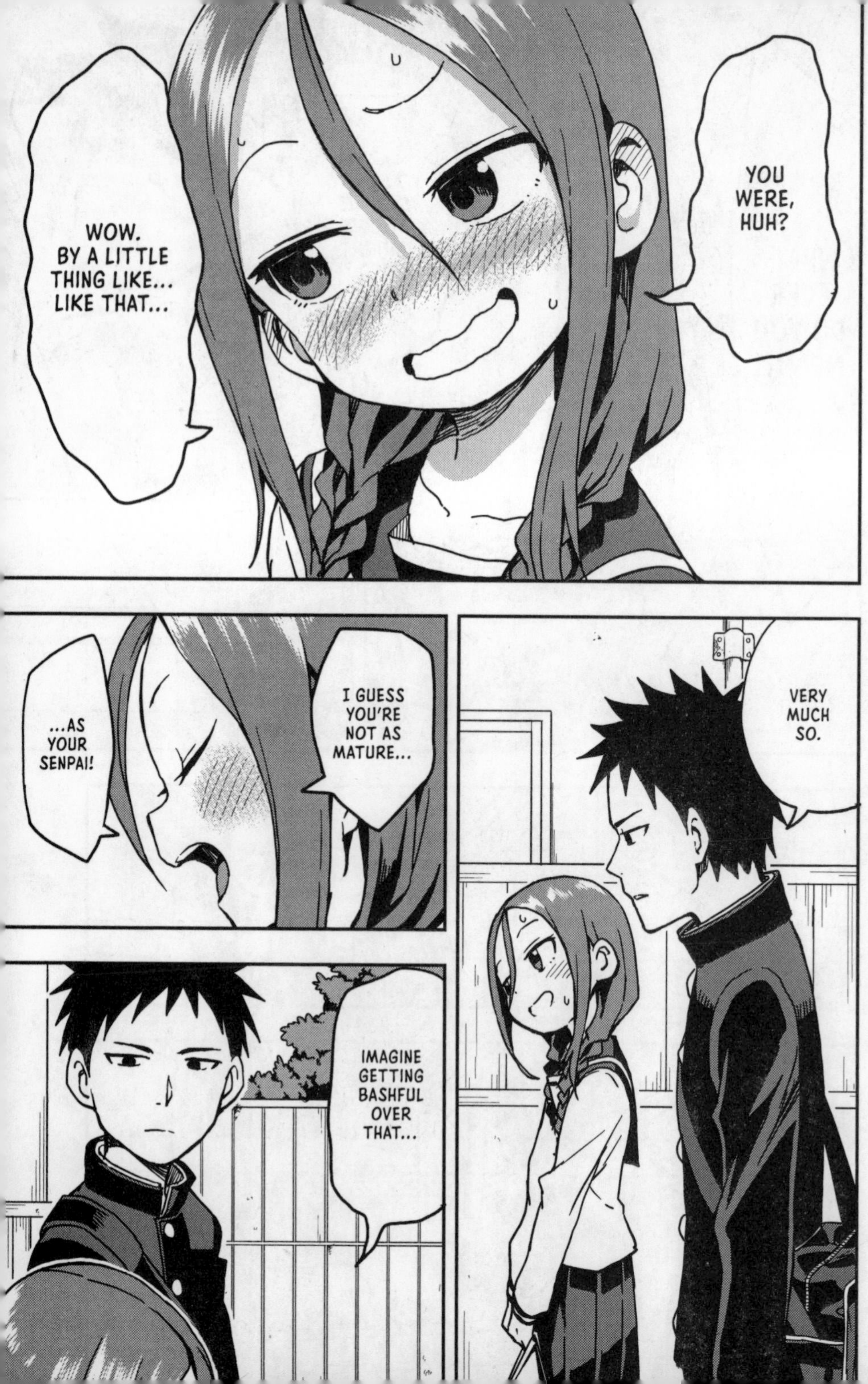
YOU WERE, HUH?
WOW. BY A LITTLE THING LIKE... LIKE THAT...
VERY MUCH SO.
I GUESS YOU'RE NOT AS MATURE...
...AS YOUR SENPAI!
IMAGINE GETTING BASHFUL OVER THAT...

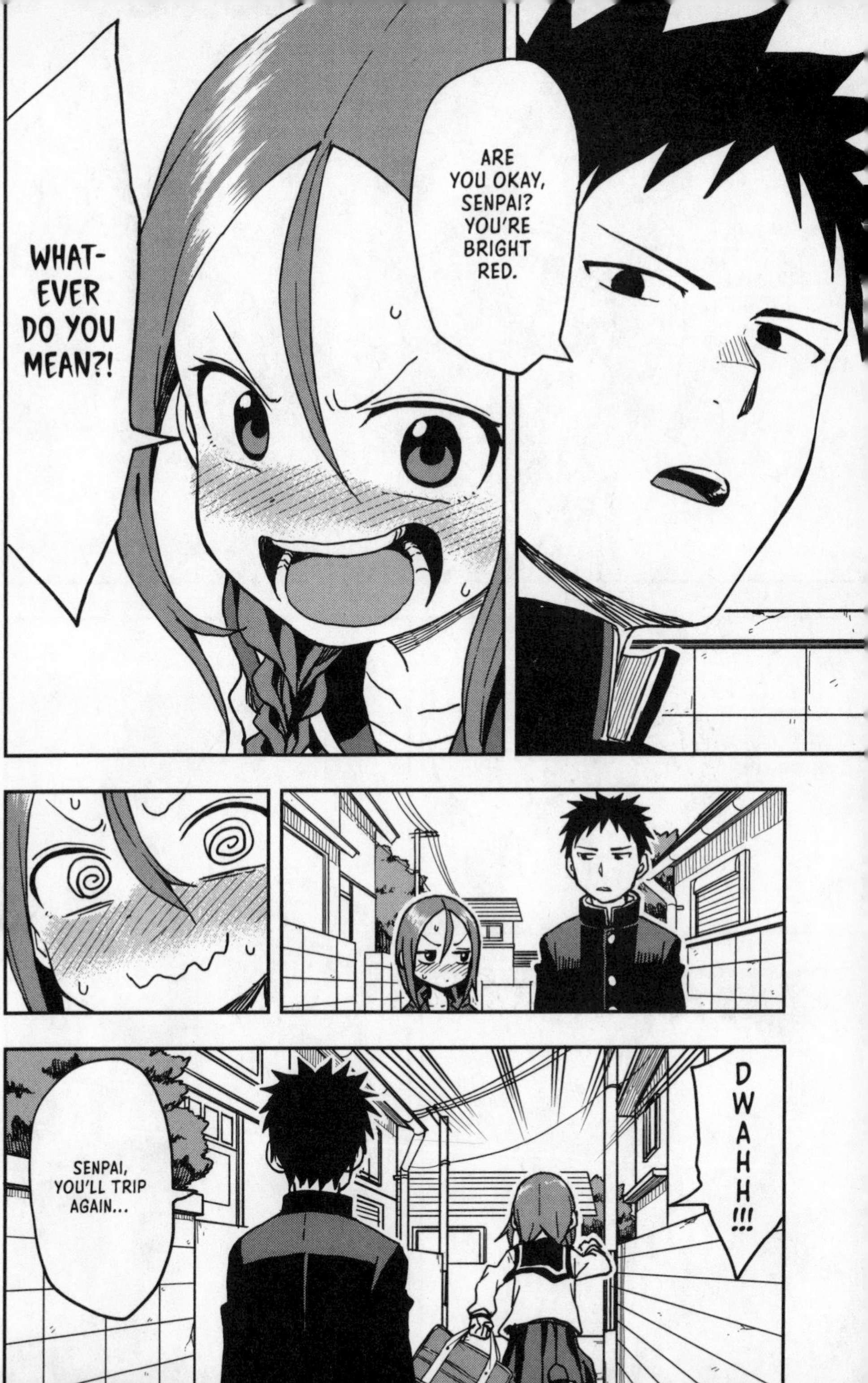
ARE YOU OKAY, SENPAI? YOU'RE BRIGHT RED.
WHAT-EVER DO YOU MEAN?!
DWAHH!!!
SENPAI, YOU'LL TRIP AGAIN...

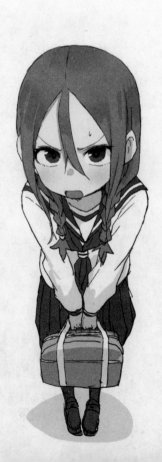

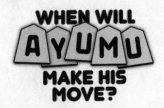

WHEN WILL AYUMU MAKE HIS MOVE?

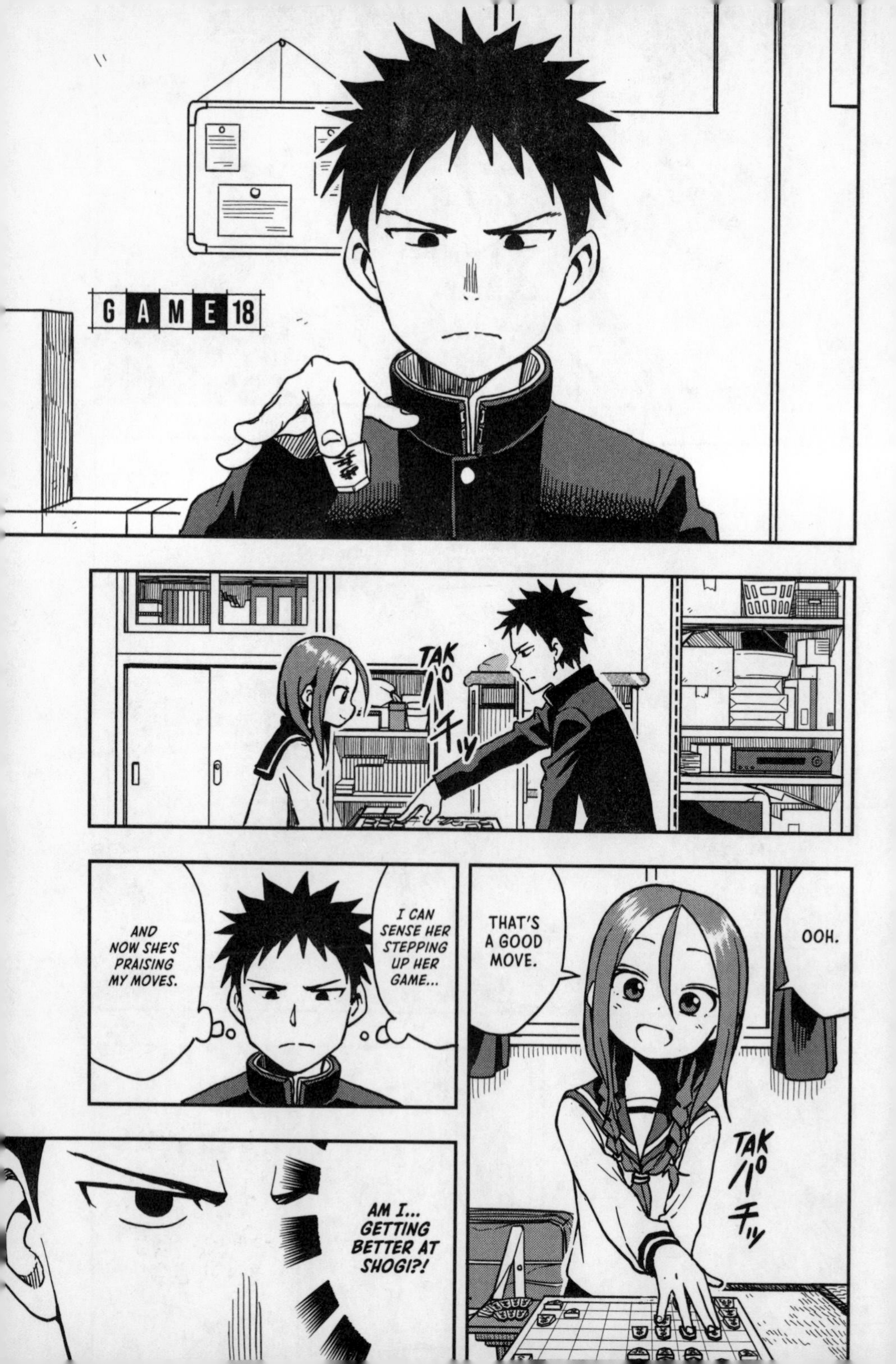
GAME 18
TAK
パチッ
OOH.
THAT'S A GOOD MOVE.
TAK
パチッ
I CAN SENSE HER STEPPING UP HER GAME...
AND NOW SHE'S PRAISING MY MOVES.
AM I... GETTING BETTER AT SHOGI?!

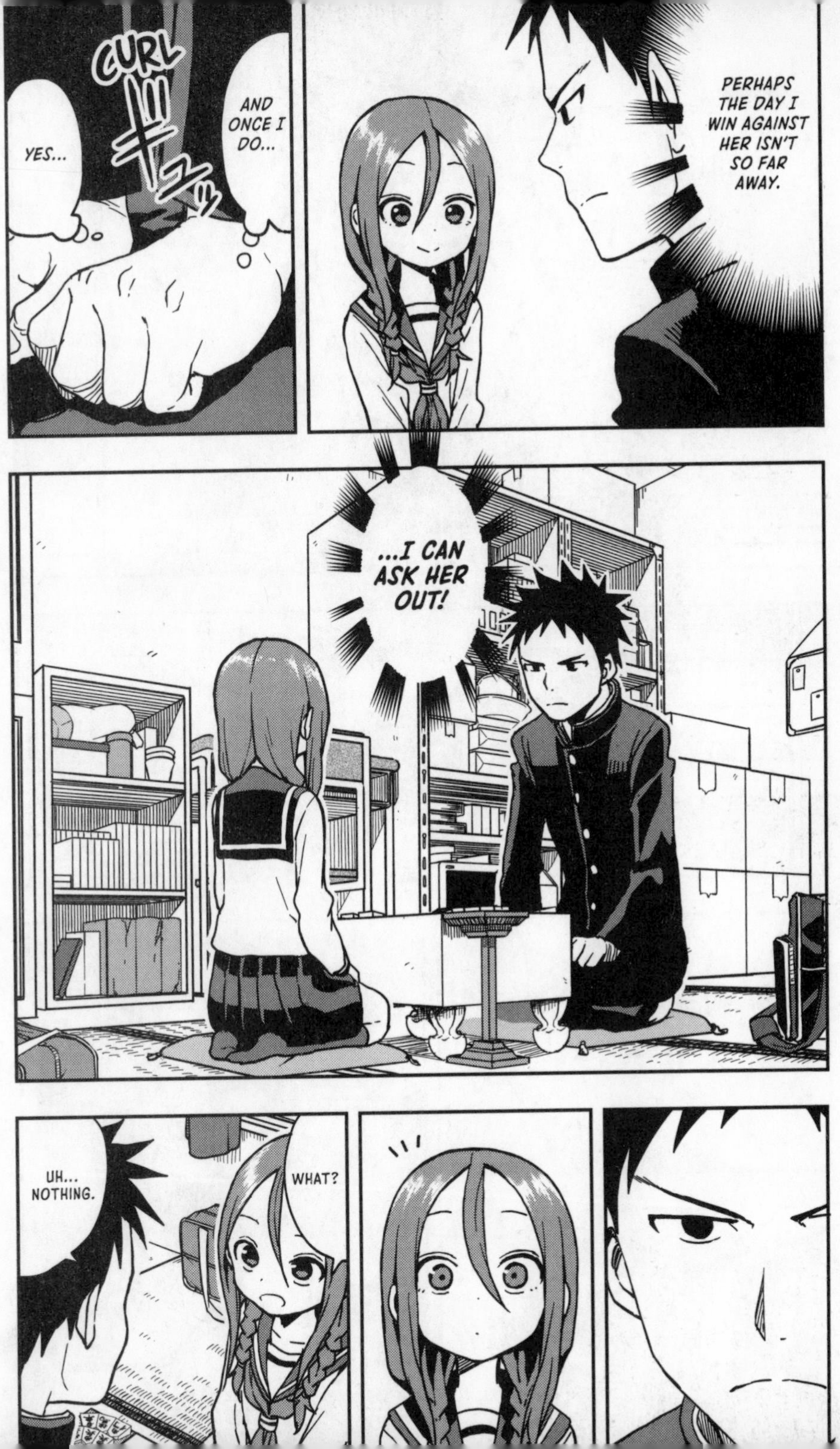
PERHAPS THE DAY I WIN AGAINST HER ISN'T SO FAR AWAY.
CURL
AND ONCE I DO...
YES...
...I CAN ASK HER OUT!
WHAT?
UH... NOTHING.

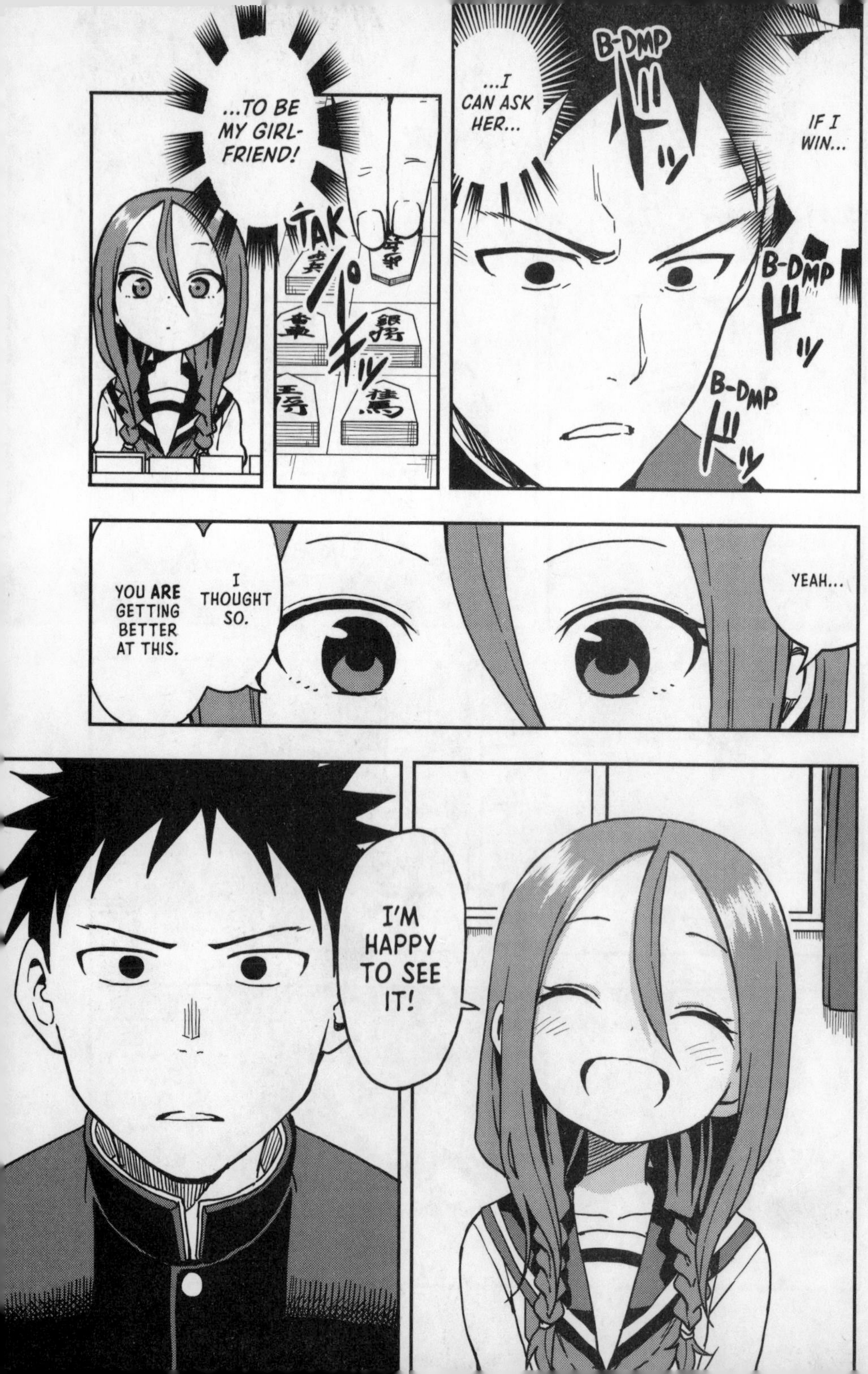

IF I WIN...
B-DMP
...I CAN ASK HER...
B-DMP
B-DMP
TAK
...TO BE MY GIRL-FRIEND!
YEAH...
I THOUGHT SO.
YOU ARE GETTING BETTER AT THIS.
I'M HAPPY TO SEE IT!

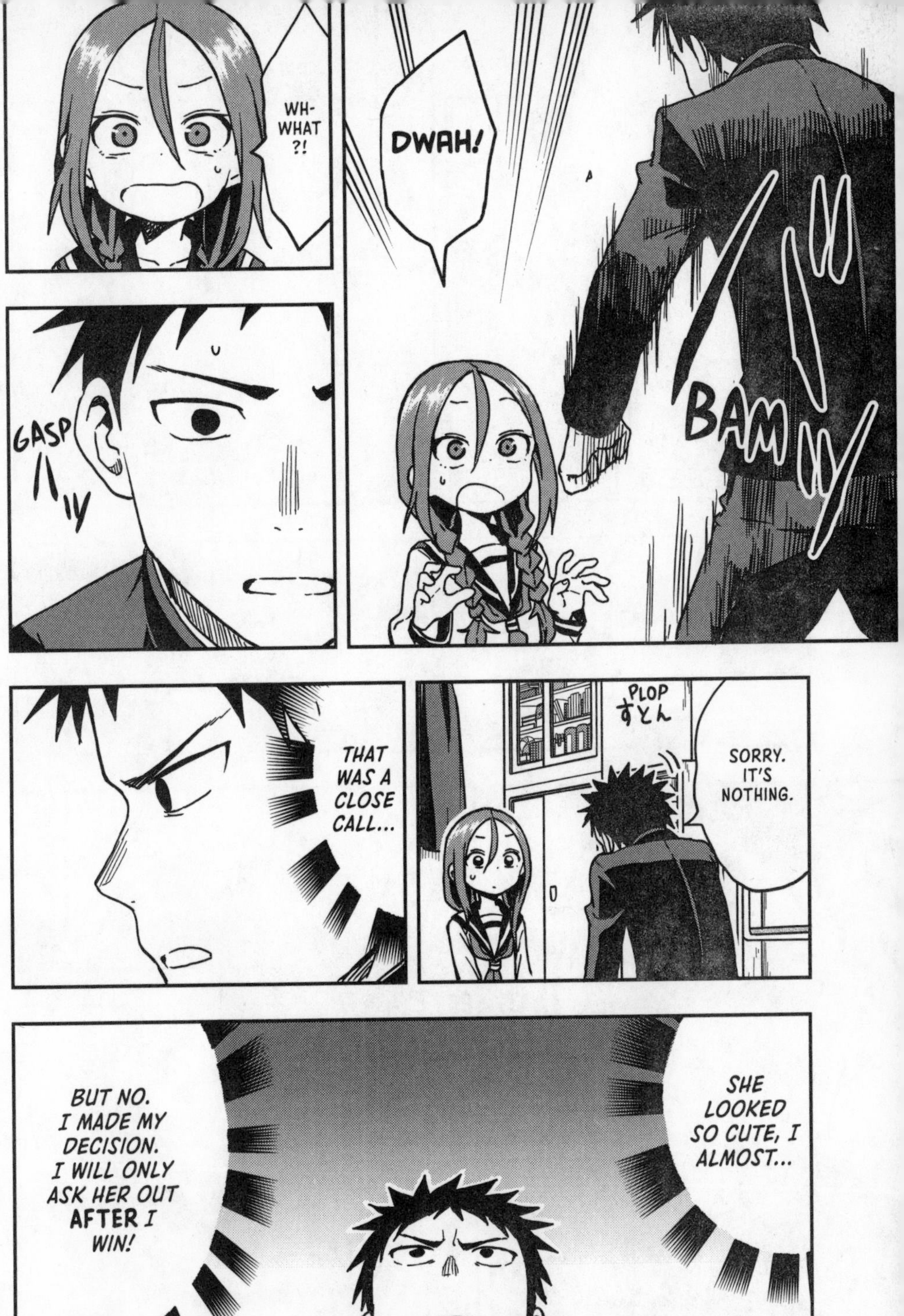
DWAH!
BAM
WH-WHAT?!
GASP
PLOP すとん
SORRY. IT'S NOTHING.
THAT WAS A CLOSE CALL...
SHE LOOKED SO CUTE, I ALMOST...
BUT NO. I MADE MY DECISION. I WILL ONLY ASK HER OUT **AFTER** I WIN!

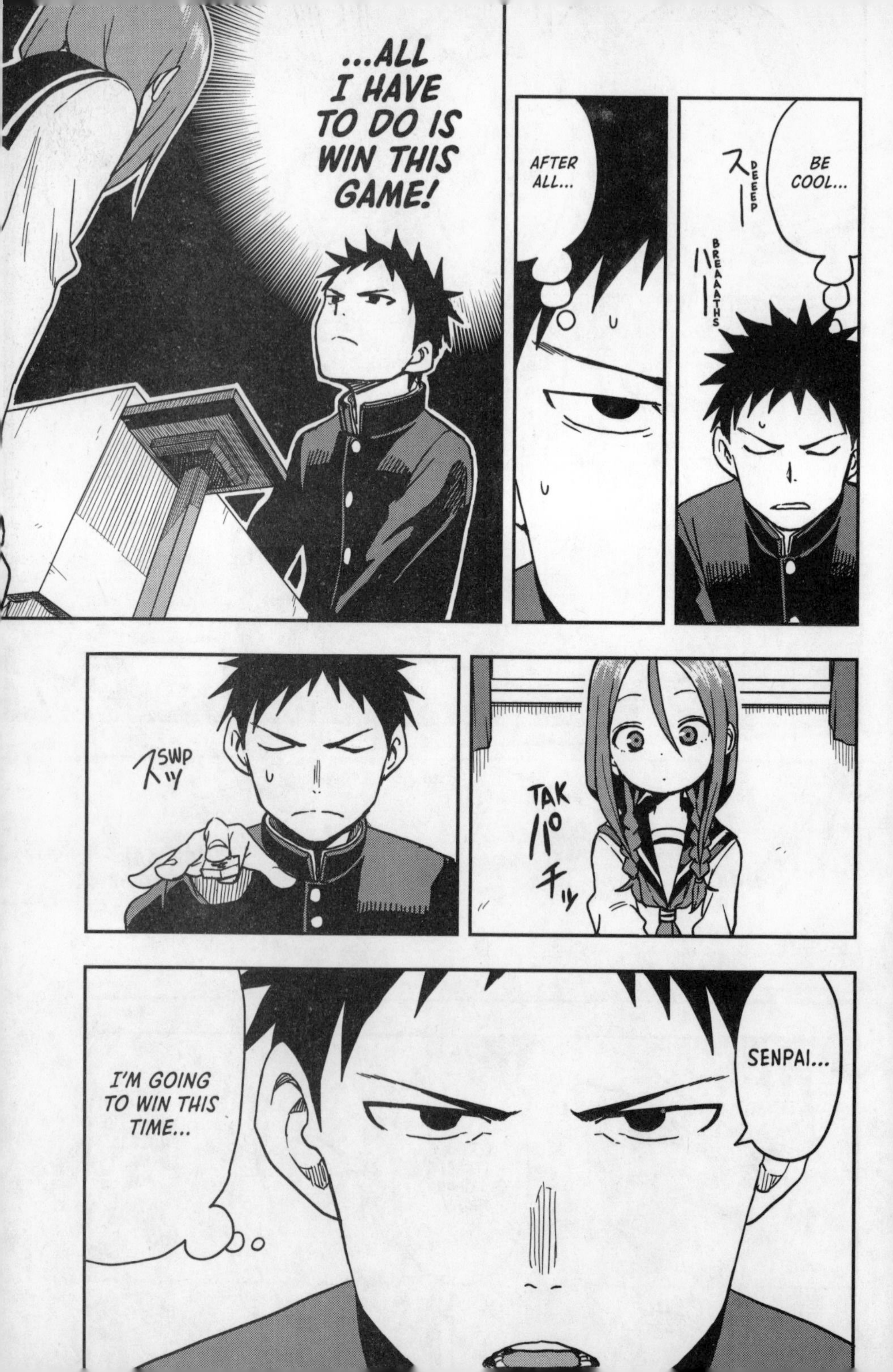
BE COOL...
スー DEEEP
ハー BREAAATHS
AFTER ALL...
...ALL I HAVE TO DO IS WIN THIS GAME!
パチッ TAK
スッ SWP
SENPAI...
I'M GOING TO WIN THIS TIME...

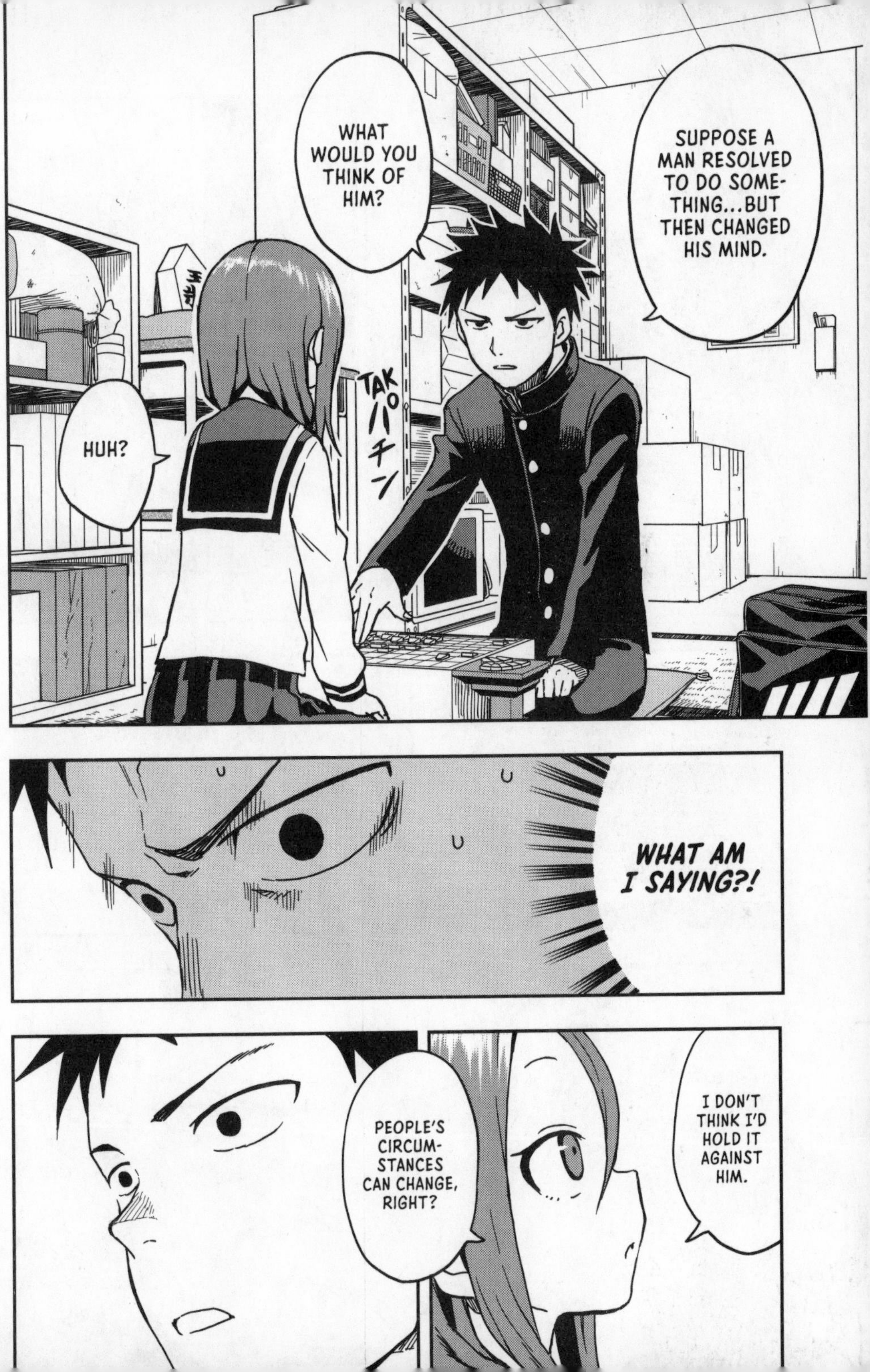
SUPPOSE A MAN RESOLVED TO DO SOME-THING...BUT THEN CHANGED HIS MIND.
WHAT WOULD YOU THINK OF HIM?
TAK
パチン
HUH?
WHAT AM I SAYING?!
I DON'T THINK I'D HOLD IT AGAINST HIM.
PEOPLE'S CIRCUM-STANCES CAN CHANGE, RIGHT?

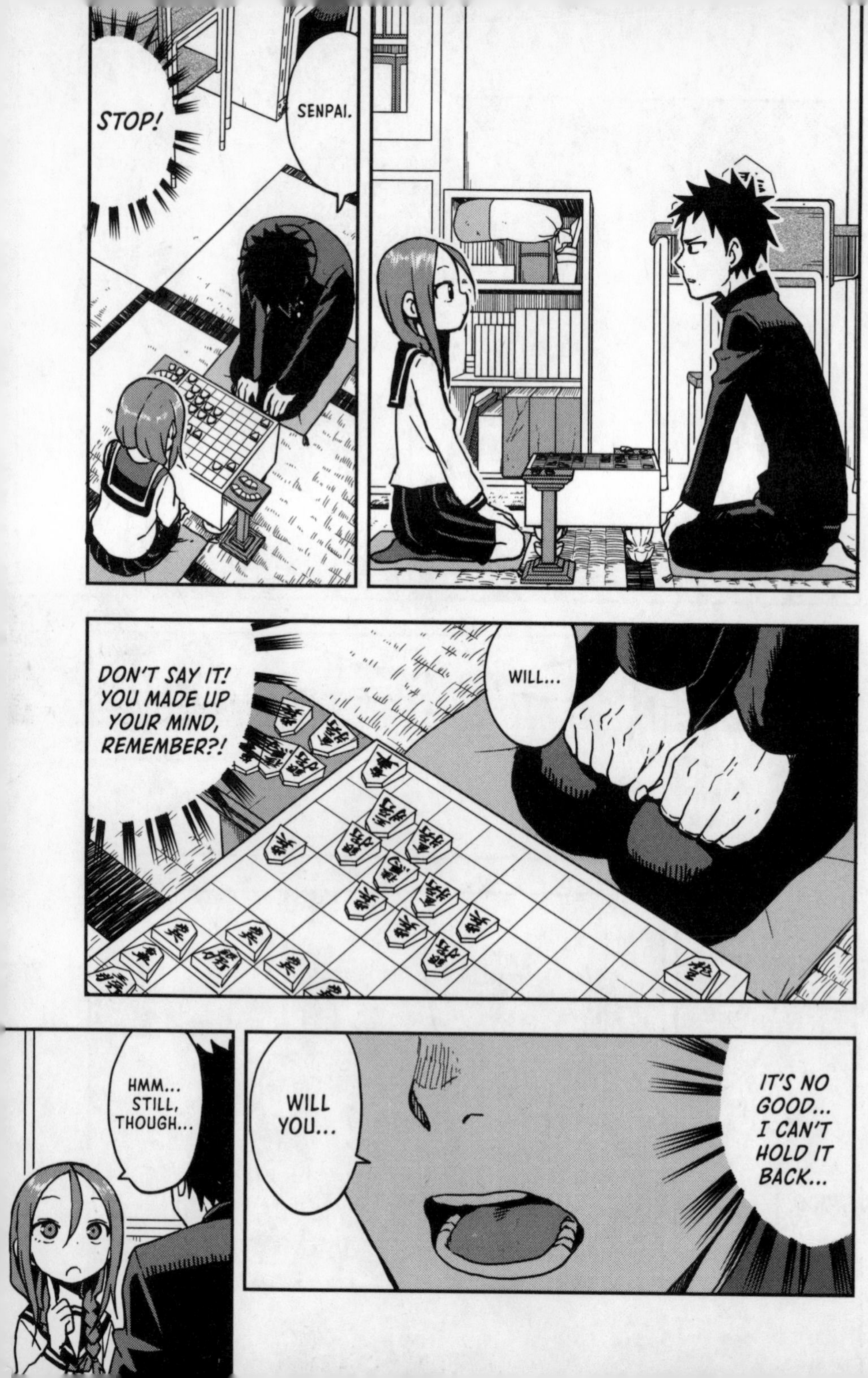
SENPAI.
STOP!
WILL...
DON'T SAY IT! YOU MADE UP YOUR MIND, REMEMBER?!
IT'S NO GOOD... I CAN'T HOLD IT BACK...
WILL YOU...
HMM... STILL, THOUGH...

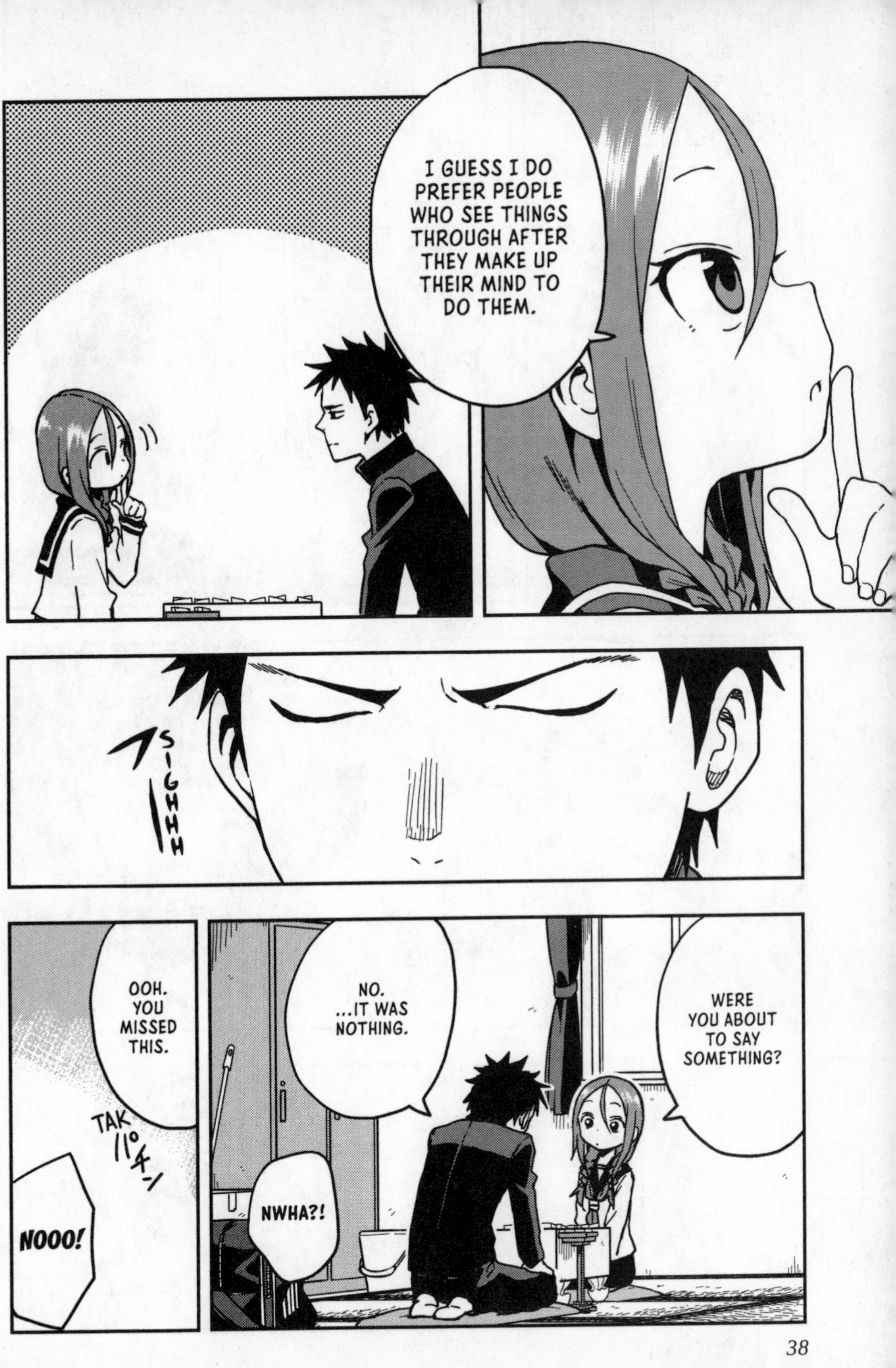
I GUESS I DO PREFER PEOPLE WHO SEE THINGS THROUGH AFTER THEY MAKE UP THEIR MIND TO DO THEM.
SIGHHH
WERE YOU ABOUT TO SAY SOMETHING?
NO. ...IT WAS NOTHING.
NWHA?!
OOH. YOU MISSED THIS.
TAK
パチン
NOOO!

GAME 18 RECORD

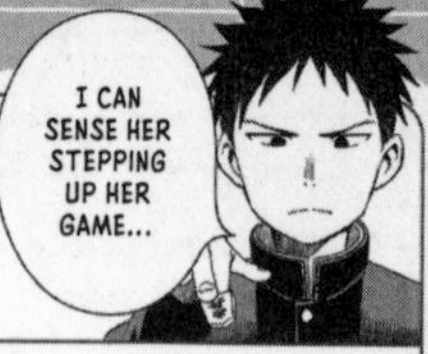
I CAN SENSE HER STEPPING UP HER GAME...

▲ BLACK (SENTE): AYUMU TANAKA △ WHITE (GOTE): URUSHI YAOTOME

(DIAGRAM SHOWS BOARD AFTER MOVE 68, △ +B×3A)

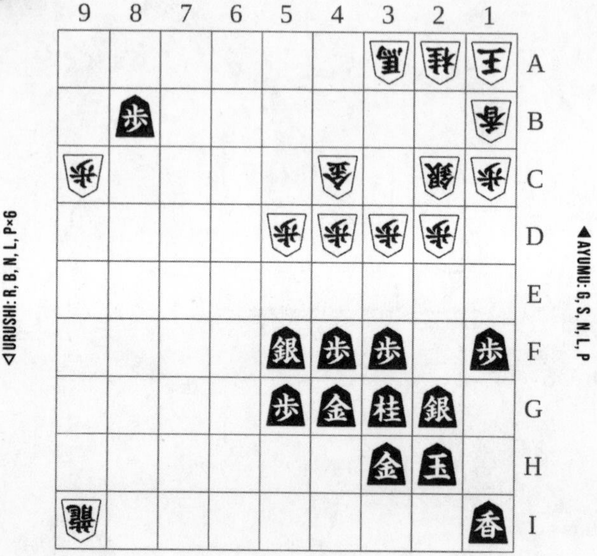
◁URUSHI: R, B, N, L, P×6
▲AYUMU: G, S, N, L, P

▲ P-7F	△ P-3D
▲ P-6F	△ P-8D
▲ R-6H	△ S-6B
▲ K-4H	△ K-4B
▲ K-3H	△ K-3B
▲ K-2H	△ P-5D
▲ S-3H	△ G6A-5B
▲ S-7H	△ B-3C
▲ S-6G	△ P-8E
▲ B-7G	△ K-2B
▲ G6I-5H	△ L-1B
▲ P-4F	△ K-1A
▲ P-3F	△ S-2B
▲ N-3G	△ P-4D
▲ G-4G	△ S-5C
▲ P-6E	△ G-3A
▲ P-2F	△ P-7D
▲ P-1F	△ B-4B
▲ S-2G	△ G-4C
▲ G-3H	△ P-6D
▲ P×6D	△ S×6D
▲ P-2E	△ P-7E
▲ P×7E	△ S×7E
▲ R-7H	△ P-8F
▲ P×8F	△ S×8F
▲ B×8F	△ B×8F
▲ R-7A+	△ R-8D
▲ P×8B	△ B-5C
▲ +R×8A	△ R×8I+
▲ +R×9A	△ +R×9I
▲ S-5F	△ B×9G+
▲ P-2D	△ P×2D
▲ P×2C	△ S×2C
▲ +R×3A	△ +B×3A

(WHITE WINS AT MOVE 68)

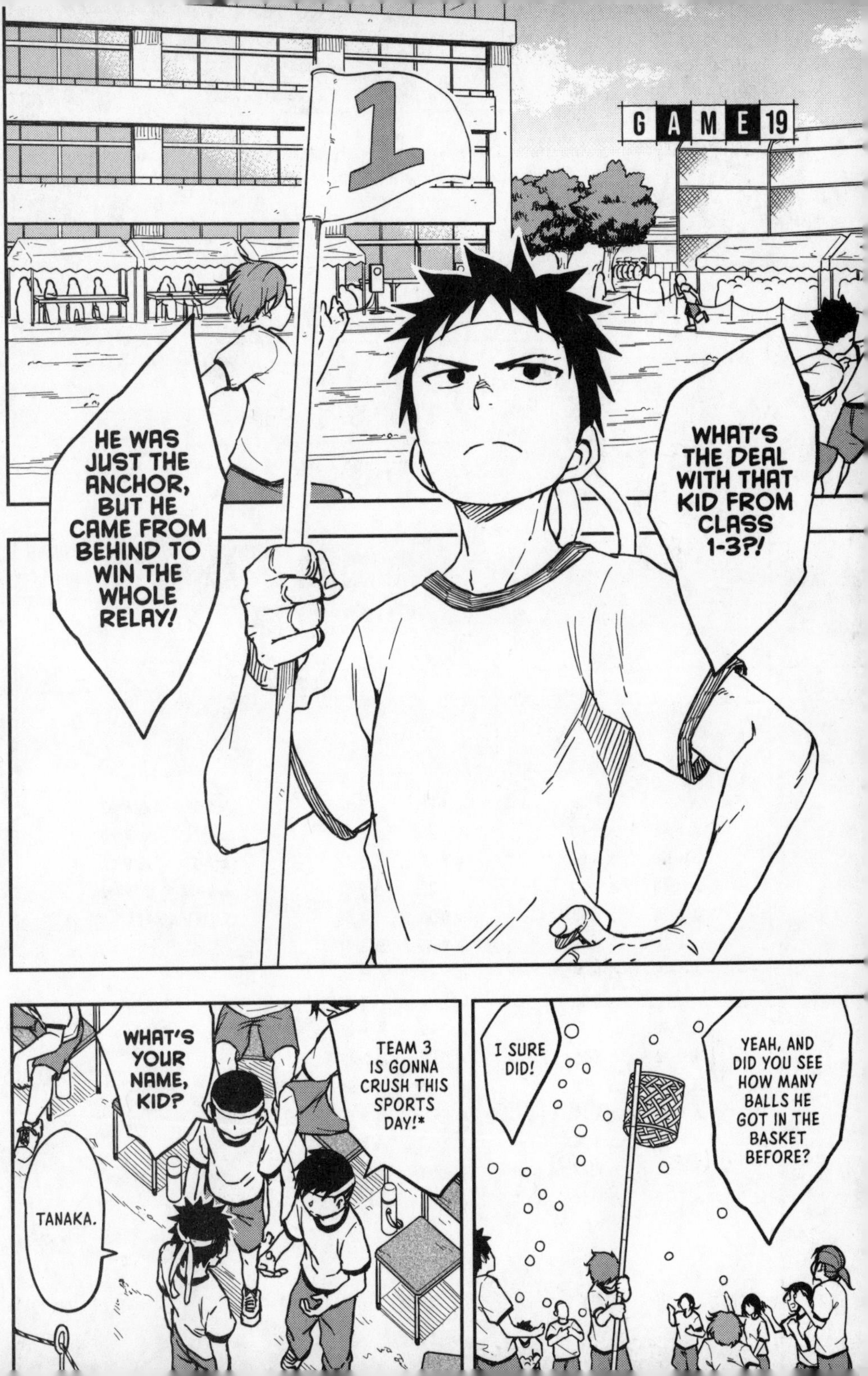
GAME 19
WHAT'S THE DEAL WITH THAT KID FROM CLASS 1-3?!
HE WAS JUST THE ANCHOR, BUT HE CAME FROM BEHIND TO WIN THE WHOLE RELAY!
YEAH, AND DID YOU SEE HOW MANY BALLS HE GOT IN THE BASKET BEFORE?
I SURE DID!
TEAM 3 IS GONNA CRUSH THIS SPORTS DAY!*
WHAT'S YOUR NAME, KID?
TANAKA.

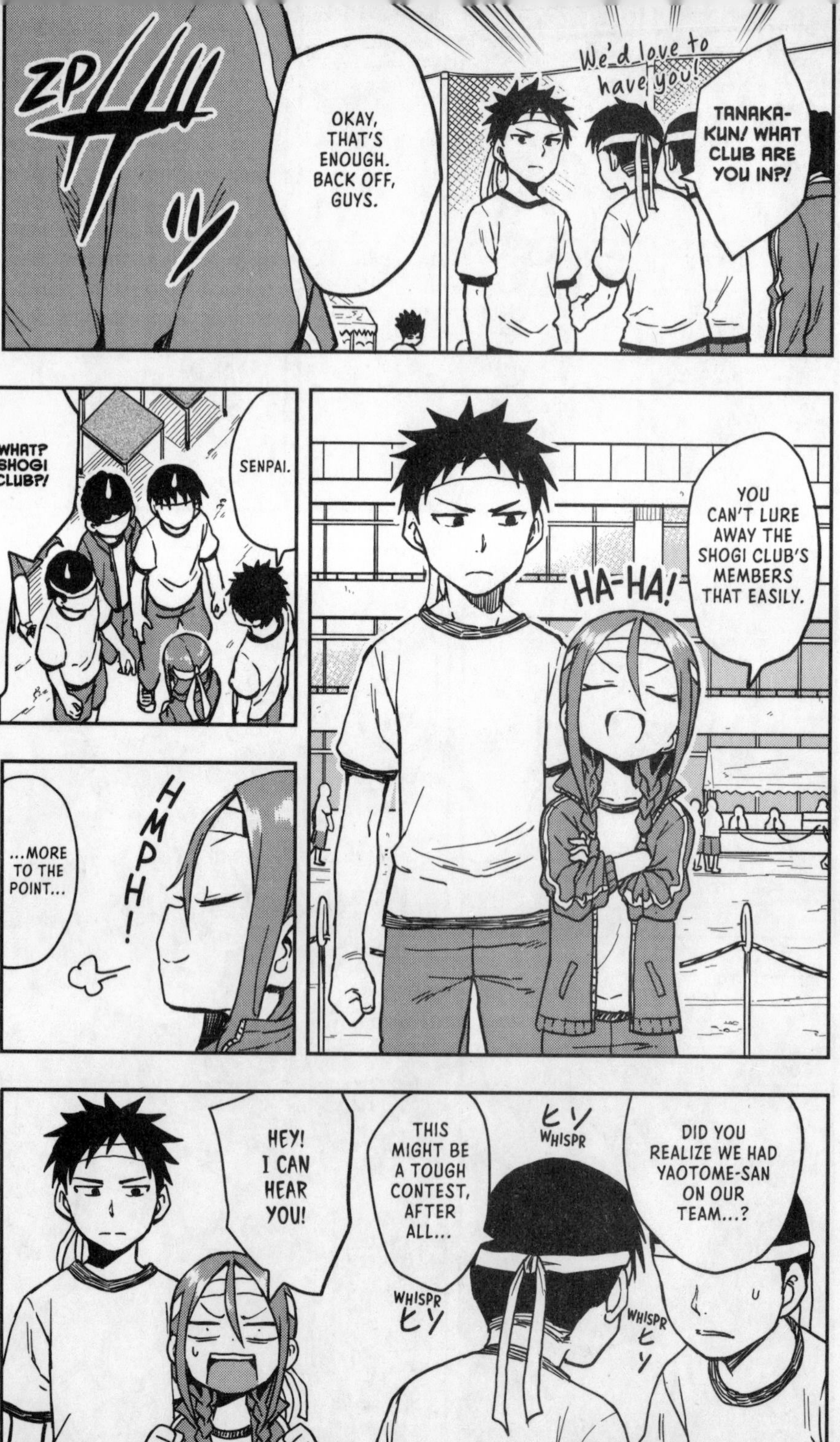
We'd love to have you!
TANAKA-KUN! WHAT CLUB ARE YOU IN?!
OKAY, THAT'S ENOUGH. BACK OFF, GUYS.
ZP
YOU CAN'T LURE AWAY THE SHOGI CLUB'S MEMBERS THAT EASILY.
HA-HA!
SENPAI.
WHAT? SHOGI CLUB?!
WHAT A WASTE!
HMPH!
...MORE TO THE POINT...
DID YOU REALIZE WE HAD YAOTOME-SAN ON OUR TEAM...?
ヒソ WHISPR
WHISPR ヒソ
THIS MIGHT BE A TOUGH CONTEST, AFTER ALL...
WHISPR ヒソ
HEY! I CAN HEAR YOU!

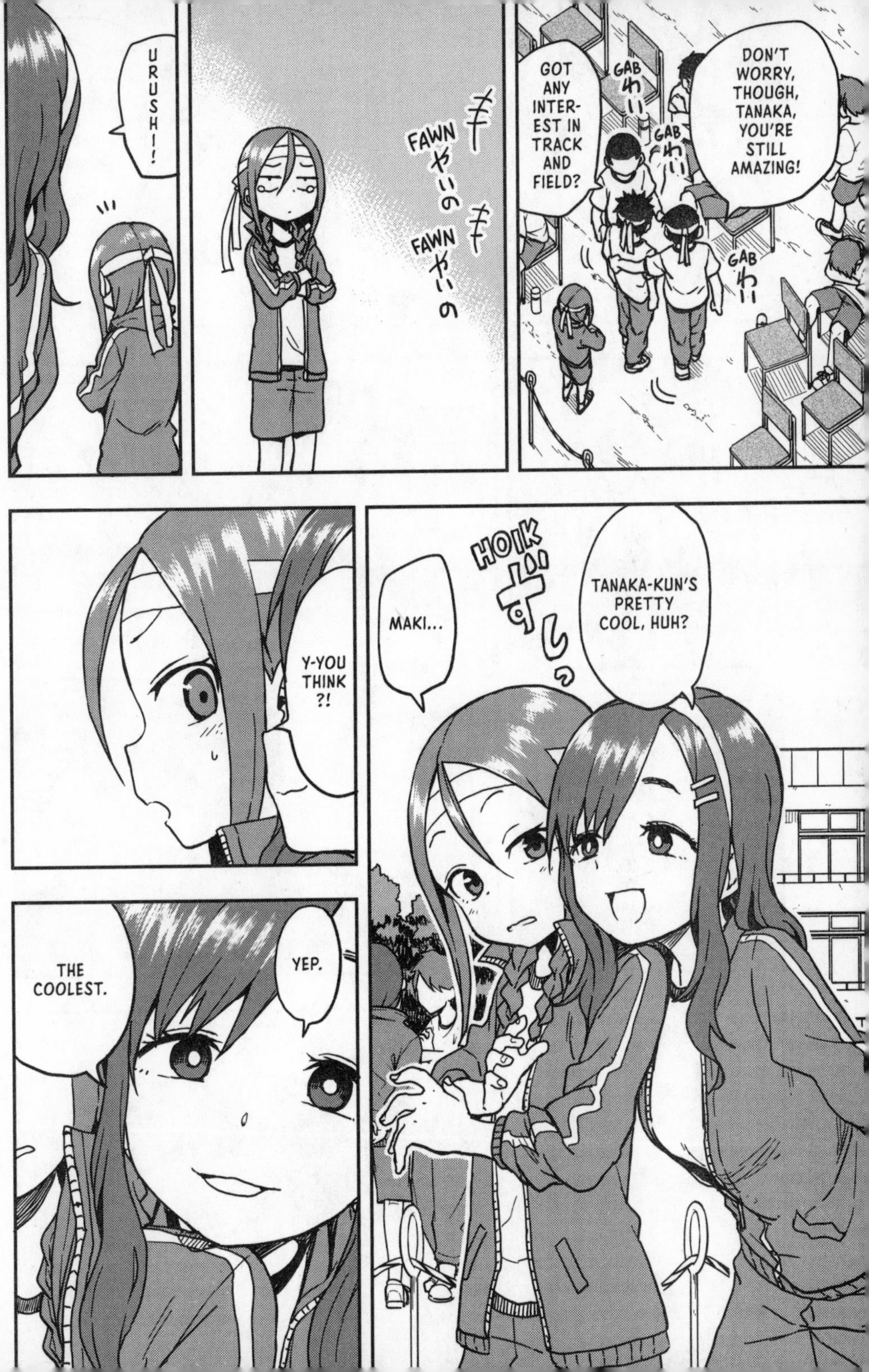
DON'T WORRY, THOUGH, TANAKA, YOU'RE STILL AMAZING!
GOT ANY INTEREST IN TRACK AND FIELD?
GAB
GAB
GAB
FAWN
FAWN
URUSH!!
TANAKA-KUN'S PRETTY COOL, HUH?
HOIK
MAKI...
Y-YOU THINK ?!
YEP.
THE COOLEST.

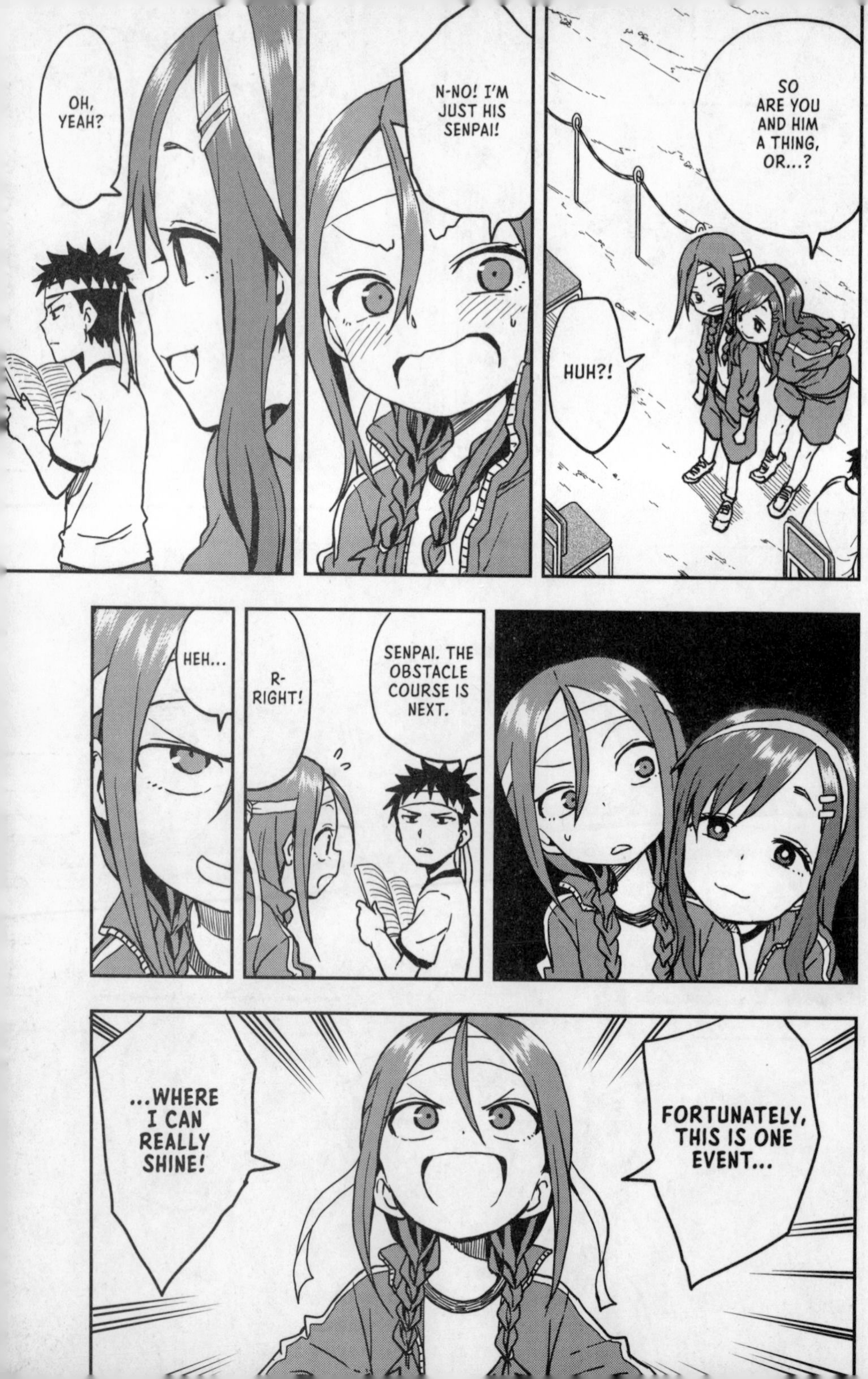
SO ARE YOU AND HIM A THING, OR...?
HUH?!
N-NO! I'M JUST HIS SENPAI!
OH, YEAH?
SENPAI. THE OBSTACLE COURSE IS NEXT.
R-RIGHT!
HEH...
FORTUNATELY, THIS IS ONE EVENT...
...WHERE I CAN REALLY SHINE!

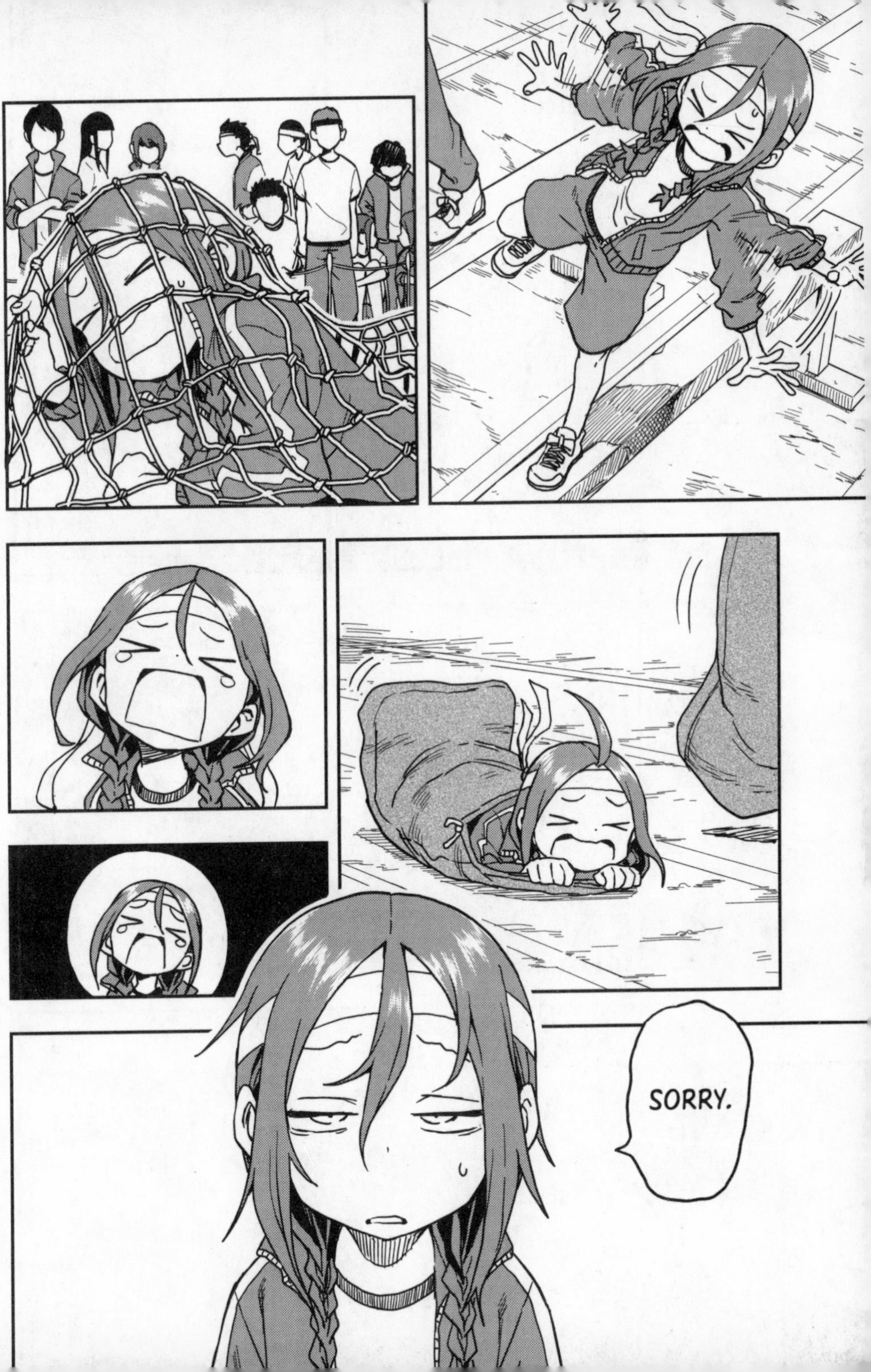
SORRY.

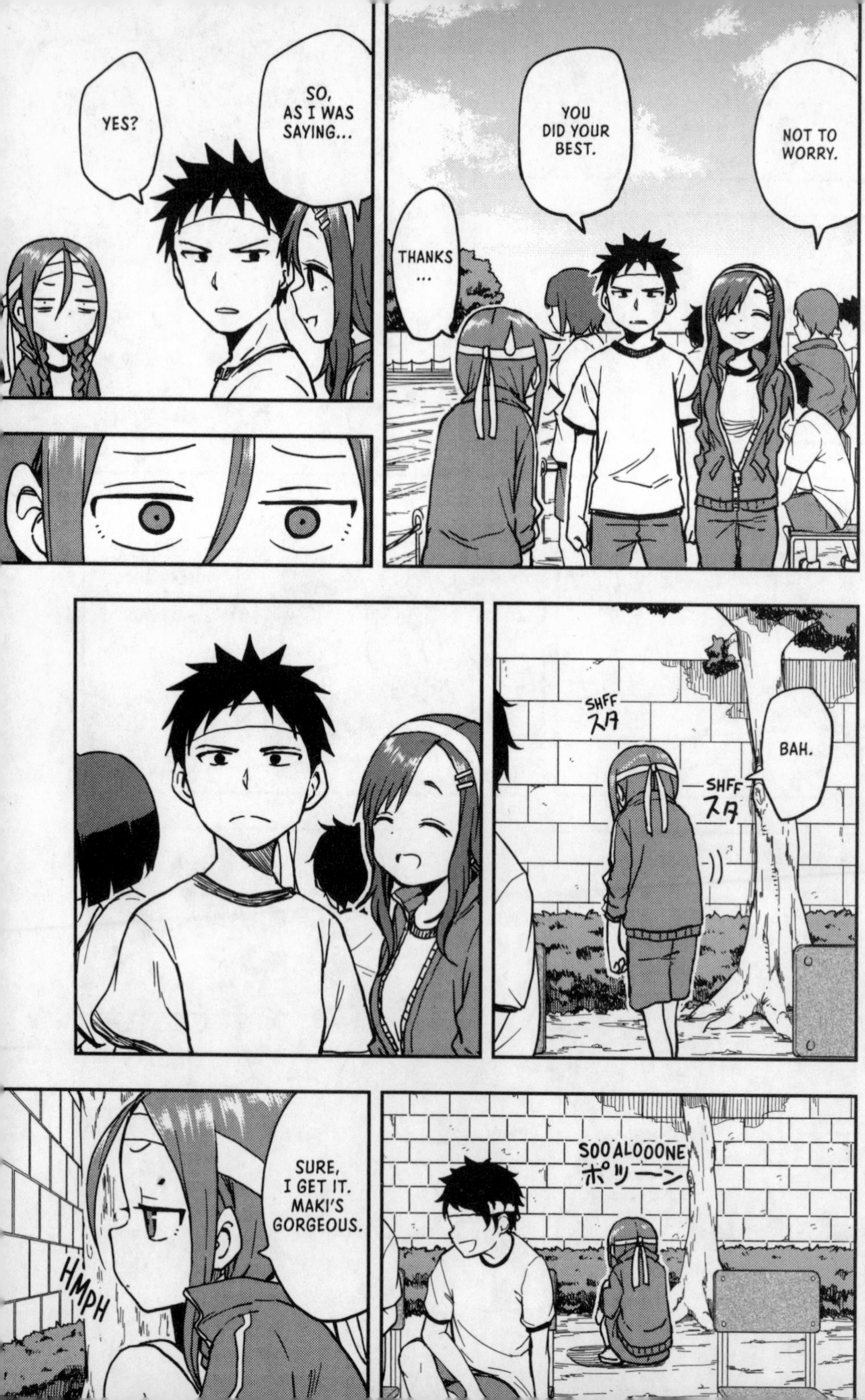
NOT TO WORRY.
YOU DID YOUR BEST.
THANKS...
SO, AS I WAS SAYING...
YES?
BAH.
SHFF
スタ
SHFF
スタ
SOO ALOOONE
ポツーン
SURE, I GET IT. MAKI'S GORGEOUS.
HMPH

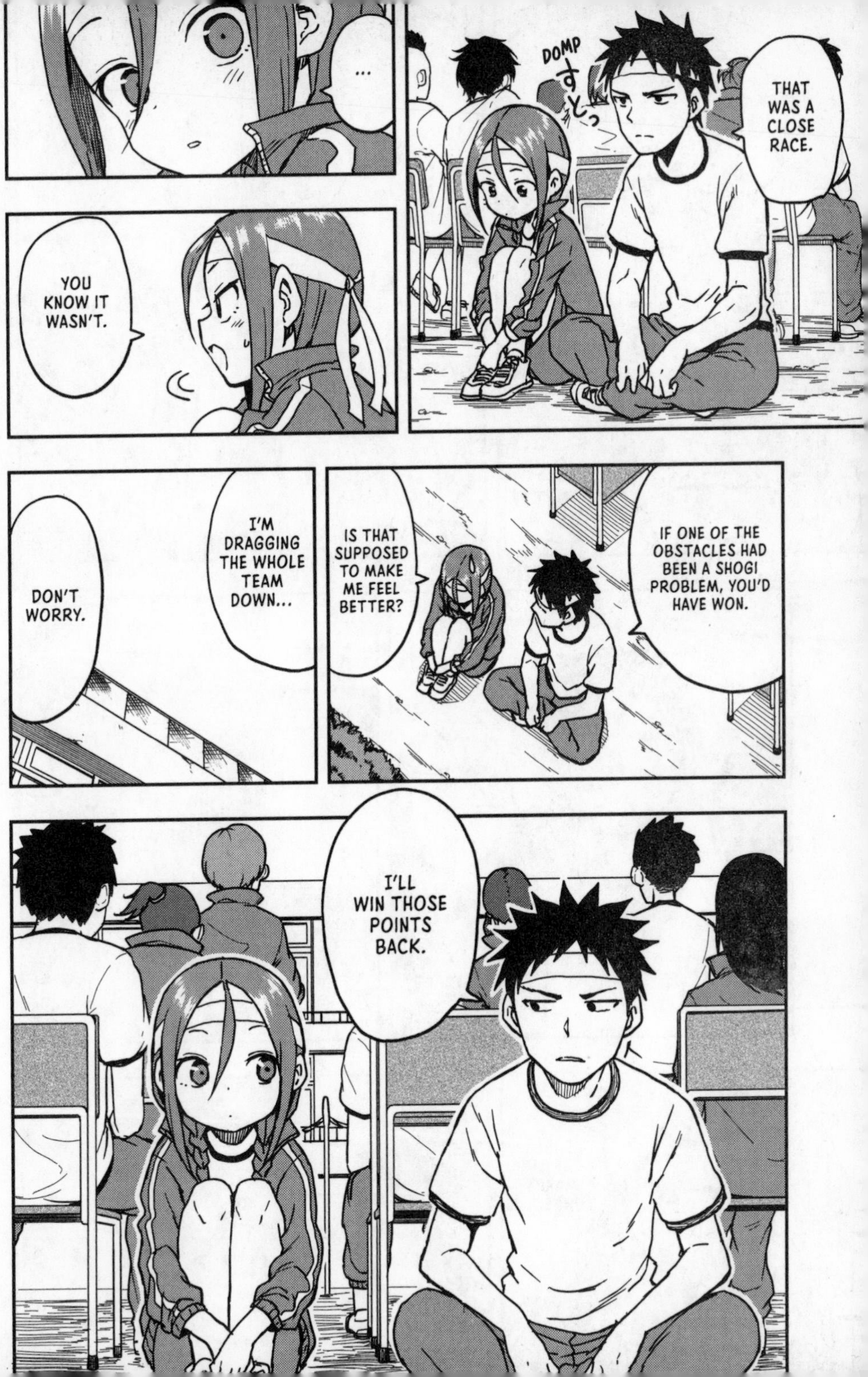
DOMP
すとっ
THAT WAS A CLOSE RACE.
...
YOU KNOW IT WASN'T.
IF ONE OF THE OBSTACLES HAD BEEN A SHOGI PROBLEM, YOU'D HAVE WON.
IS THAT SUPPOSED TO MAKE ME FEEL BETTER?
I'M DRAGGING THE WHOLE TEAM DOWN...
DON'T WORRY.
I'LL WIN THOSE POINTS BACK.

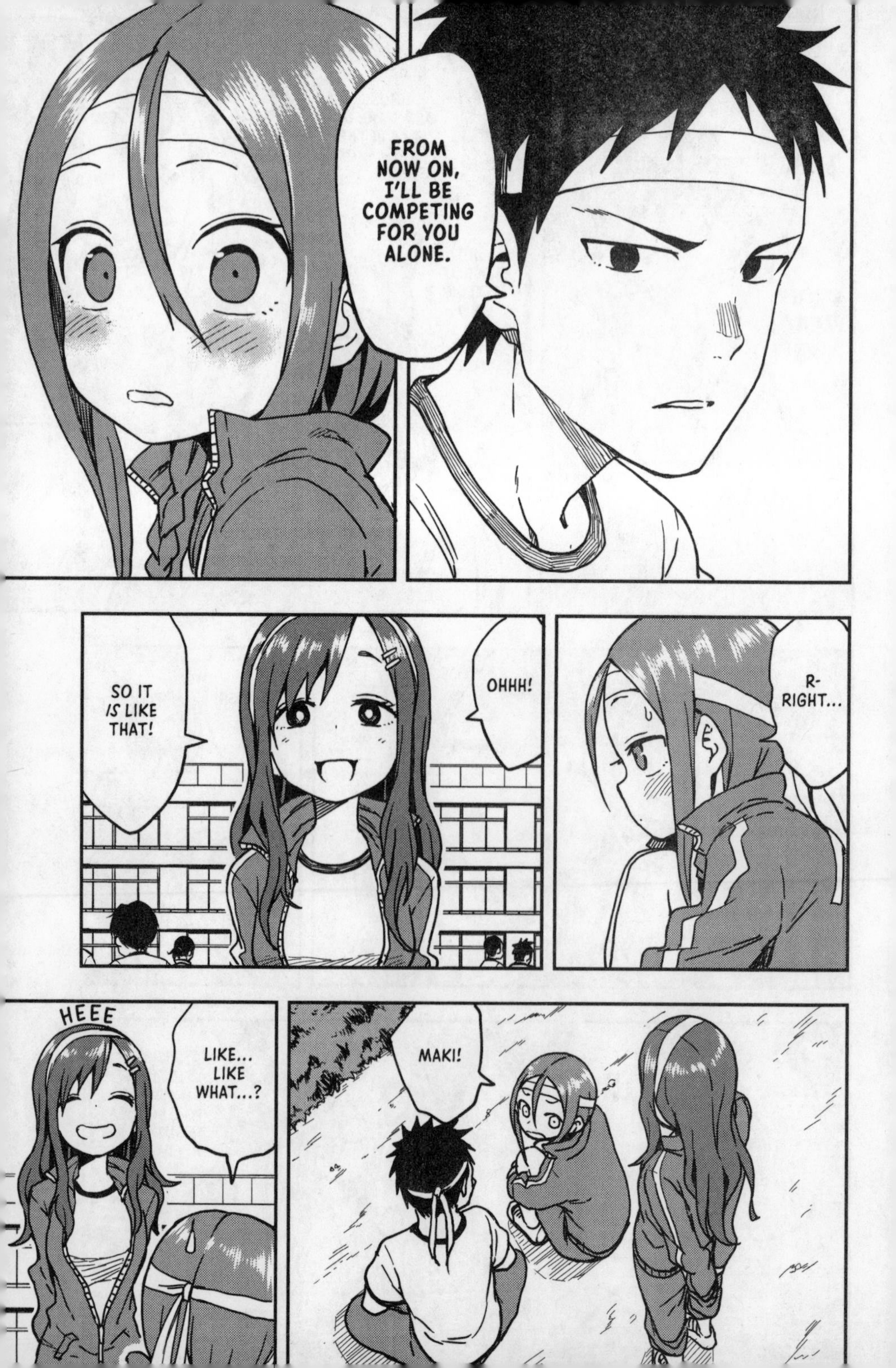
FROM NOW ON, I'LL BE COMPETING FOR YOU ALONE.
R- RIGHT...
OHHH!
SO IT *IS* LIKE THAT!
MAKI!
LIKE... LIKE WHAT...?
HEEE

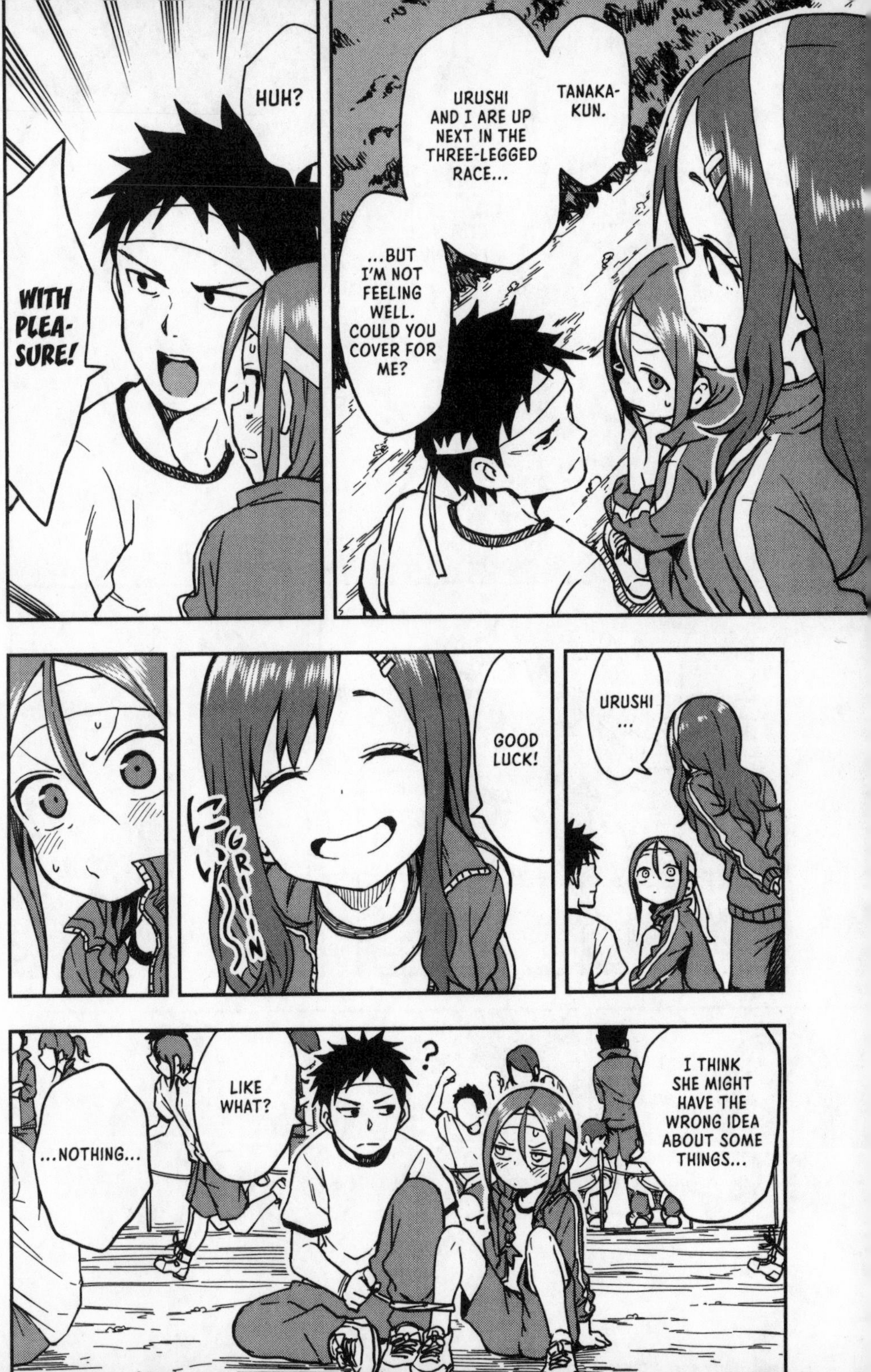
TANAKA-KUN.
URUSHI AND I ARE UP NEXT IN THE THREE-LEGGED RACE...
...BUT I'M NOT FEELING WELL. COULD YOU COVER FOR ME?
HUH?
WITH PLEA-SURE!
URUSHI ...
GOOD LUCK!
GRIIIN
I THINK SHE MIGHT HAVE THE WRONG IDEA ABOUT SOME THINGS...
LIKE WHAT?
...NOTHING...

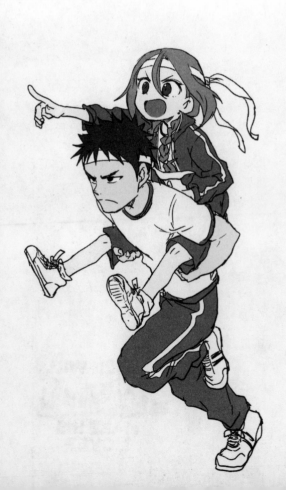

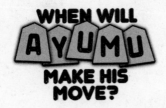
WHEN WILL AYUMU MAKE HIS MOVE?

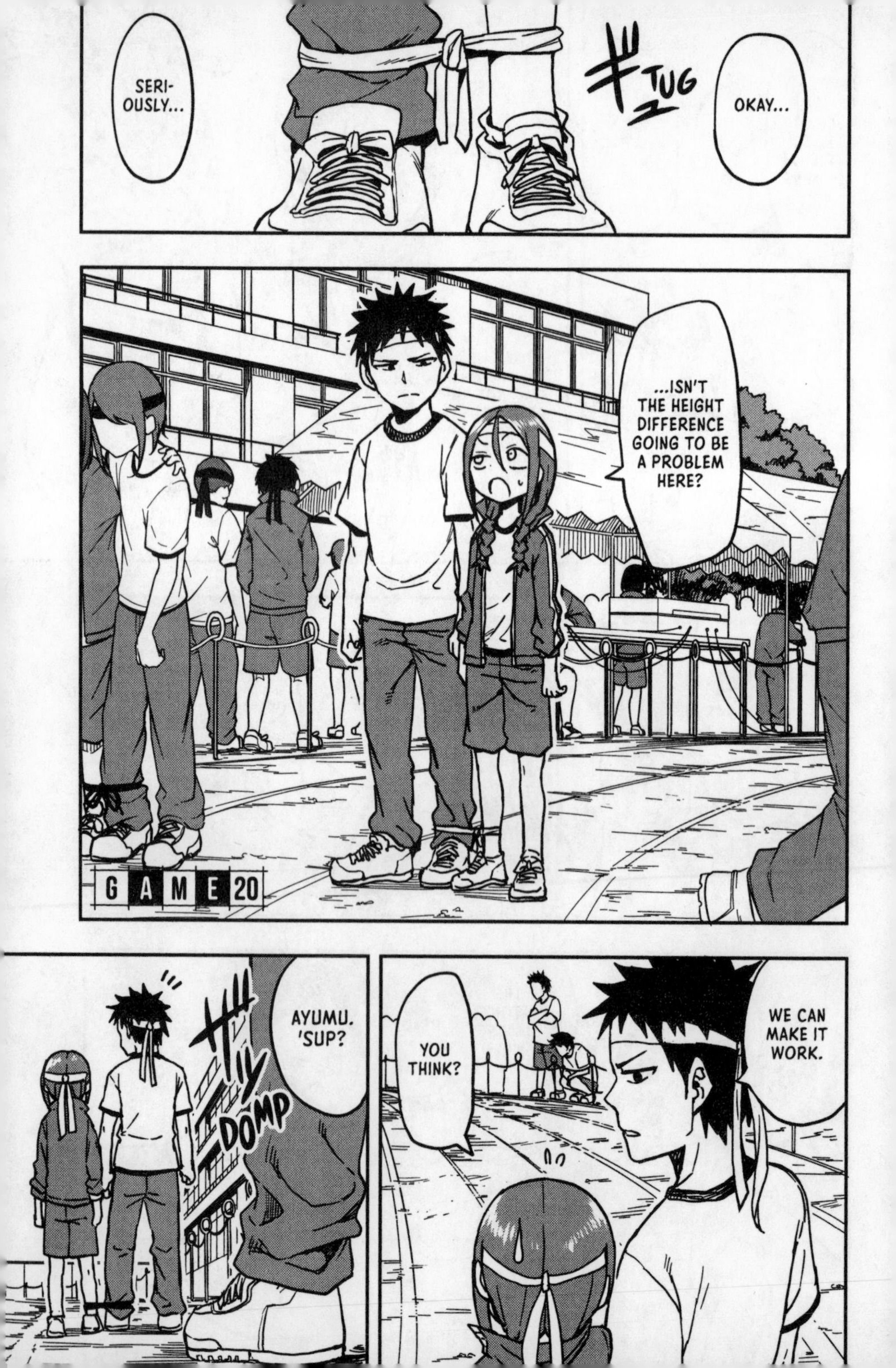
OKAY...
TUG
SERI-OUSLY...
...ISN'T THE HEIGHT DIFFERENCE GOING TO BE A PROBLEM HERE?
GAME 20
WE CAN MAKE IT WORK.
YOU THINK?
AYUMU. 'SUP?
DOMP

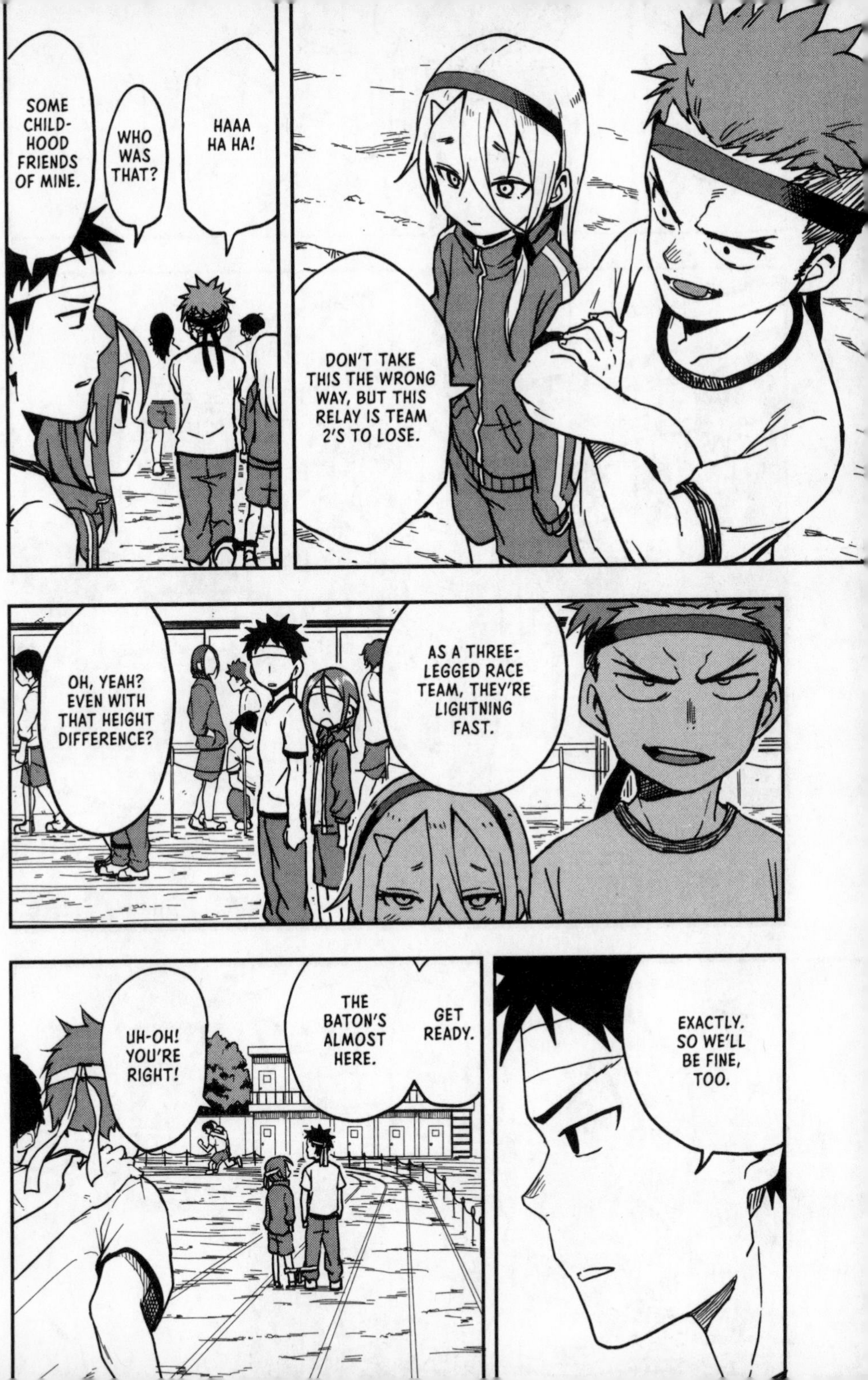
DON'T TAKE THIS THE WRONG WAY, BUT THIS RELAY IS TEAM 2'S TO LOSE.
HAAAA HA HA!
WHO WAS THAT?
SOME CHILD-HOOD FRIENDS OF MINE.
AS A THREE-LEGGED RACE TEAM, THEY'RE LIGHTNING FAST.
OH, YEAH? EVEN WITH THAT HEIGHT DIFFERENCE?
EXACTLY. SO WE'LL BE FINE, TOO.
GET READY.
THE BATON'S ALMOST HERE.
UH-OH! YOU'RE RIGHT!

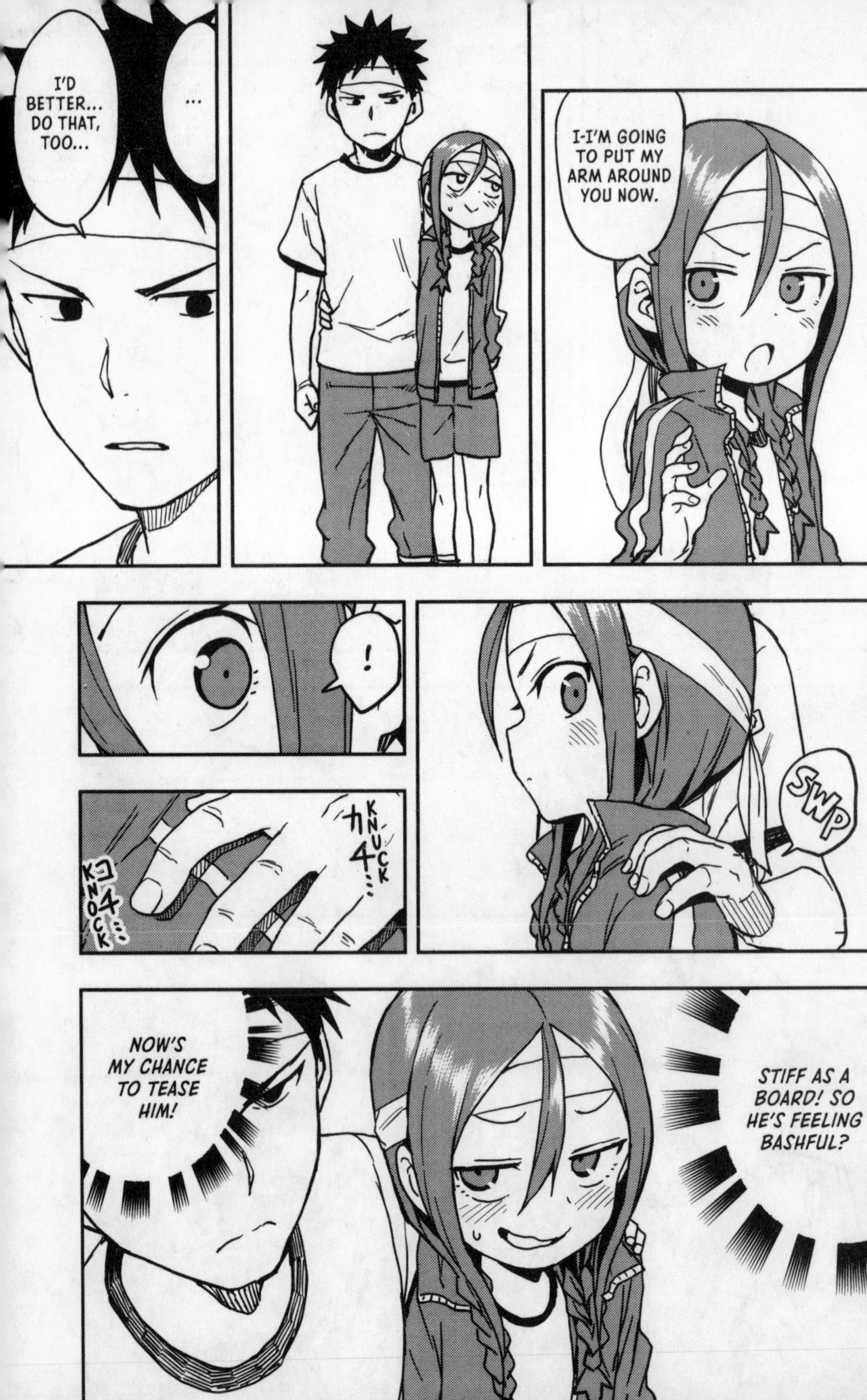
I-I'M GOING TO PUT MY ARM AROUND YOU NOW.
...
I'D BETTER... DO THAT, TOO...
SWP
!
KNUCK...
KNOCK...
STIFF AS A BOARD! SO HE'S FEELING BASHFUL?
NOW'S MY CHANCE TO TEASE HIM!

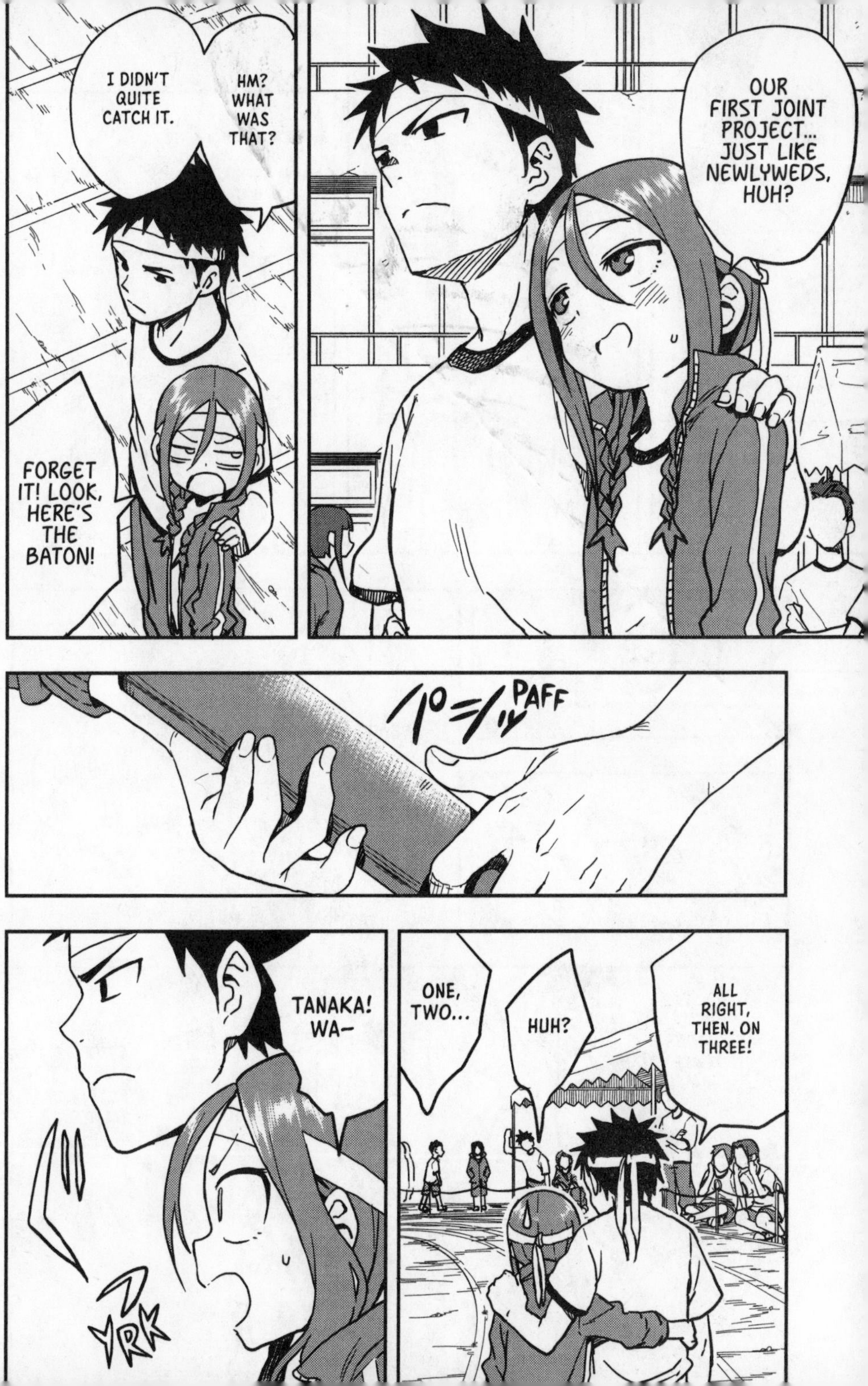
OUR FIRST JOINT PROJECT... JUST LIKE NEWLYWEDS, HUH?
HM? WHAT WAS THAT?
I DIDN'T QUITE CATCH IT.
FORGET IT! LOOK, HERE'S THE BATON!
PAFF
ALL RIGHT, THEN. ON THREE!
HUH?
ONE, TWO...
TANAKA! WA-
YRK

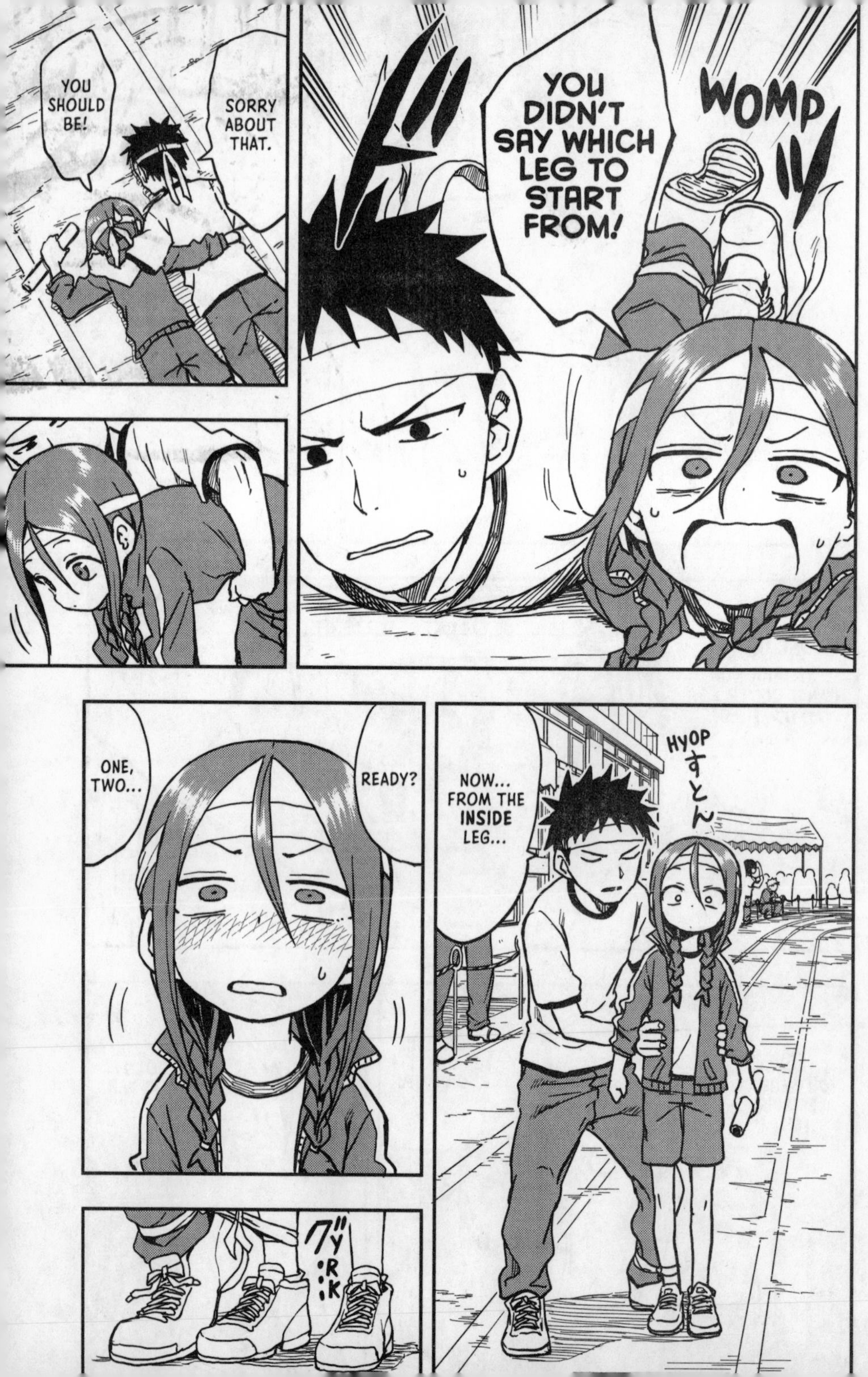
WOMP
YOU DIDN'T SAY WHICH LEG TO START FROM!
SORRY ABOUT THAT.
YOU SHOULD BE!
HYOP すとん
NOW... FROM THE INSIDE LEG...
READY?
ONE, TWO...
グッ YRK

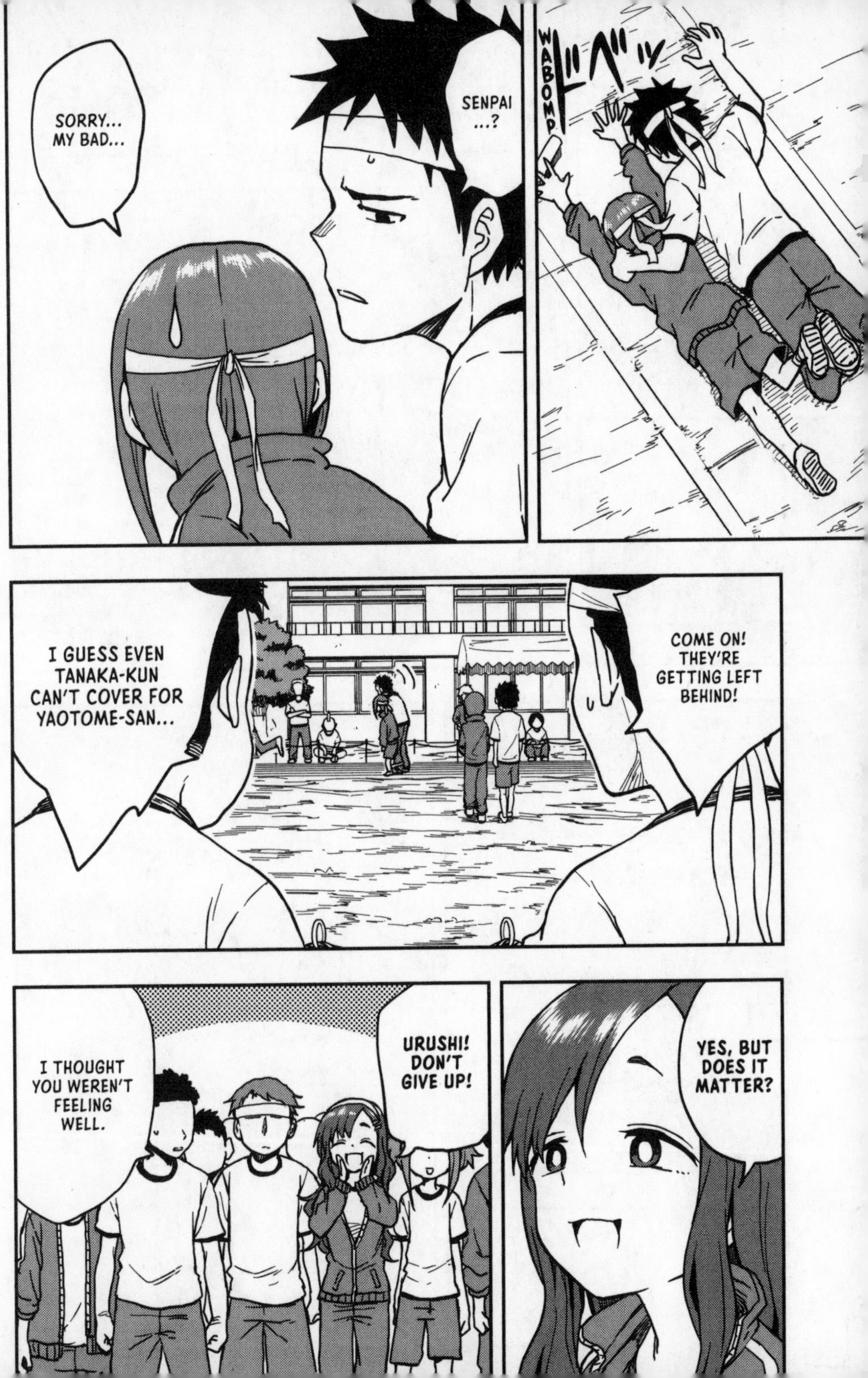
WABOMP
SENPAI ...?
SORRY... MY BAD...
COME ON! THEY'RE GETTING LEFT BEHIND!
I GUESS EVEN TANAKA-KUN CAN'T COVER FOR YAOTOME-SAN...
YES, BUT DOES IT MATTER?
URUSHI! DON'T GIVE UP!
I THOUGHT YOU WEREN'T FEELING WELL.

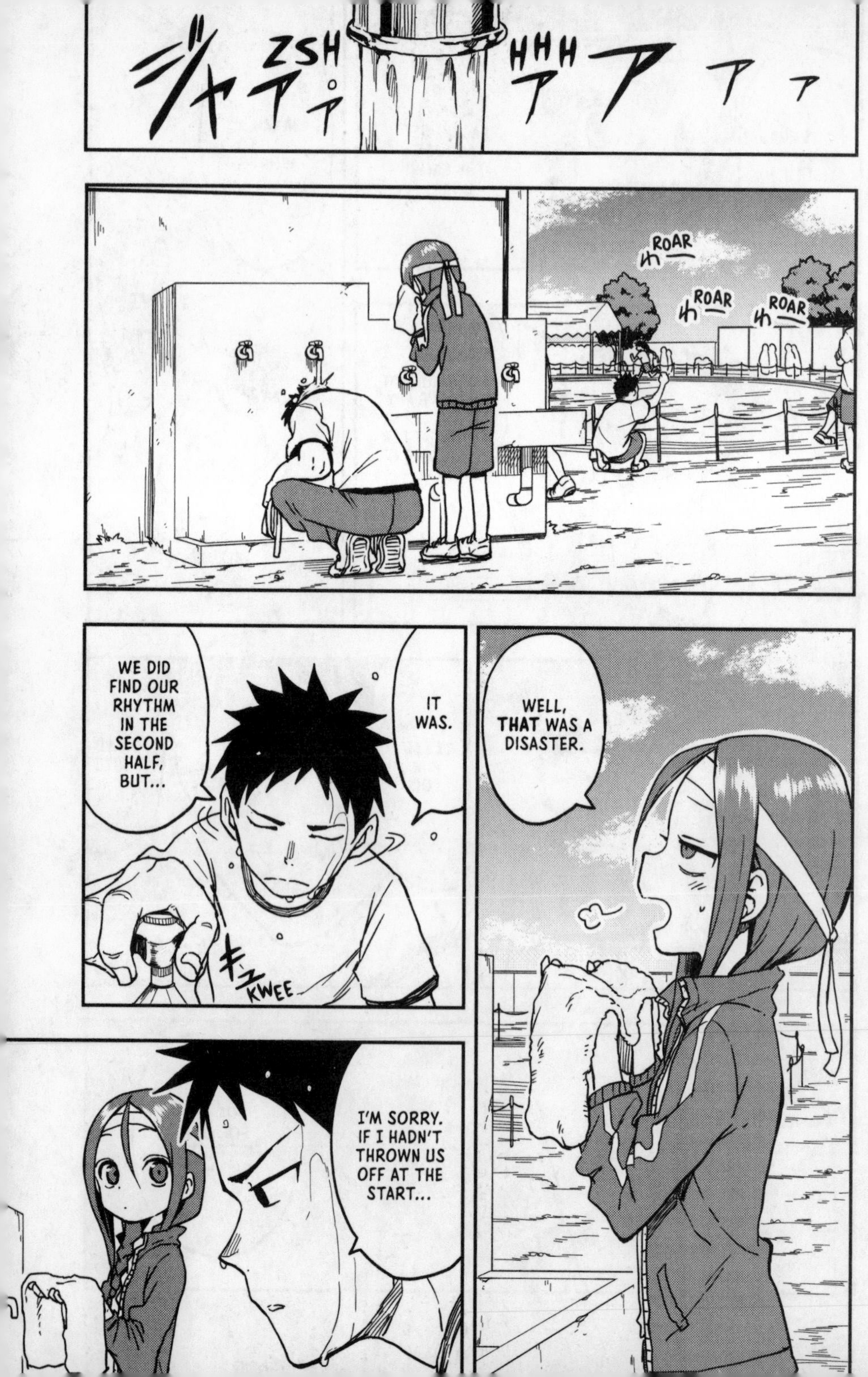
ジャアァアアアァ
ZSHHHH
ROAR
ROAR
ROAR
WELL, THAT WAS A DISASTER.
IT WAS.
WE DID FIND OUR RHYTHM IN THE SECOND HALF, BUT...
KWEE
I'M SORRY. IF I HADN'T THROWN US OFF AT THE START...

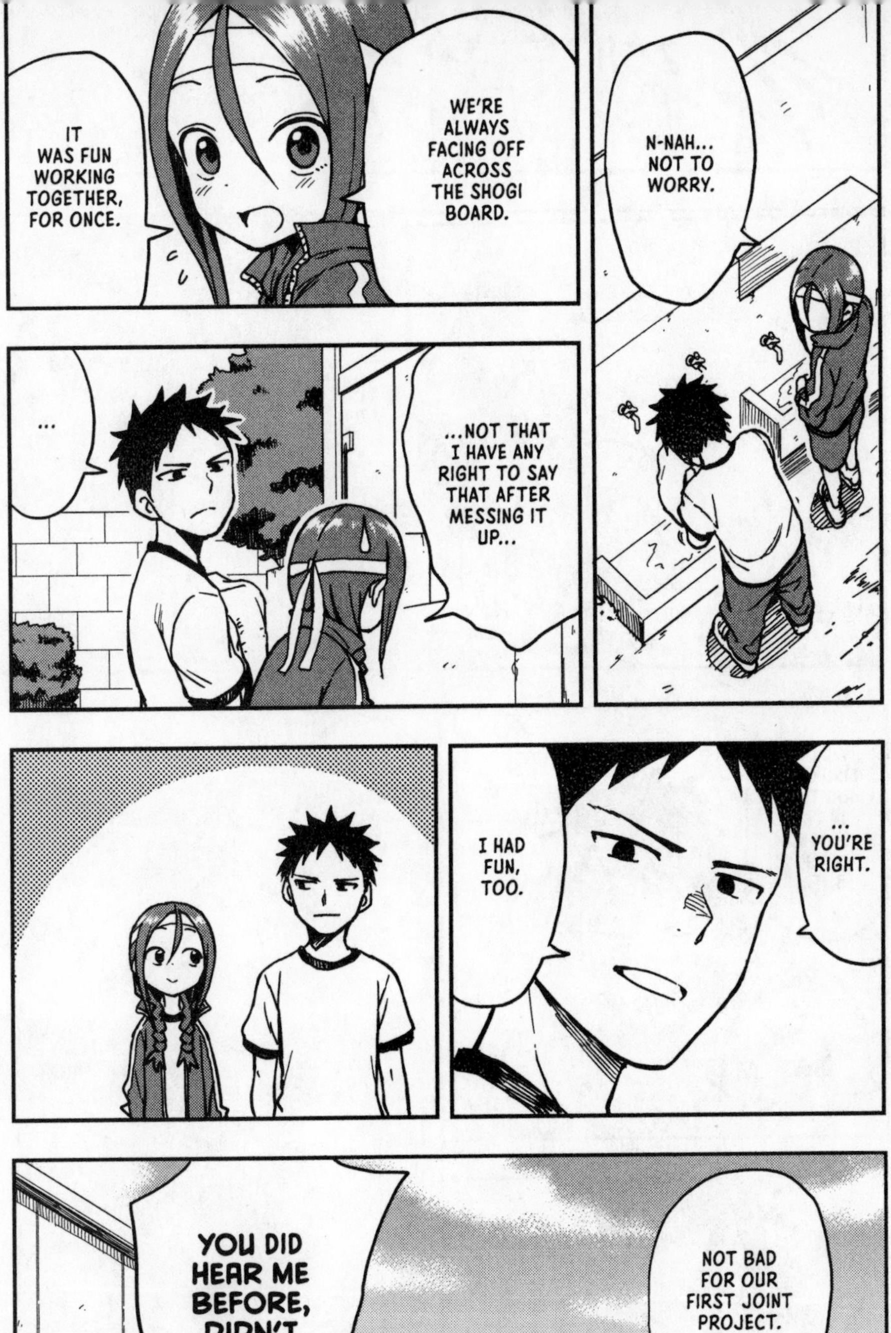
N-NAH... NOT TO WORRY.
WE'RE ALWAYS FACING OFF ACROSS THE SHOGI BOARD.
IT WAS FUN WORKING TOGETHER, FOR ONCE.
...NOT THAT I HAVE ANY RIGHT TO SAY THAT AFTER MESSING IT UP...
...
... YOU'RE RIGHT.
I HAD FUN, TOO.
NOT BAD FOR OUR FIRST JOINT PROJECT.
YOU DID HEAR ME BEFORE, DIDN'T YOU?!

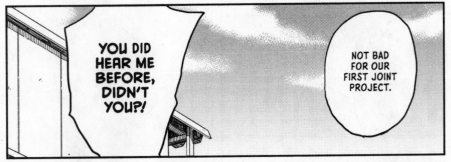

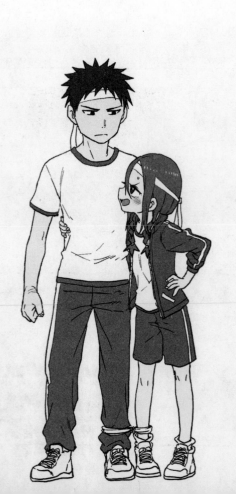

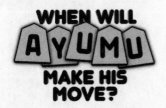
WHEN WILL AYUMU MAKE HIS MOVE?

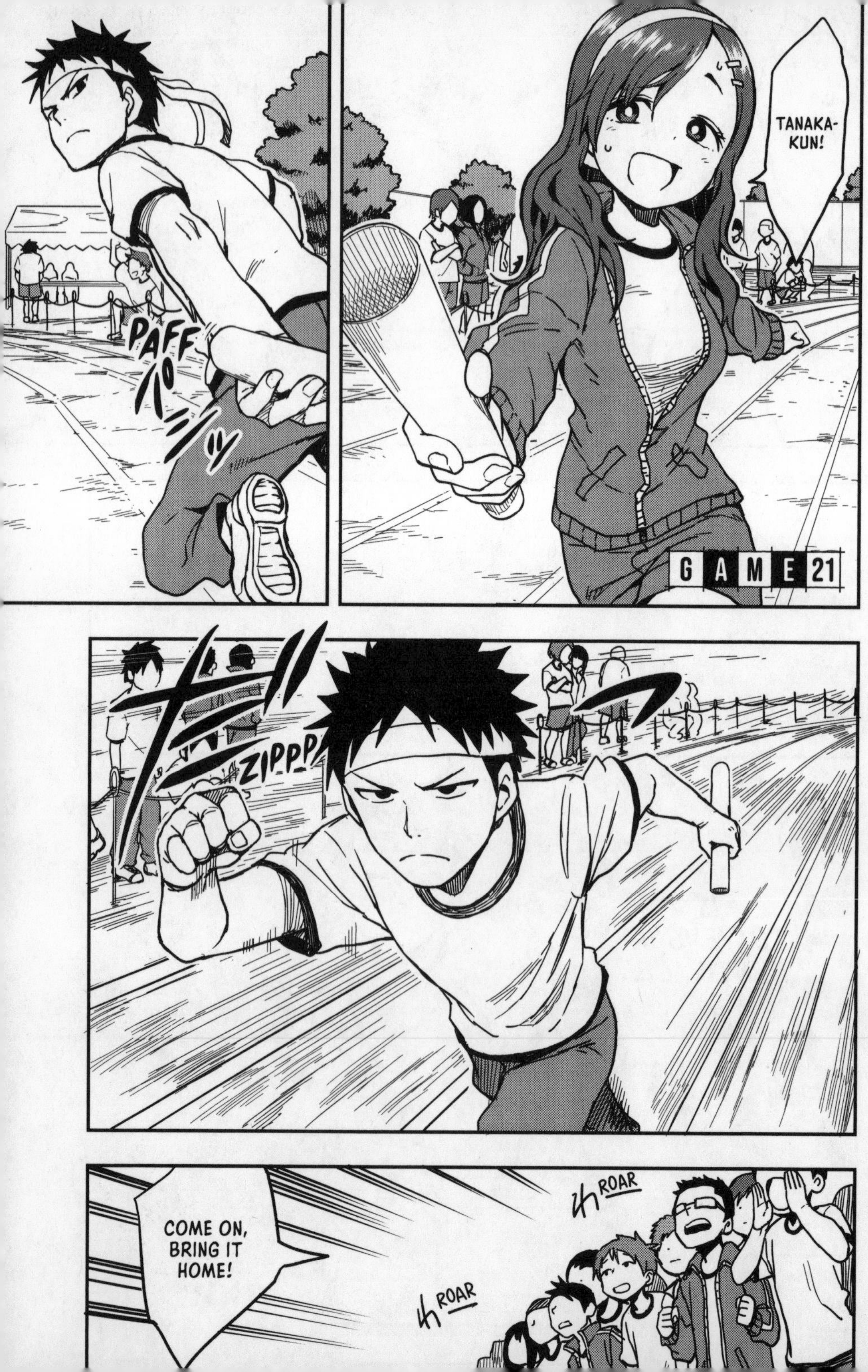
TANAKA-KUN!
GAME 21
PAFF
ZIPPP
COME ON, BRING IT HOME!
ROAR
ROAR

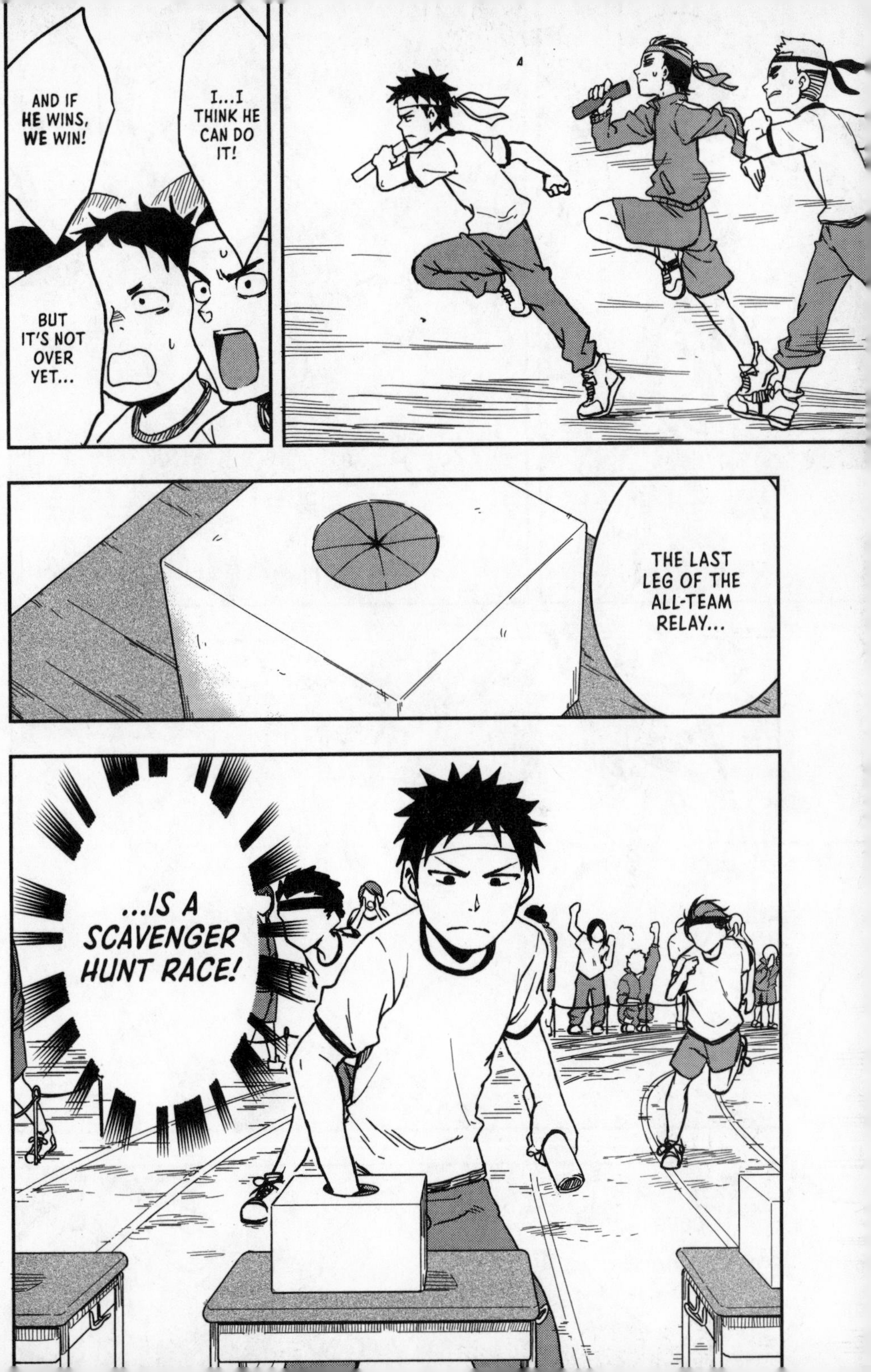
I...I THINK HE CAN DO IT!
AND IF HE WINS, WE WIN!
BUT IT'S NOT OVER YET...
THE LAST LEG OF THE ALL-TEAM RELAY...
...IS A SCAVENGER HUNT RACE!

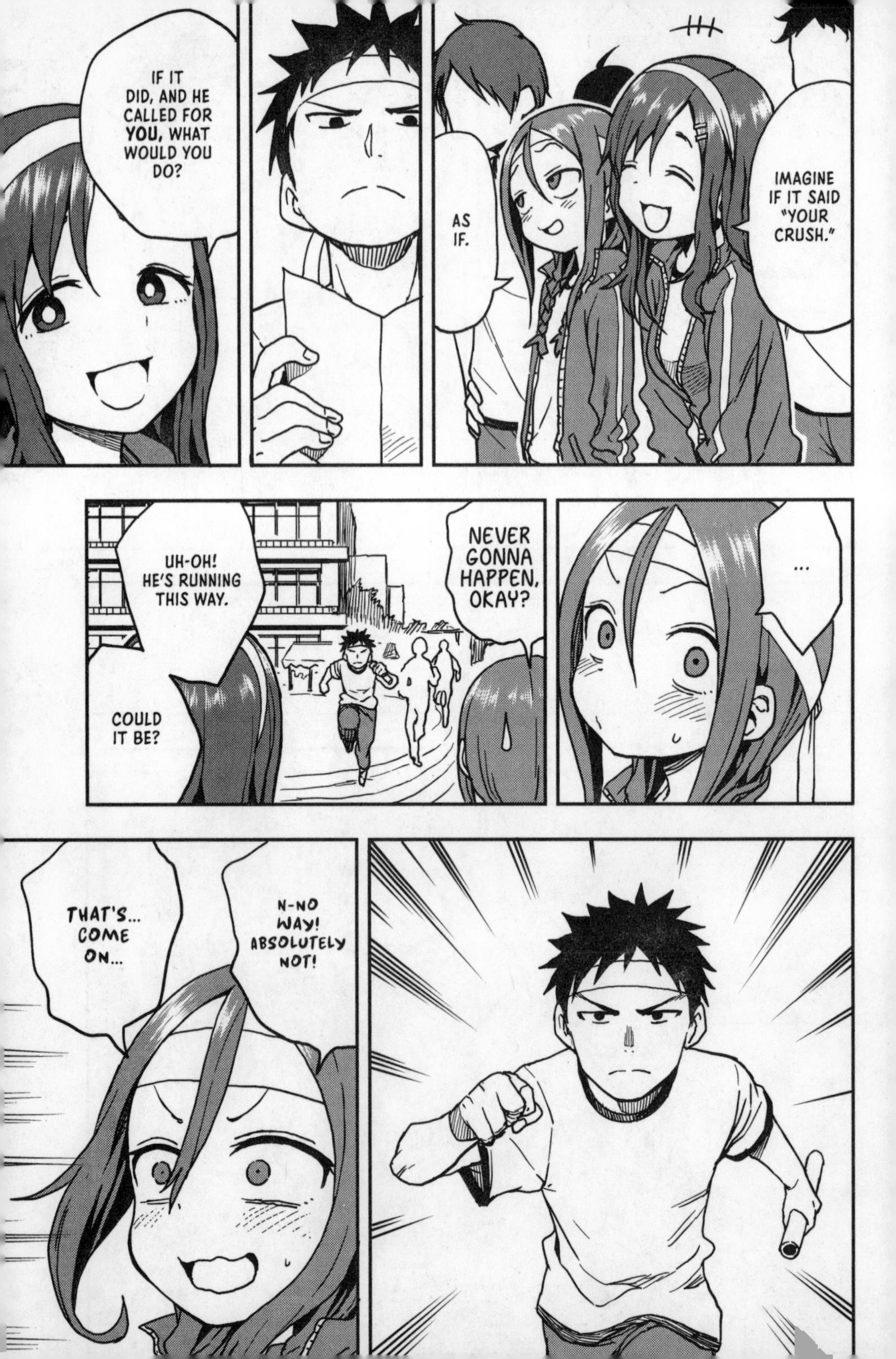
IMAGINE IF IT SAID "YOUR CRUSH."
AS IF.
IF IT DID, AND HE CALLED FOR YOU, WHAT WOULD YOU DO?
...
NEVER GONNA HAPPEN, OKAY?
UH-OH! HE'S RUNNING THIS WAY.
COULD IT BE?
N-NO WAY! ABSOLUTELY NOT!
THAT'S... COME ON...

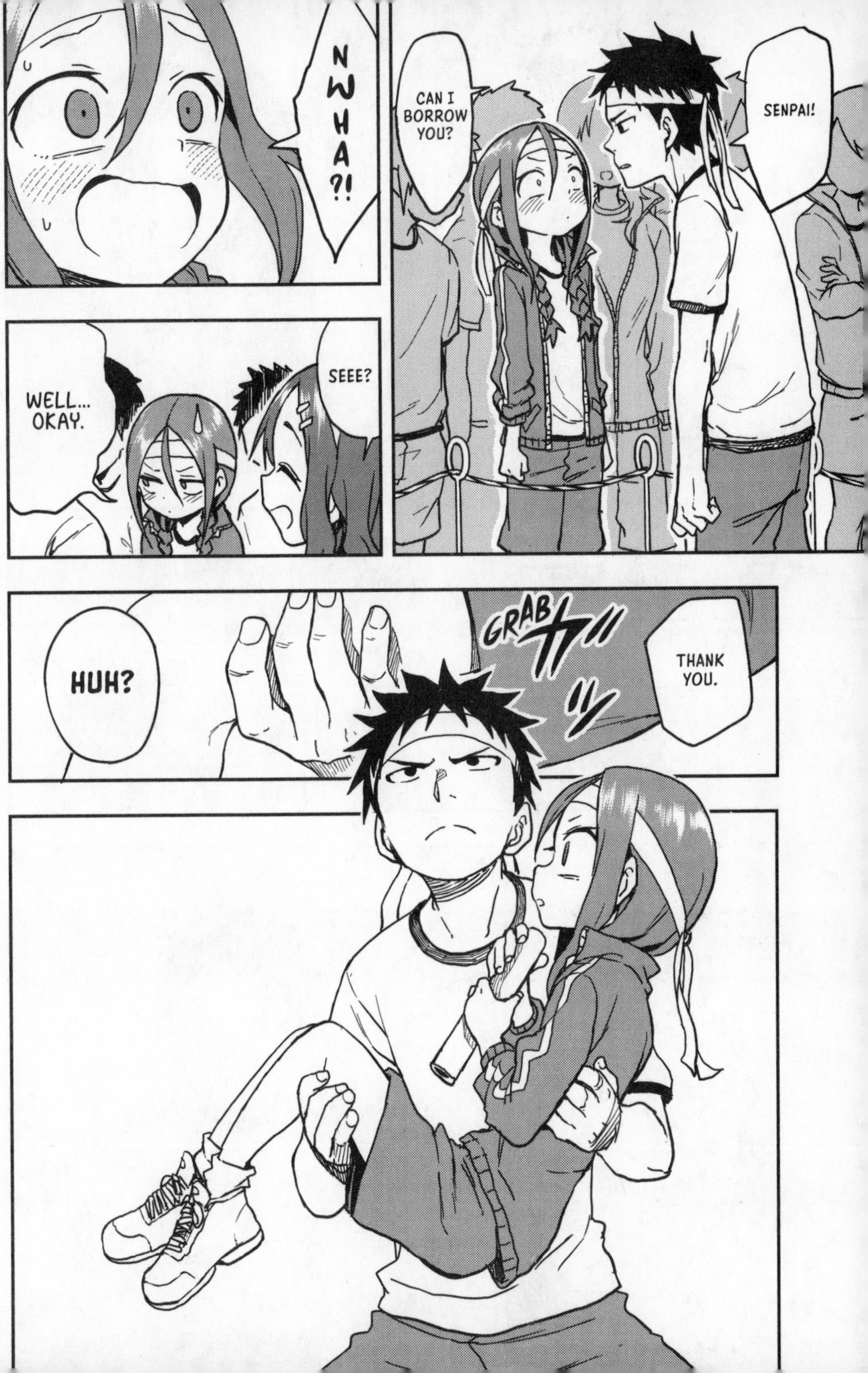
SENPAI!
CAN I BORROW YOU?
NWHA?!
SEEE?
WELL... OKAY.
THANK YOU.
GRAB
HUH?

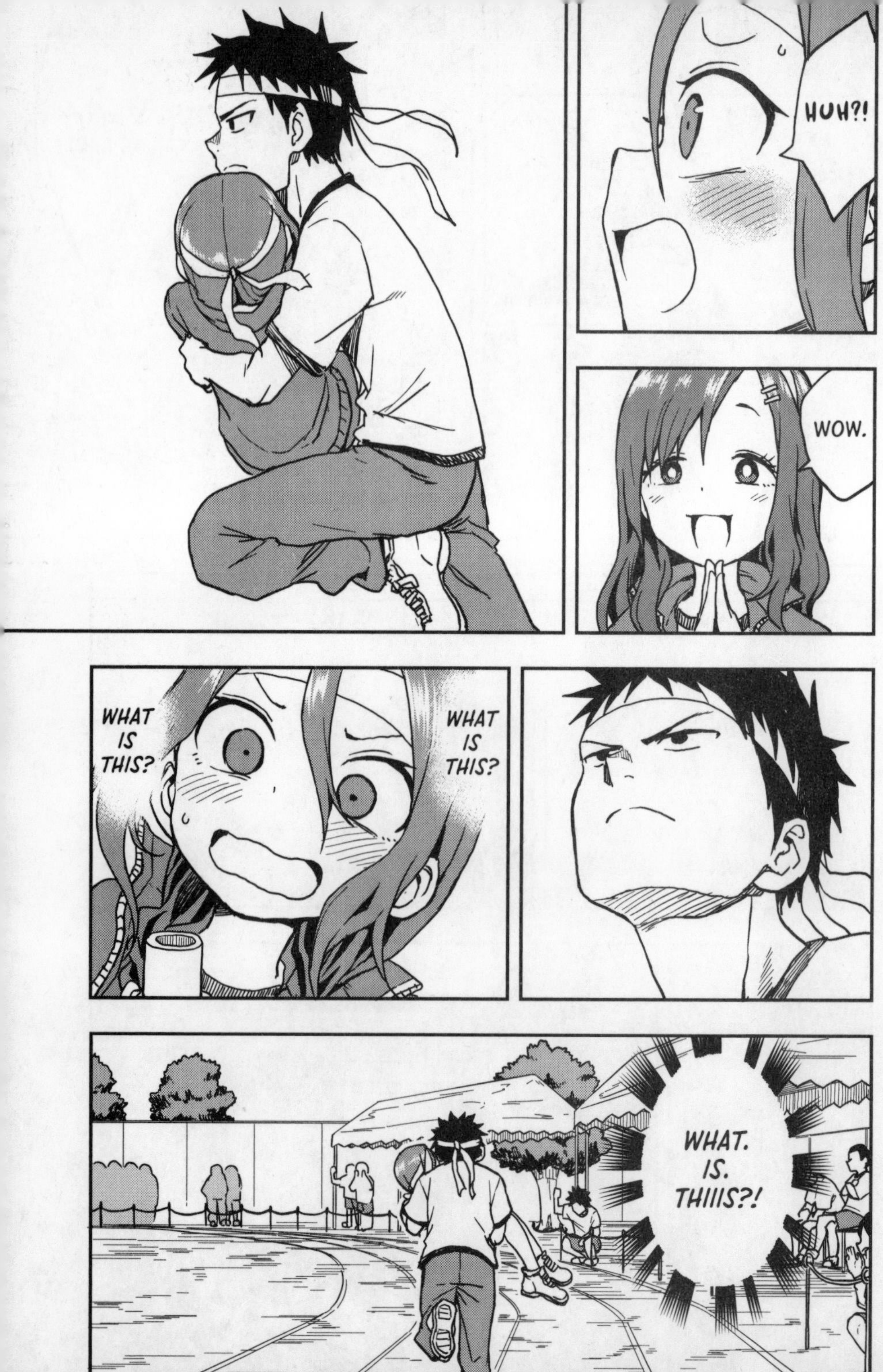
HUH?!
WOW.
WHAT IS THIS?
WHAT IS THIS?
WHAT. IS. THIIIS?!

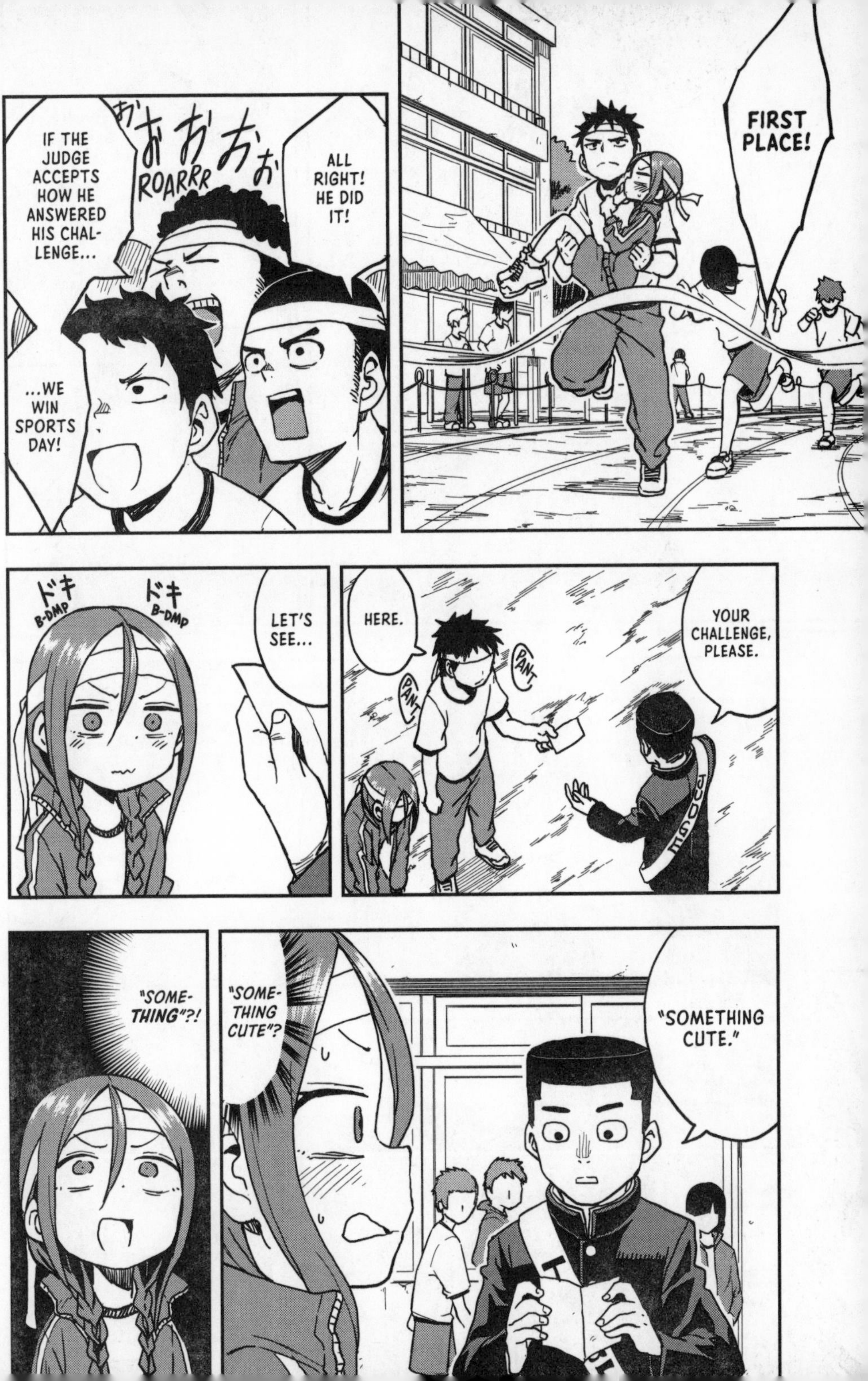
FIRST PLACE!
ALL RIGHT! HE DID IT!
おおおおお
ROARRR
IF THE JUDGE ACCEPTS HOW HE ANSWERED HIS CHALLENGE...
...WE WIN SPORTS DAY!
YOUR CHALLENGE, PLEASE.
PANT
PANT
HERE.
LET'S SEE...
ドキ B-DMP
ドキ B-DMP
"SOMETHING CUTE."
"SOMETHING CUTE"?
"SOMETHING"?!

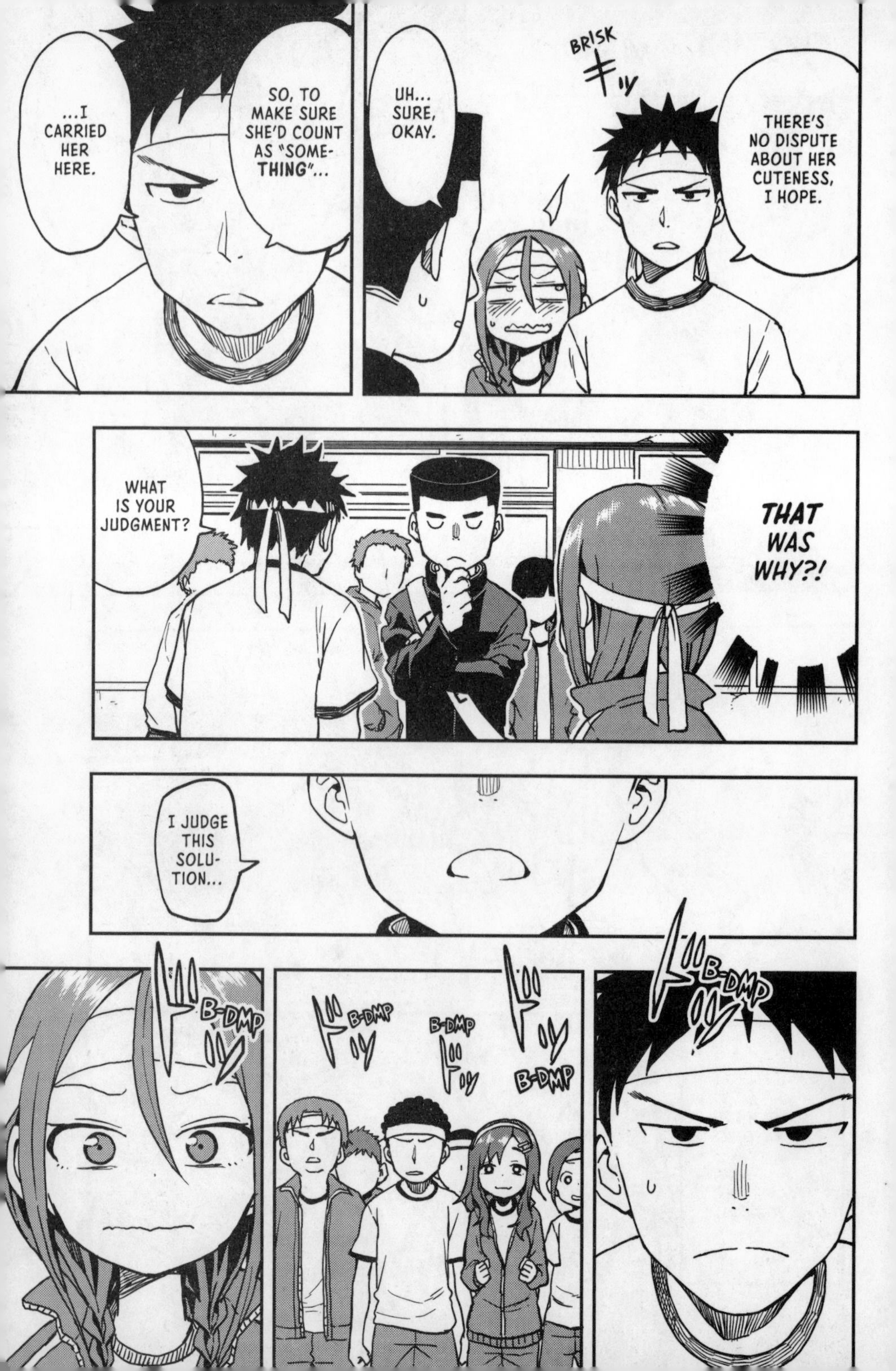
BRISK
THERE'S NO DISPUTE ABOUT HER CUTENESS, I HOPE.
UH... SURE, OKAY.
SO, TO MAKE SURE SHE'D COUNT AS "SOME-THING"...
...I CARRIED HER HERE.
THAT WAS WHY?!
WHAT IS YOUR JUDGMENT?
I JUDGE THIS SOLU-TION...
B-DMP
B-DMP
B-DMP
B-DMP
B-DMP

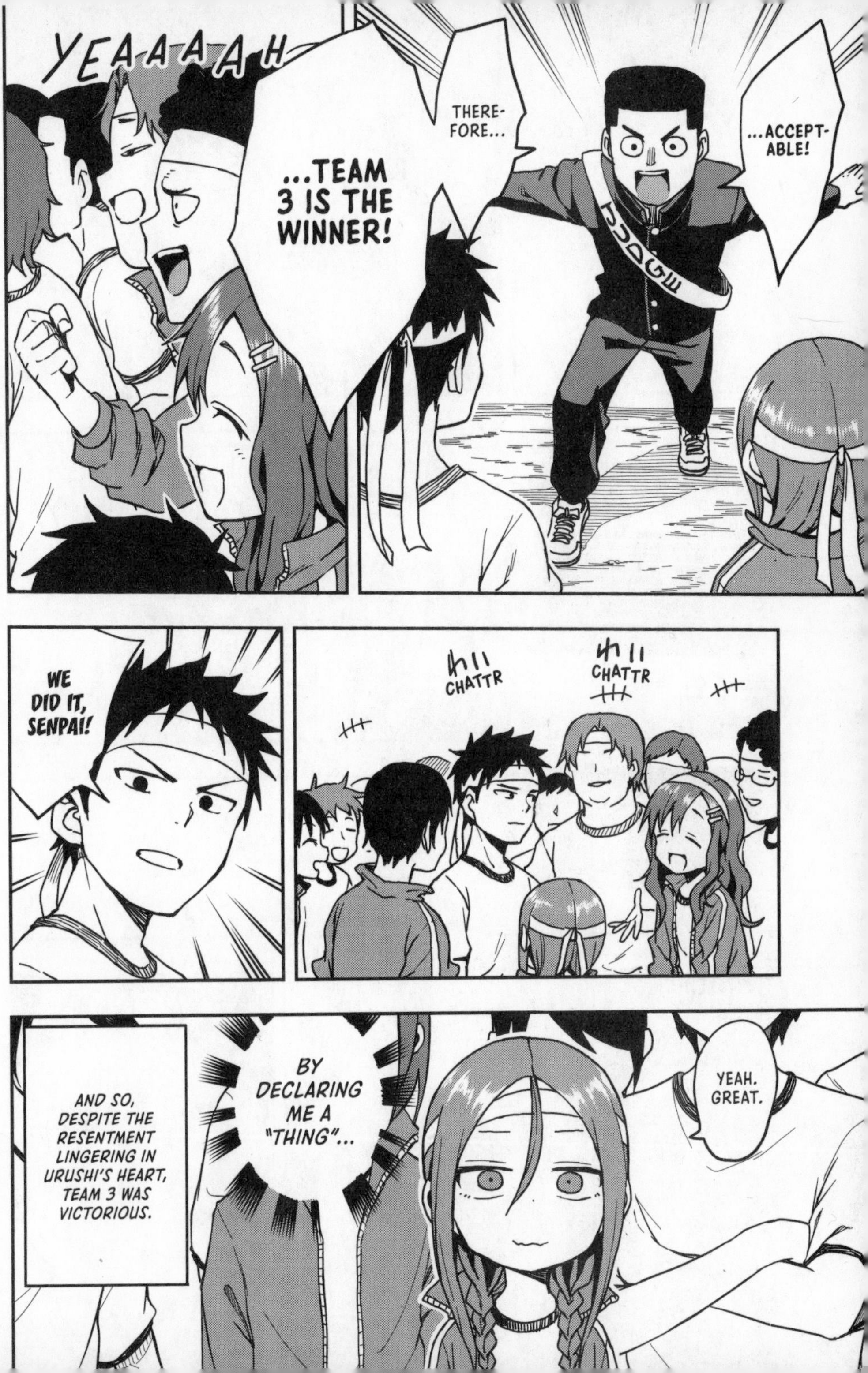
...ACCEPTABLE!
THEREFORE...
...TEAM 3 IS THE WINNER!
YEAAAAAH
CHATTR
CHATTR
WE DID IT, SENPAI!
YEAH. GREAT.
BY DECLARING ME A "THING"...
AND SO, DESPITE THE RESENTMENT LINGERING IN URUSHI'S HEART, TEAM 3 WAS VICTORIOUS.

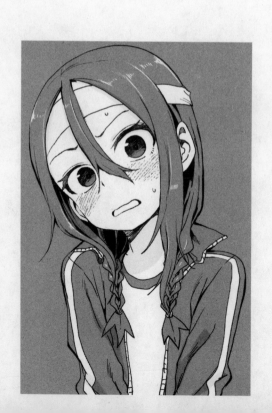

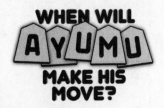

WHEN WILL AYUMU MAKE HIS MOVE?

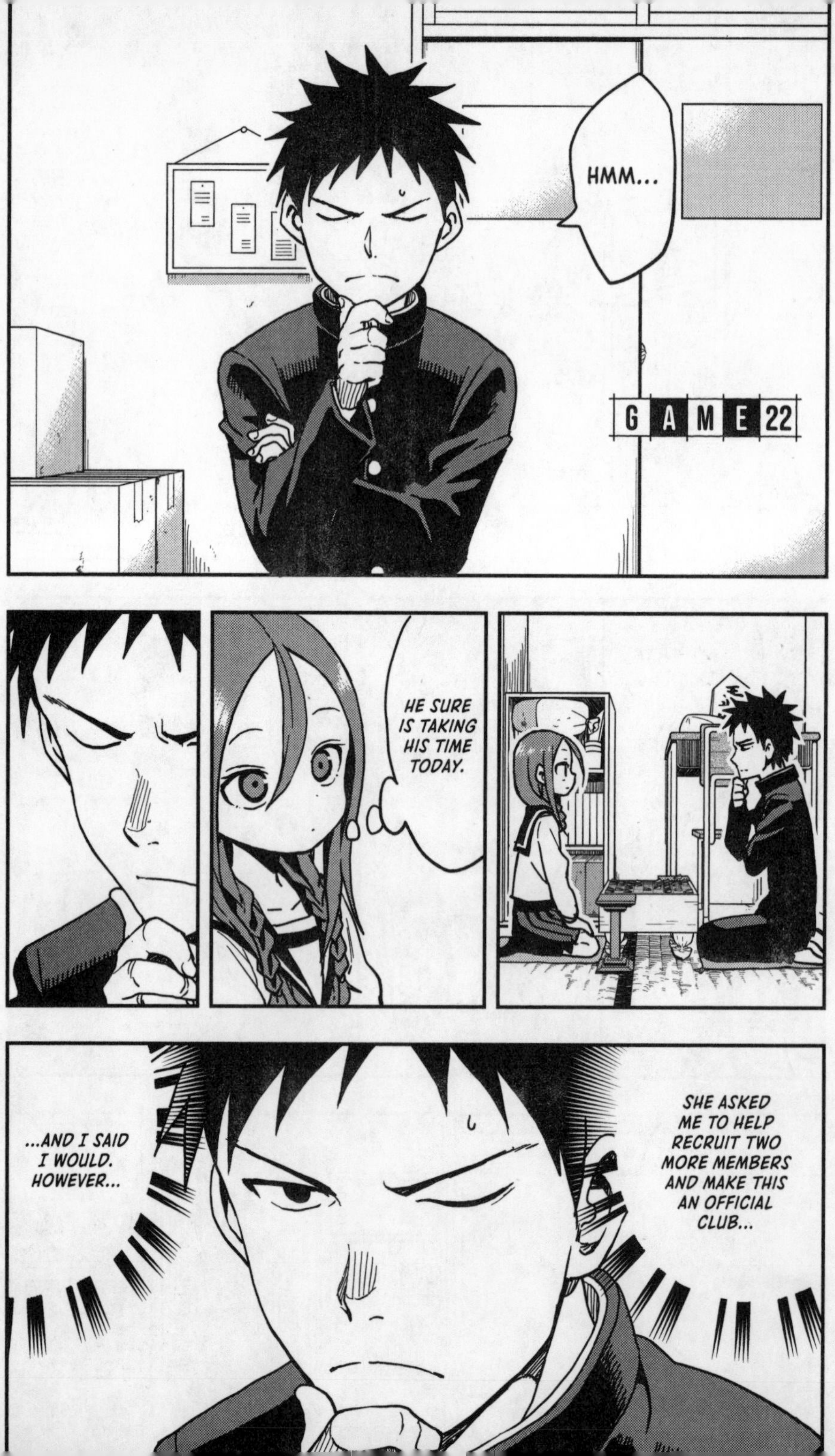
HMM...
GAME 22
HE SURE IS TAKING HIS TIME TODAY.
SHE ASKED ME TO HELP RECRUIT TWO MORE MEMBERS AND MAKE THIS AN OFFICIAL CLUB...
...AND I SAID I WOULD. HOWEVER...

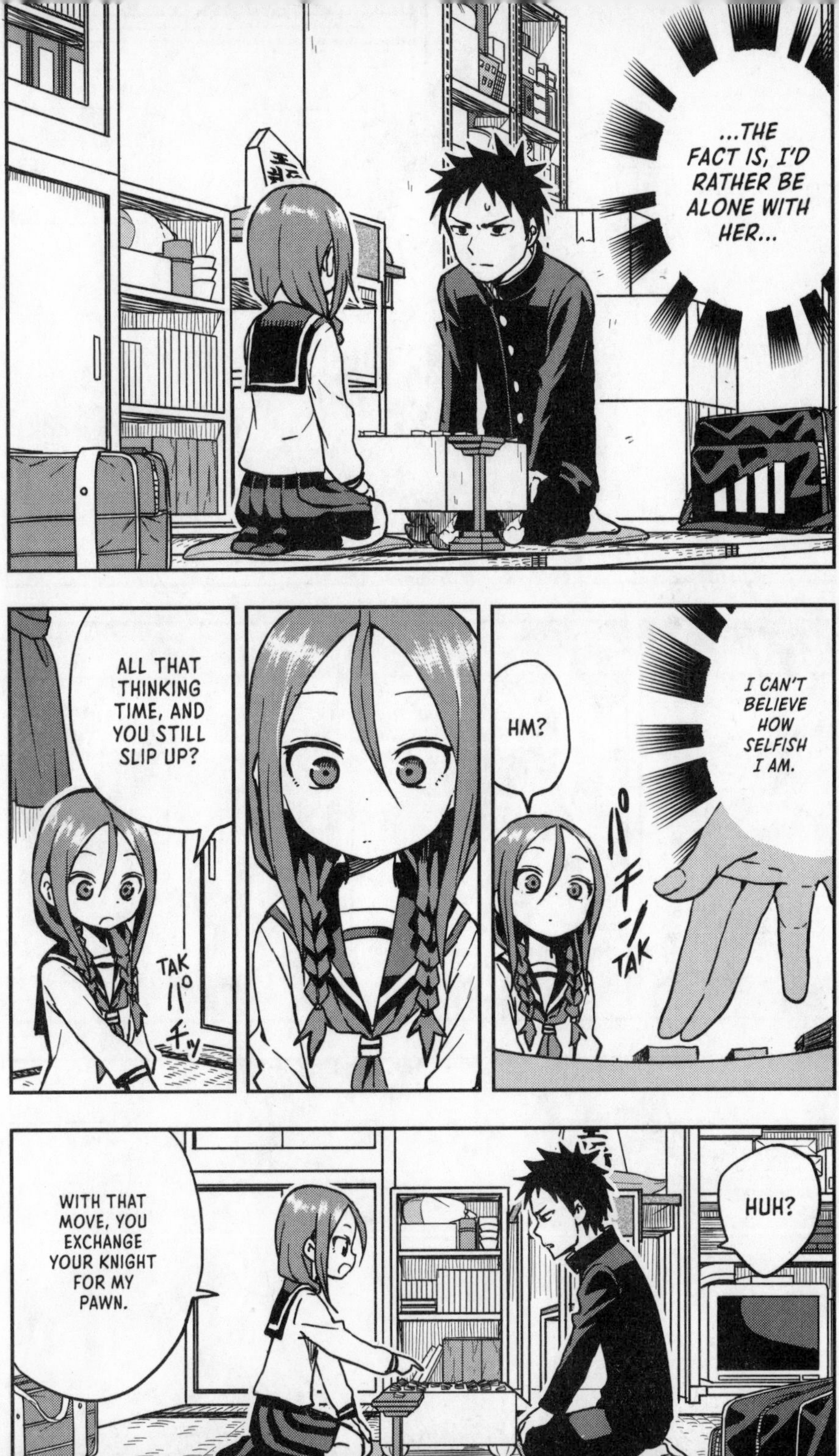
...THE FACT IS, I'D RATHER BE ALONE WITH HER...
I CAN'T BELIEVE HOW SELFISH I AM.
パチーン
TAK
HM?
ALL THAT THINKING TIME, AND YOU STILL SLIP UP?
TAK
パチッ
HUH?
WITH THAT MOVE, YOU EXCHANGE YOUR KNIGHT FOR MY PAWN.

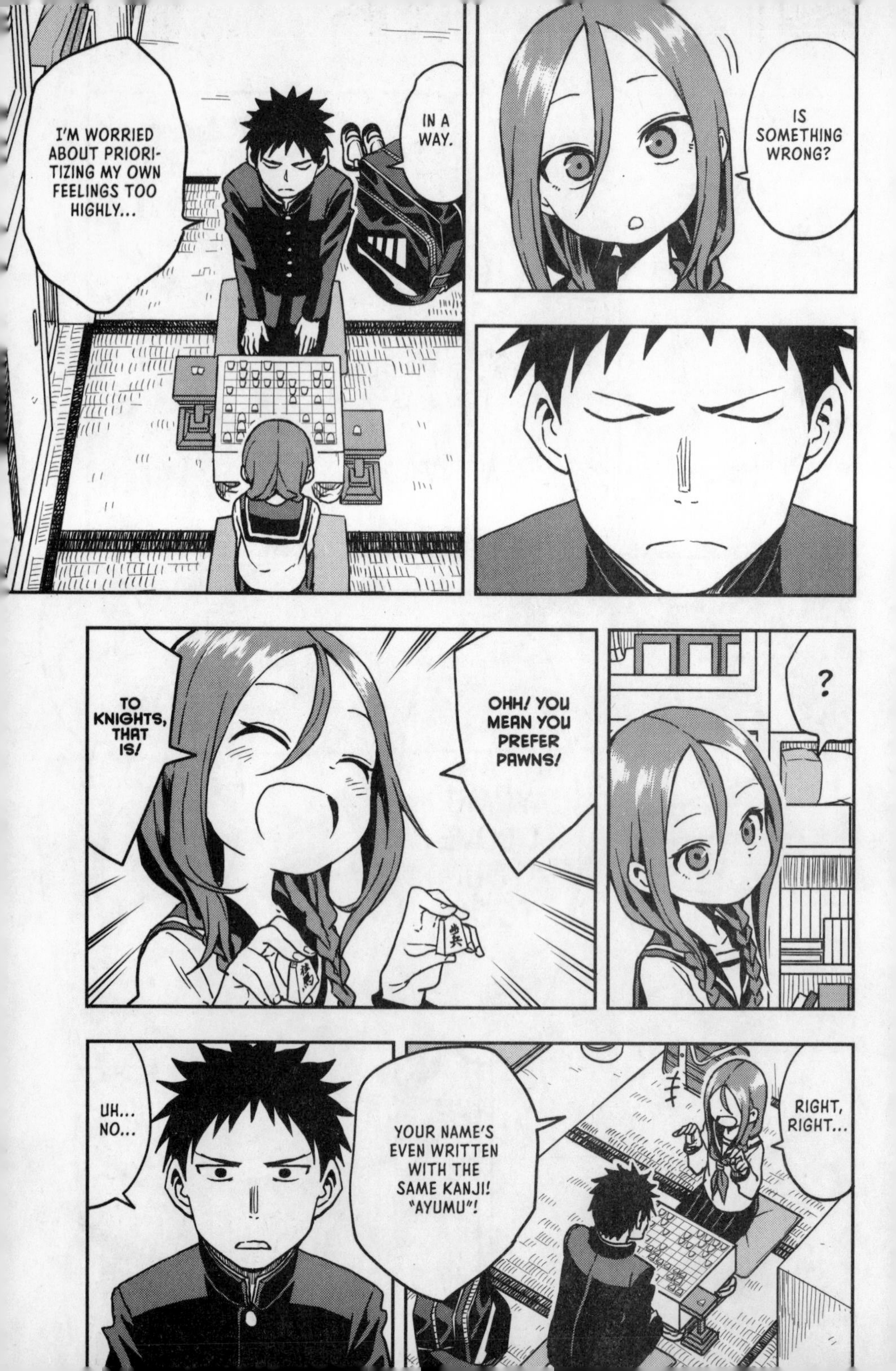
IS SOMETHING WRONG?
IN A WAY.
I'M WORRIED ABOUT PRIORITIZING MY OWN FEELINGS TOO HIGHLY...
?
OHH! YOU MEAN YOU PREFER PAWNS!
TO KNIGHTS, THAT IS!
RIGHT, RIGHT...
YOUR NAME'S EVEN WRITTEN WITH THE SAME KANJI! "AYUMU"!
UH... NO...

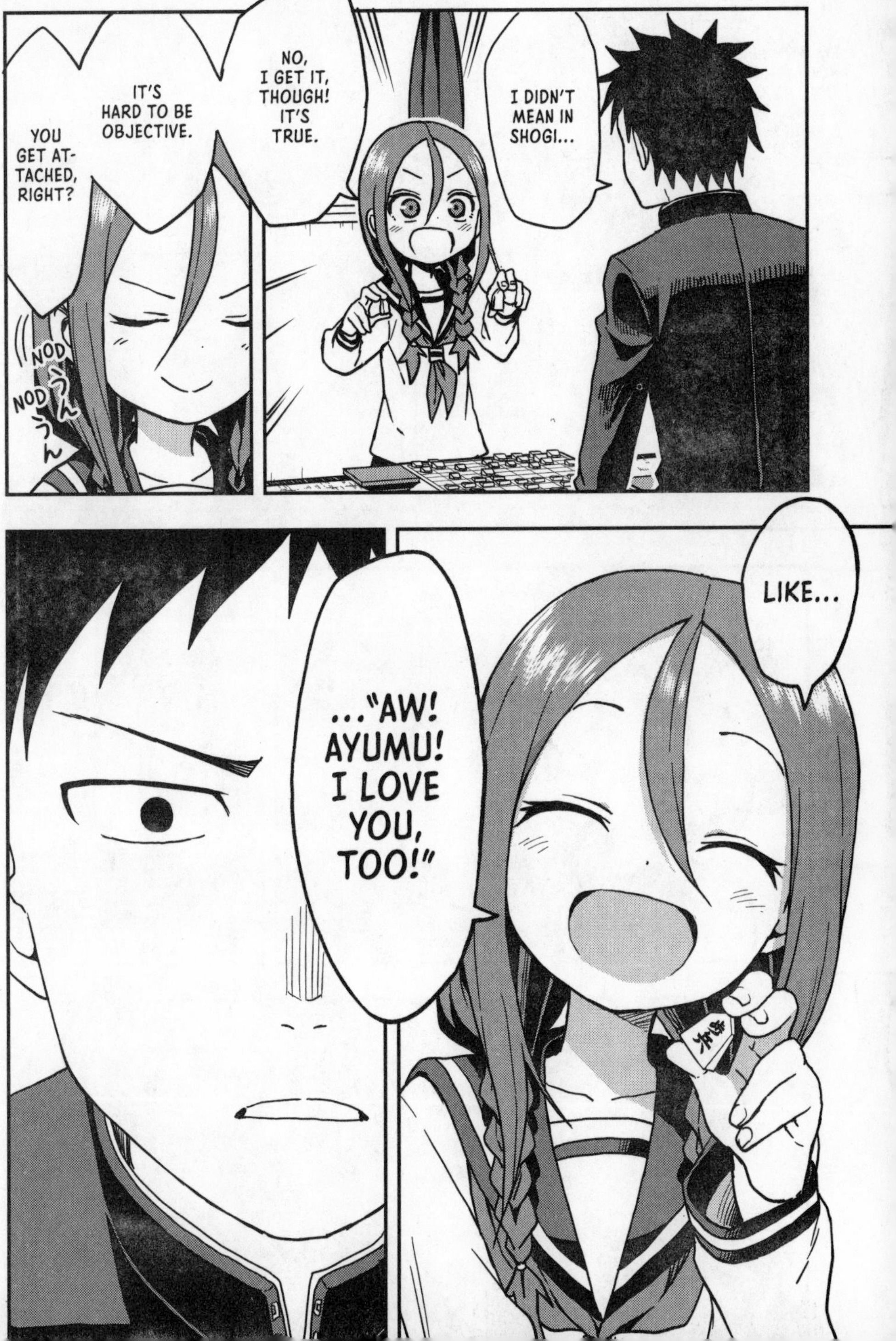
I DIDN'T MEAN IN SHOGI...
NO, I GET IT, THOUGH! IT'S TRUE.
IT'S HARD TO BE OBJECTIVE.
YOU GET AT-TACHED, RIGHT?
NOD うん
NOD うん
LIKE...
..."AW! AYUMU! I LOVE YOU, TOO!"

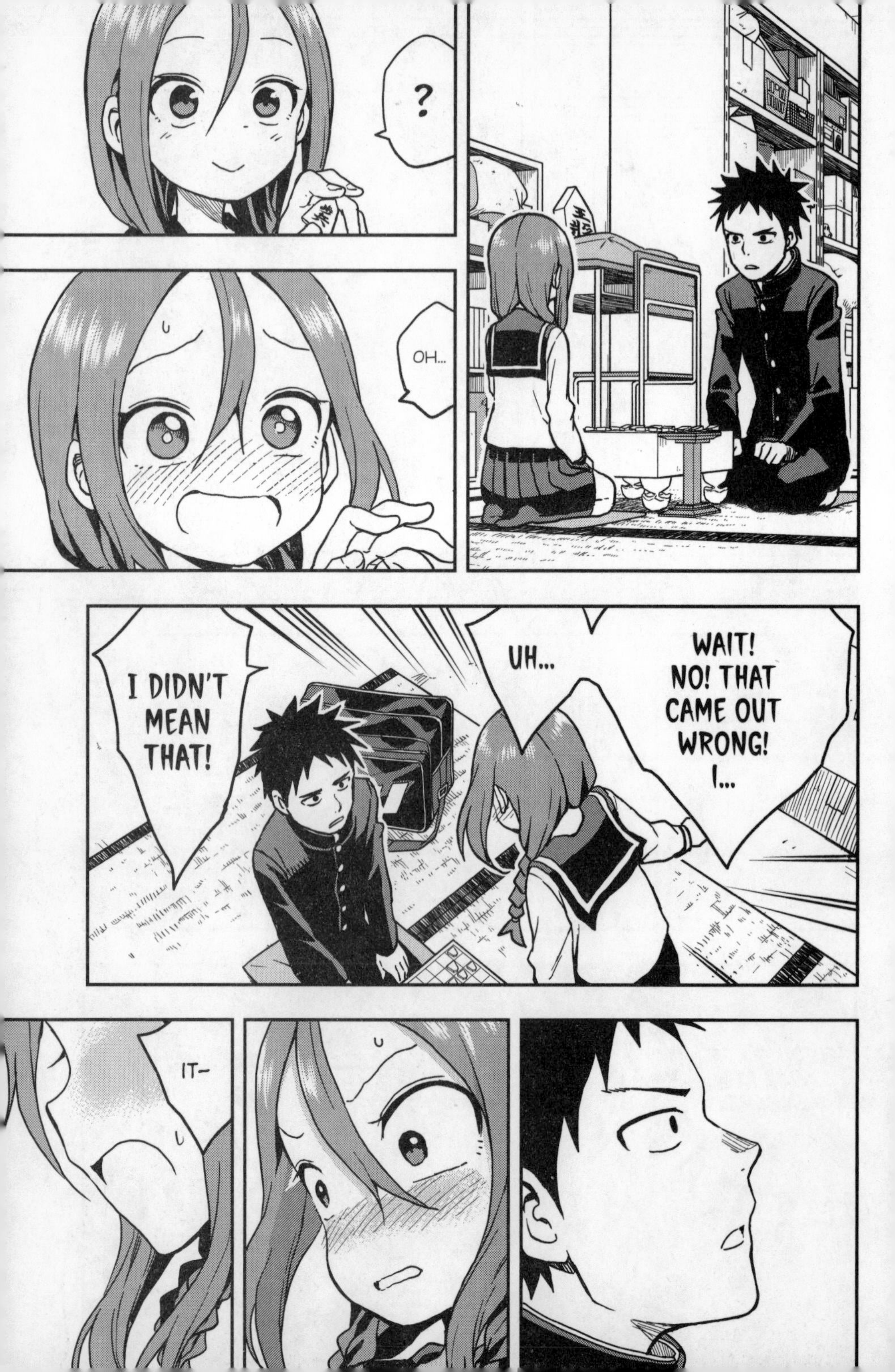
?
OH...
WAIT! NO! THAT CAME OUT WRONG! I...
UH...
I DIDN'T MEAN THAT!
IT–

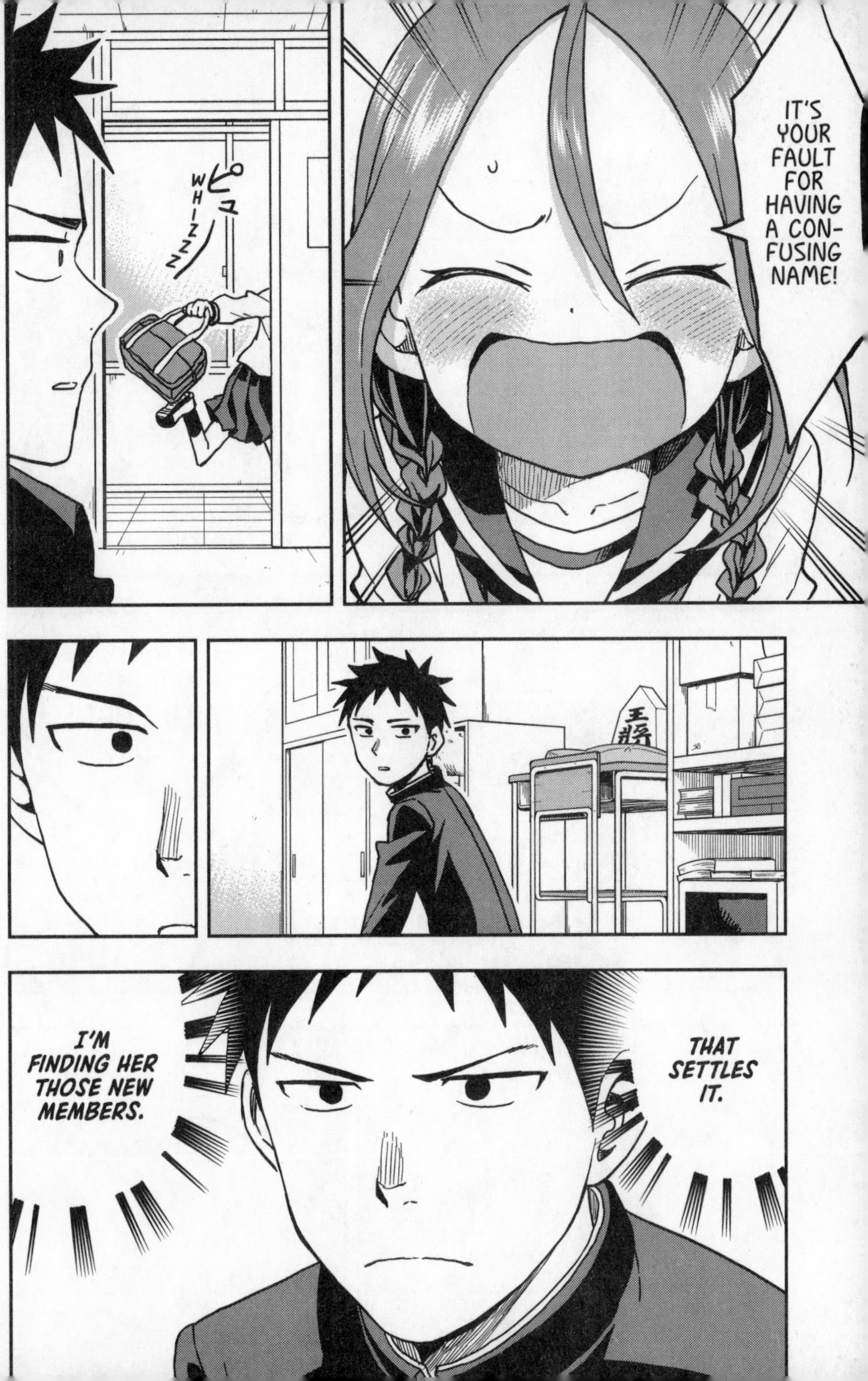
IT'S YOUR FAULT FOR HAVING A CON-FUSING NAME!
ピュ
WHIZZZ
THAT SETTLES IT.
I'M FINDING HER THOSE NEW MEMBERS.

GAME 22 RECORD

▲ BLACK (SENTE): AYUMU TANAKA △ WHITE (GOTE): URUSHI YAOTOME

(DIAGRAM SHOWS BOARD AFTER MOVE 30, △ S-6E)

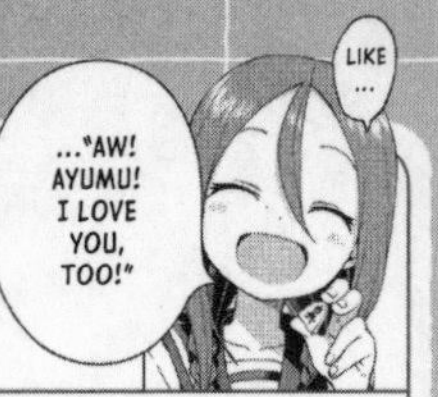

LIKE ...
..."AW! AYUMU! I LOVE YOU, TOO!"

◁URUSHI: N

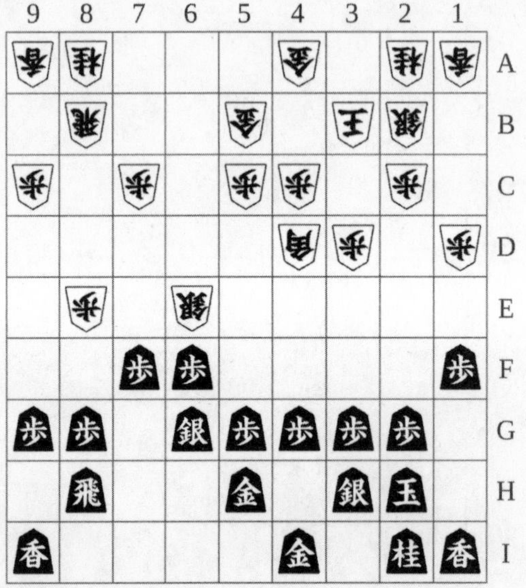

▲AYUMU: B, P

▲ P-7F	△ P-3D
▲ R-6H	△ P-8D
▲ B×2B+	△ S×2B
▲ K-4H	△ S-6B
▲ K-3H	△ K-4B
▲ K-2H	△ K-3B
▲ R-8H	△ P-8E
▲ S-6H	△ P-6D
▲ S-3H	△ P-1D
▲ P-1F	△ S-6C
▲ P-6F	△ G6A-5B
▲ S-6G	△ S-5D
▲ G6I-5H	△ B×4D
▲ N-7G	△ P-6E
▲ NX6E	△ SX6E

(RECORD ENDS AT TURN 30)

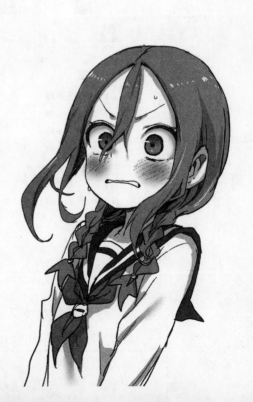

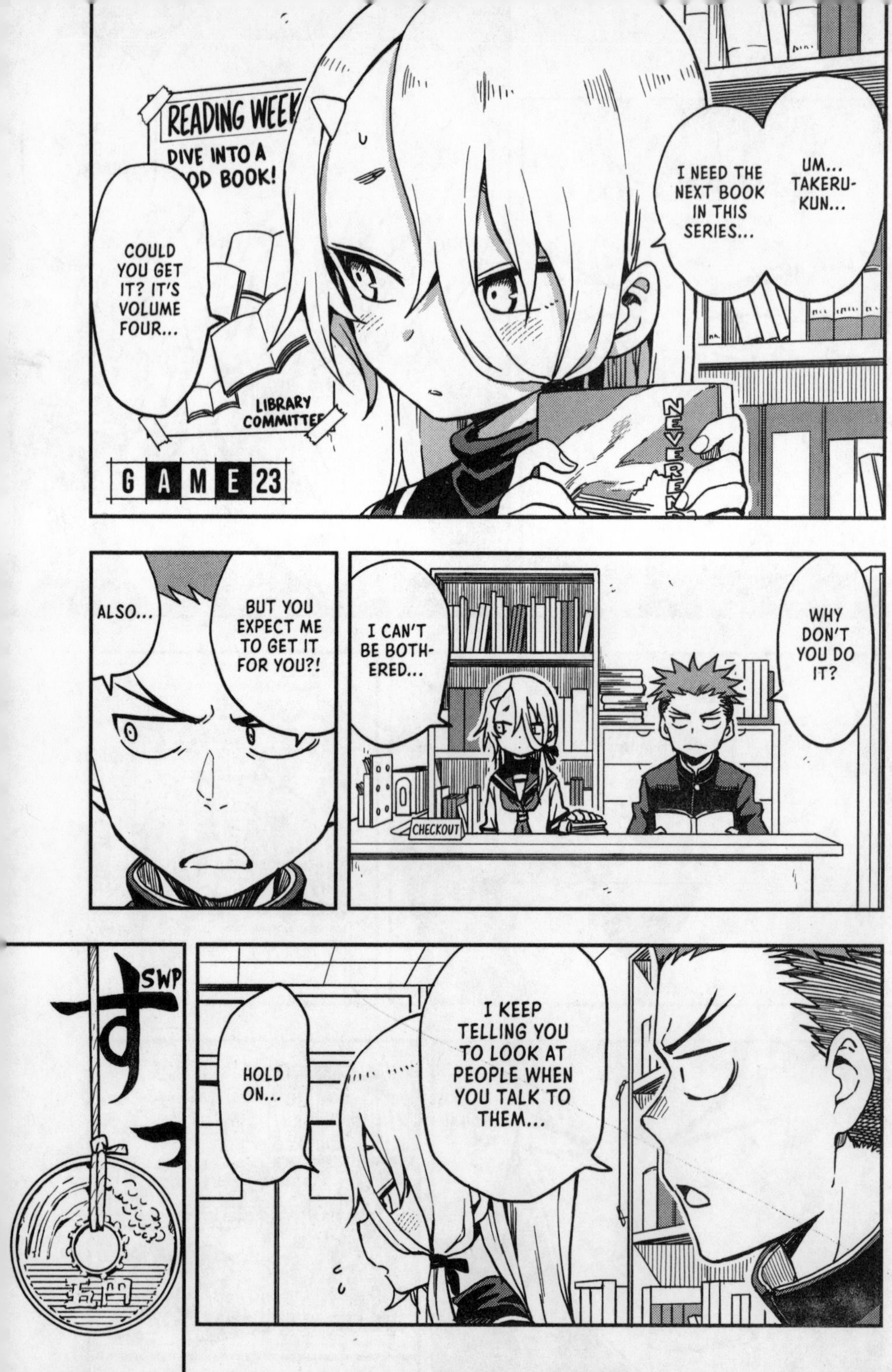
GAME 23
UM... TAKERU-KUN...
I NEED THE NEXT BOOK IN THIS SERIES...
READING WEEK
DIVE INTO A
OD BOOK!
LIBRARY COMMITTEE
COULD YOU GET IT? IT'S VOLUME FOUR...
WHY DON'T YOU DO IT?
I CAN'T BE BOTHERED...
CHECKOUT
BUT YOU EXPECT ME TO GET IT FOR YOU?!
ALSO...
I KEEP TELLING YOU TO LOOK AT PEOPLE WHEN YOU TALK TO THEM...
HOLD ON...
すっ
SWP

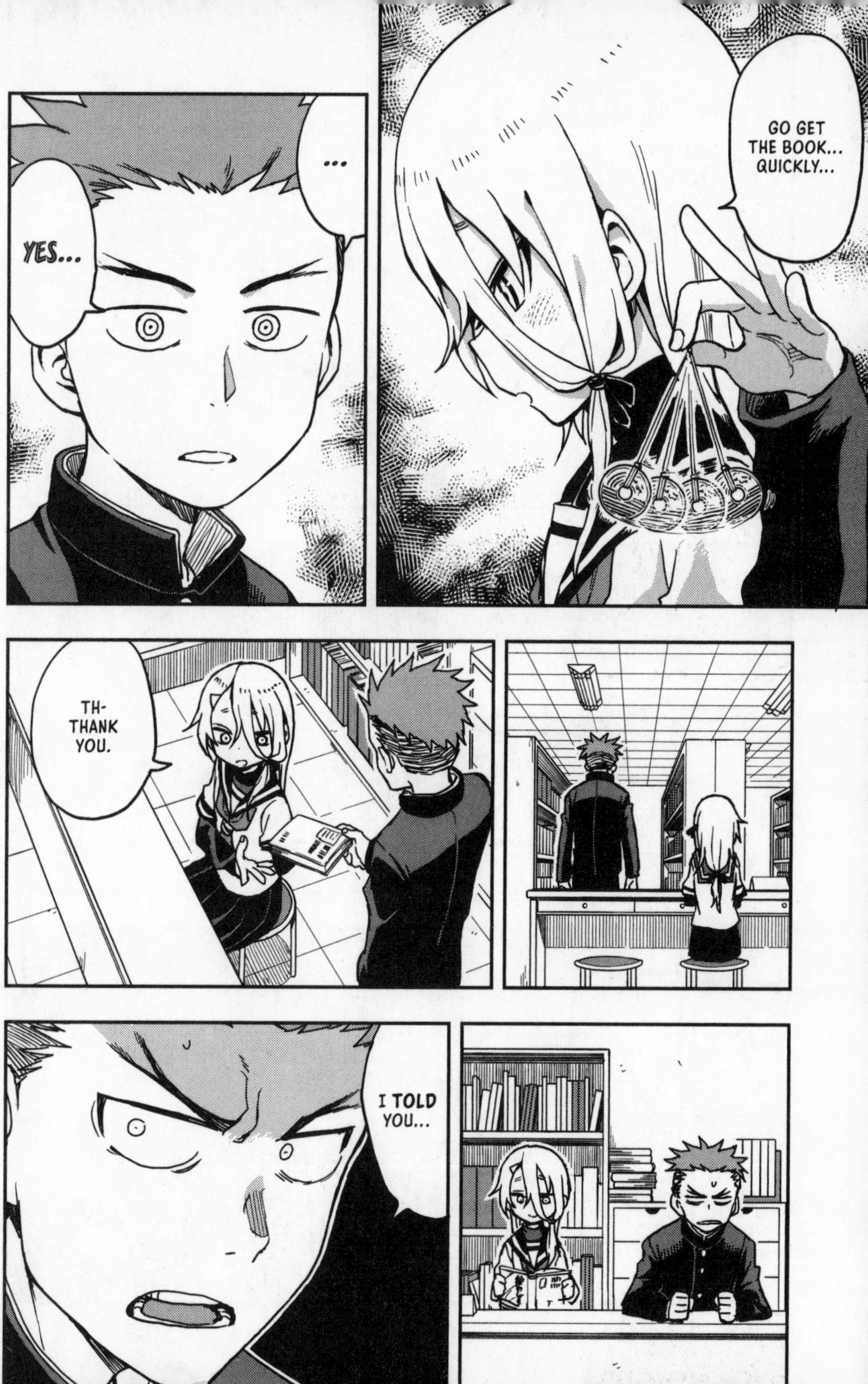
GO GET THE BOOK... QUICKLY...
...
YES...
TH- THANK YOU.
I TOLD YOU...

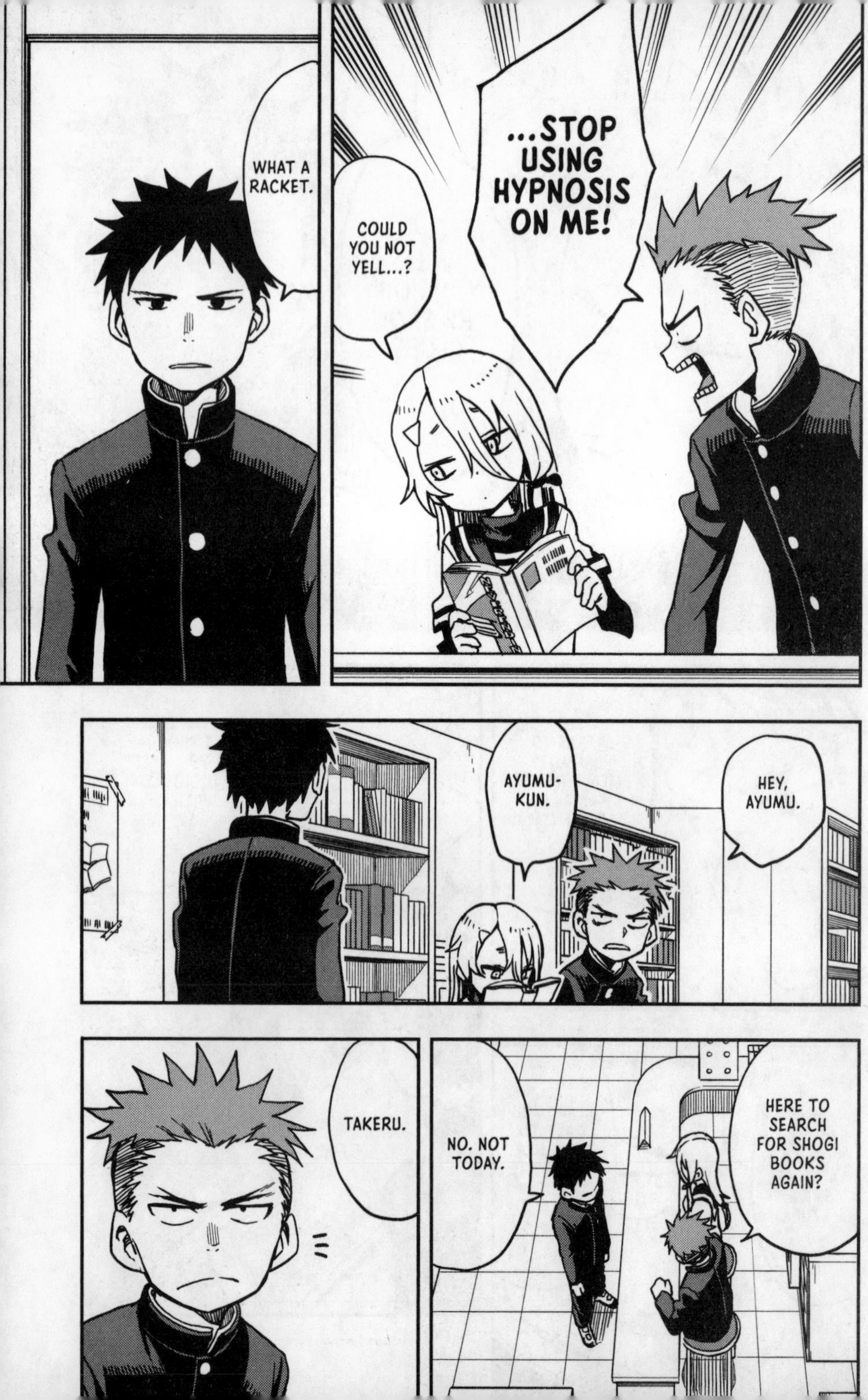
...STOP USING HYPNOSIS ON ME!
COULD YOU NOT YELL...?
WHAT A RACKET.
HEY, AYUMU.
AYUMU-KUN.
HERE TO SEARCH FOR SHOGI BOOKS AGAIN?
NO. NOT TODAY.
TAKERU.

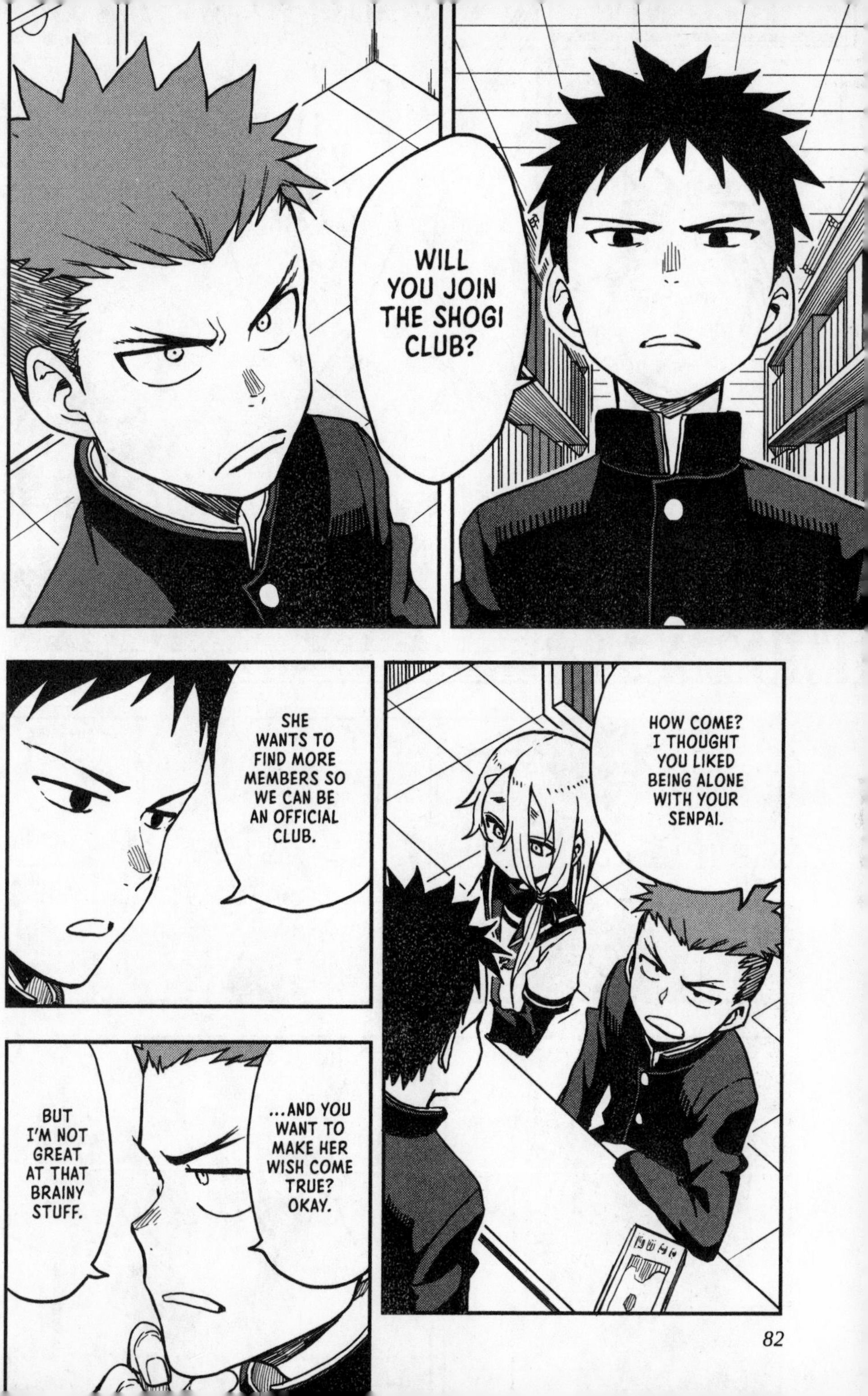
WILL YOU JOIN THE SHOGI CLUB?
HOW COME? I THOUGHT YOU LIKED BEING ALONE WITH YOUR SENPAI.
SHE WANTS TO FIND MORE MEMBERS SO WE CAN BE AN OFFICIAL CLUB.
...AND YOU WANT TO MAKE HER WISH COME TRUE? OKAY.
BUT I'M NOT GREAT AT THAT BRAINY STUFF.

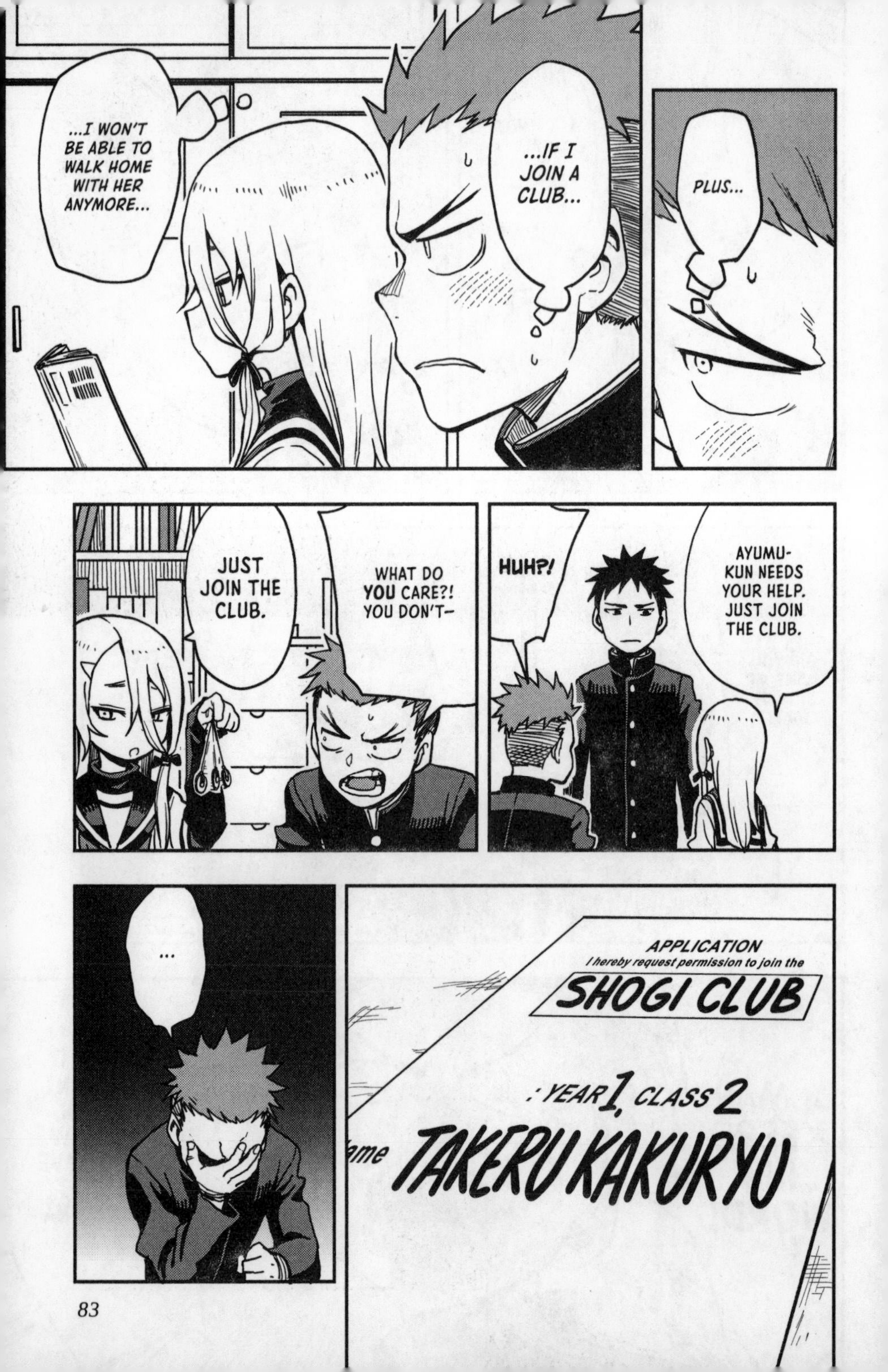
PLUS...
...IF I JOIN A CLUB...
...I WON'T BE ABLE TO WALK HOME WITH HER ANYMORE...
AYUMU-KUN NEEDS YOUR HELP. JUST JOIN THE CLUB.
HUH?!
WHAT DO YOU CARE?! YOU DON'T–
JUST JOIN THE CLUB.
APPLICATION
I hereby request permission to join the
SHOGI CLUB
: YEAR 1, CLASS 2
Name TAKERU KAKURYU
...

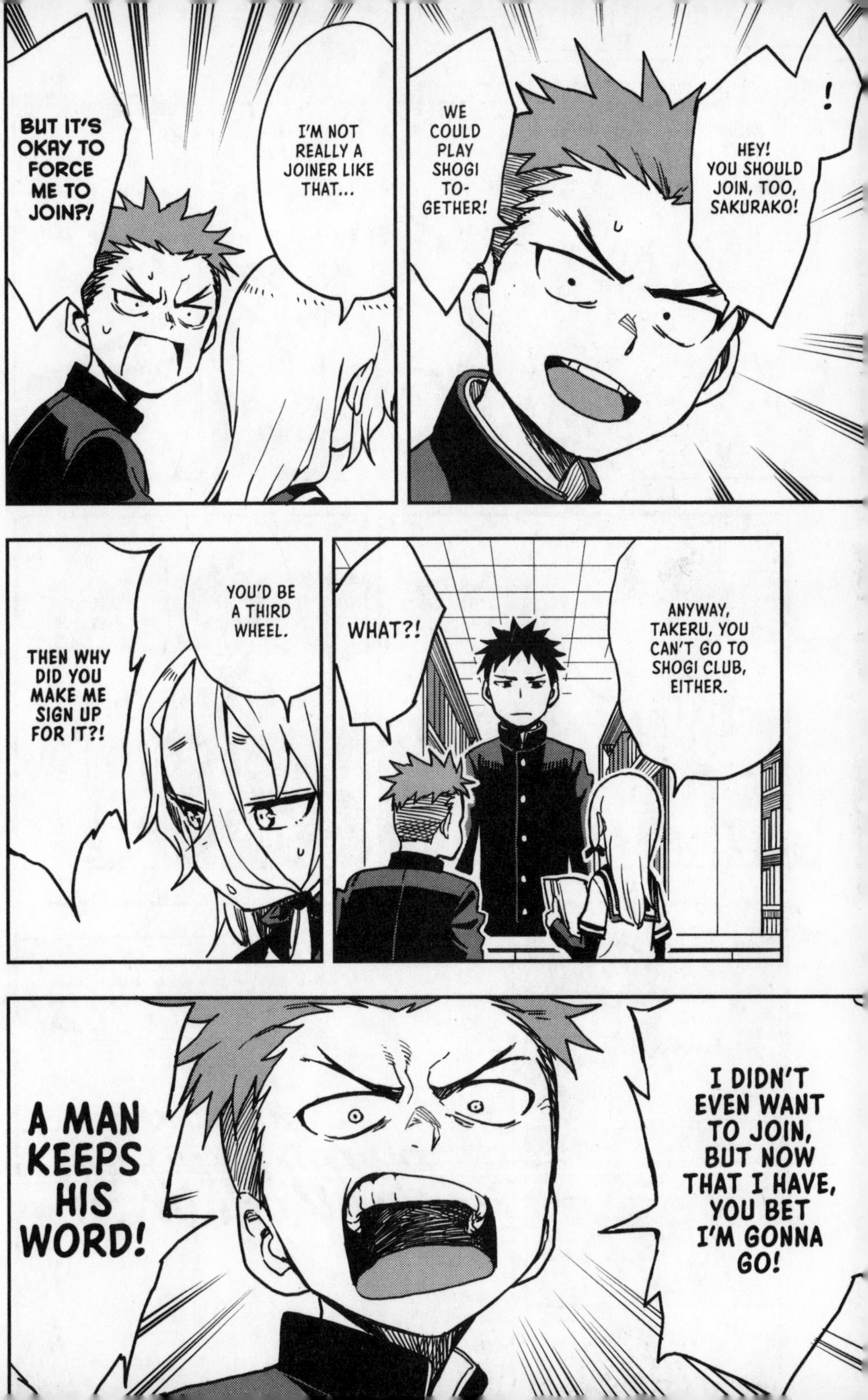
!
HEY! YOU SHOULD JOIN, TOO, SAKURAKO!
WE COULD PLAY SHOGI TO-GETHER!
I'M NOT REALLY A JOINER LIKE THAT...
BUT IT'S OKAY TO FORCE ME TO JOIN?!
ANYWAY, TAKERU, YOU CAN'T GO TO SHOGI CLUB, EITHER.
WHAT?!
YOU'D BE A THIRD WHEEL.
THEN WHY DID YOU MAKE ME SIGN UP FOR IT?!
I DIDN'T EVEN WANT TO JOIN, BUT NOW THAT I HAVE, YOU BET I'M GONNA GO!
A MAN KEEPS HIS WORD!

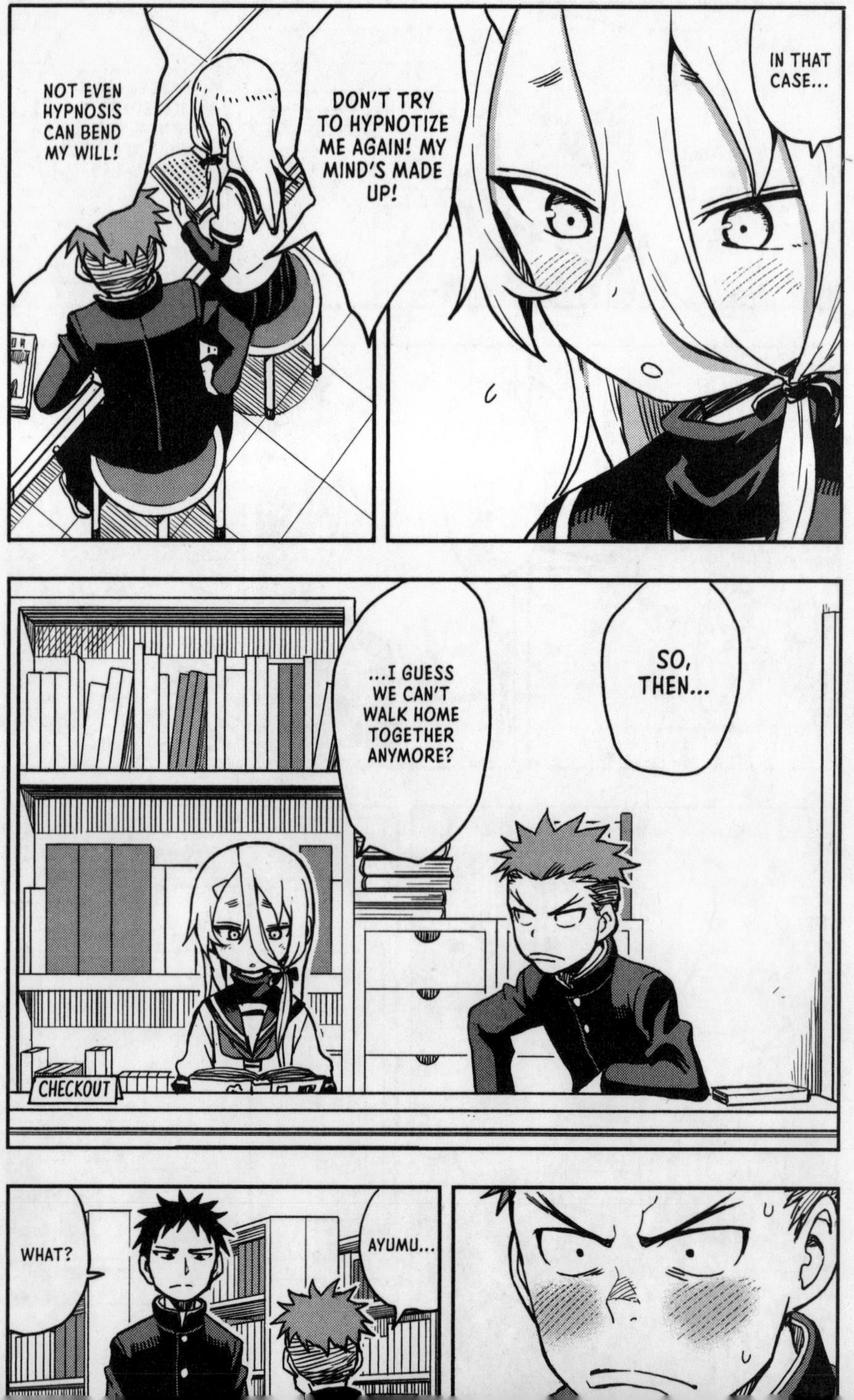
IN THAT CASE...
DON'T TRY TO HYPNOTIZE ME AGAIN! MY MIND'S MADE UP!
NOT EVEN HYPNOSIS CAN BEND MY WILL!
SO, THEN...
...I GUESS WE CAN'T WALK HOME TOGETHER ANYMORE?
CHECKOUT
AYUMU...
WHAT?

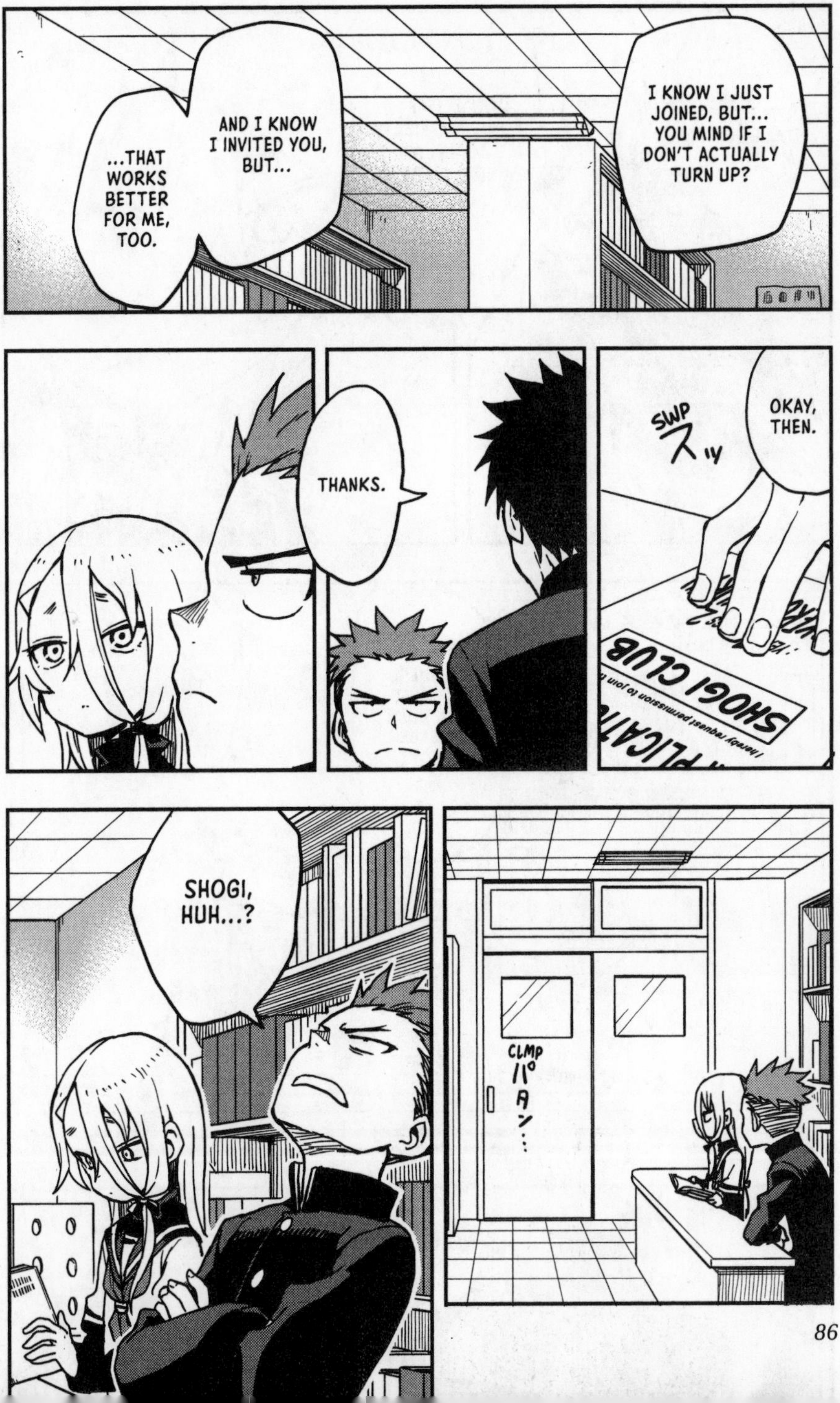
I KNOW I JUST JOINED, BUT... YOU MIND IF I DON'T ACTUALLY TURN UP?
AND I KNOW I INVITED YOU, BUT...
...THAT WORKS BETTER FOR ME, TOO.
OKAY, THEN.
SWP
SHOGI CLUB
THANKS.
CLMP
SHOGI, HUH...?

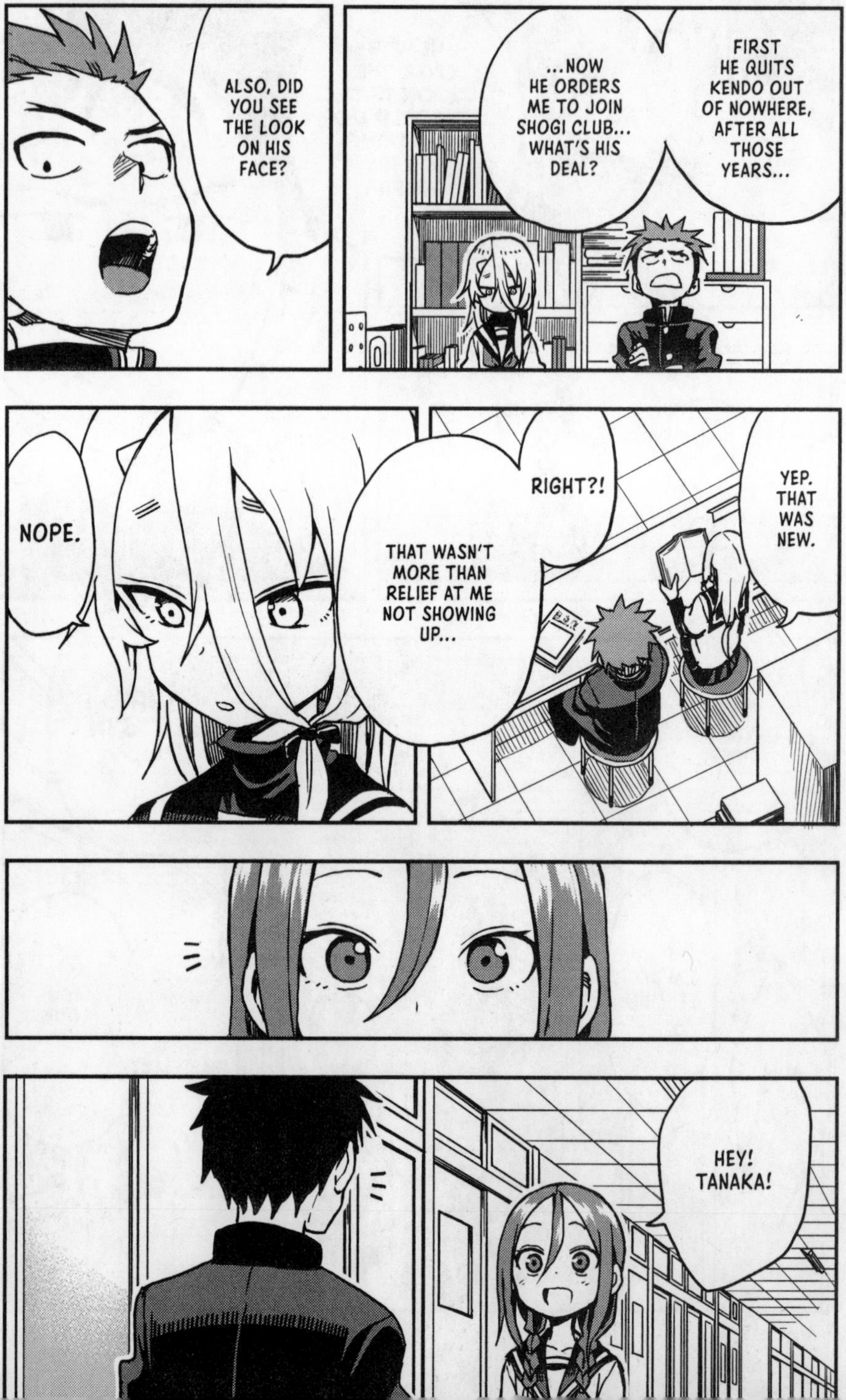
FIRST HE QUITS KENDO OUT OF NOWHERE, AFTER ALL THOSE YEARS...
...NOW HE ORDERS ME TO JOIN SHOGI CLUB... WHAT'S HIS DEAL?
ALSO, DID YOU SEE THE LOOK ON HIS FACE?
YEP. THAT WAS NEW.
RIGHT?!
THAT WASN'T MORE THAN RELIEF AT ME NOT SHOWING UP...
NOPE.
HEY! TANAKA!

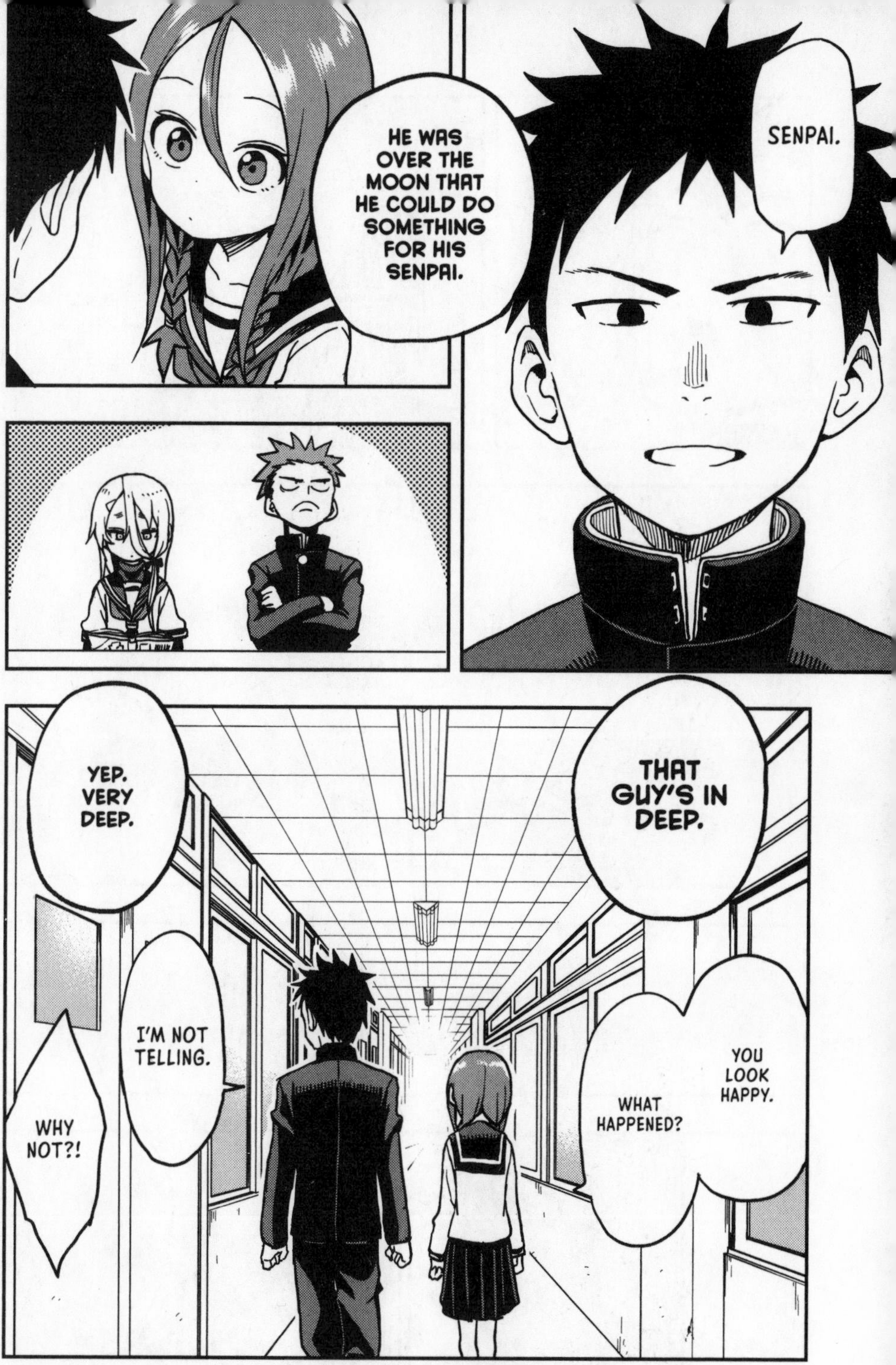
SENPAI.
HE WAS OVER THE MOON THAT HE COULD DO SOMETHING FOR HIS SENPAI.
THAT GUY'S IN DEEP.
YEP. VERY DEEP.
YOU LOOK HAPPY. WHAT HAPPENED?
I'M NOT TELLING.
WHY NOT?!

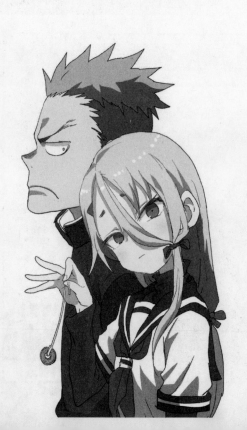

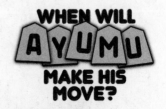

WHEN WILL AYUMU MAKE HIS MOVE?

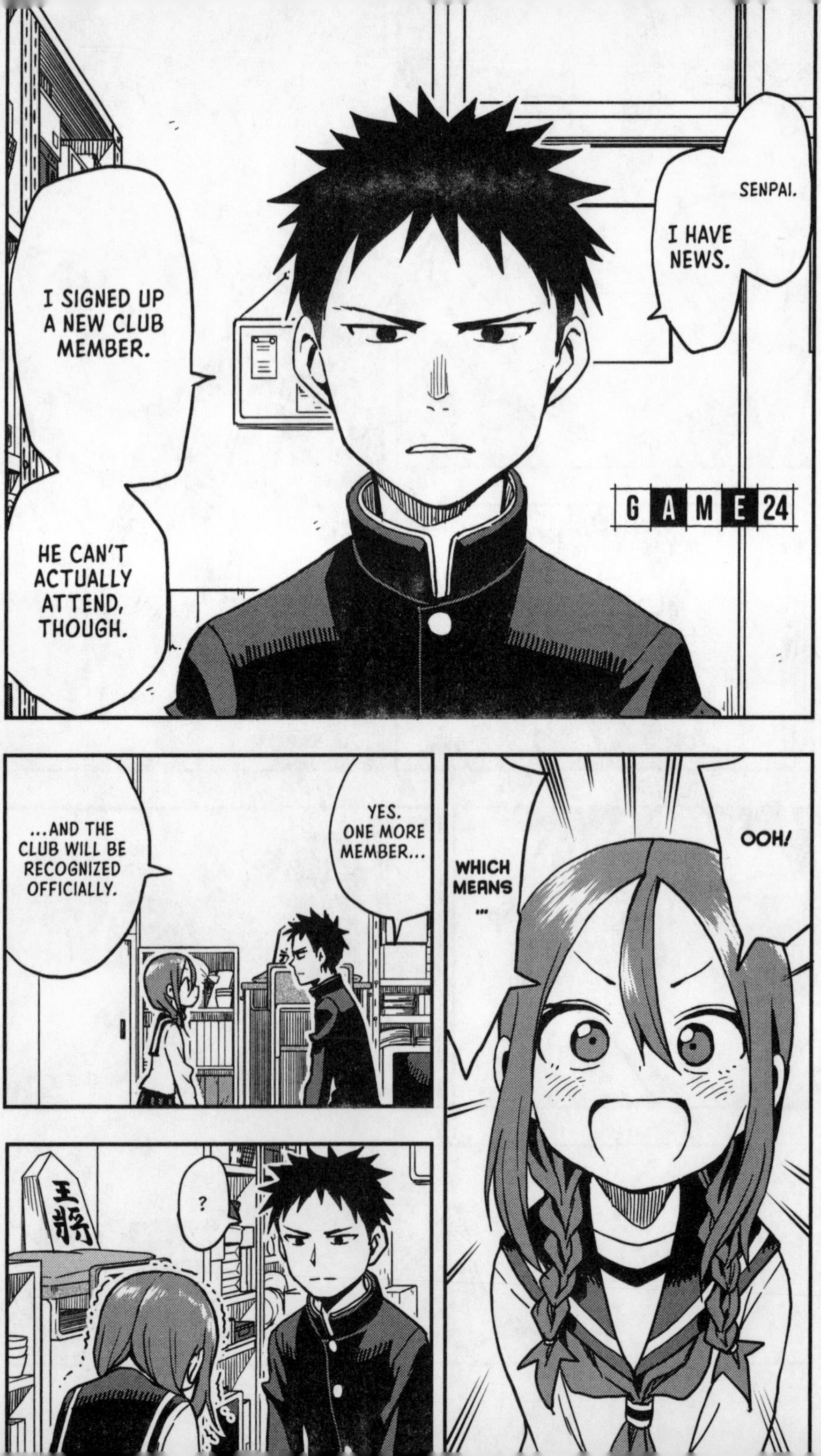
SENPAI.
I HAVE NEWS.
I SIGNED UP A NEW CLUB MEMBER.
HE CAN'T ACTUALLY ATTEND, THOUGH.
GAME 24
OOH!
WHICH MEANS...
YES. ONE MORE MEMBER...
...AND THE CLUB WILL BE RECOGNIZED OFFICIALLY.
?

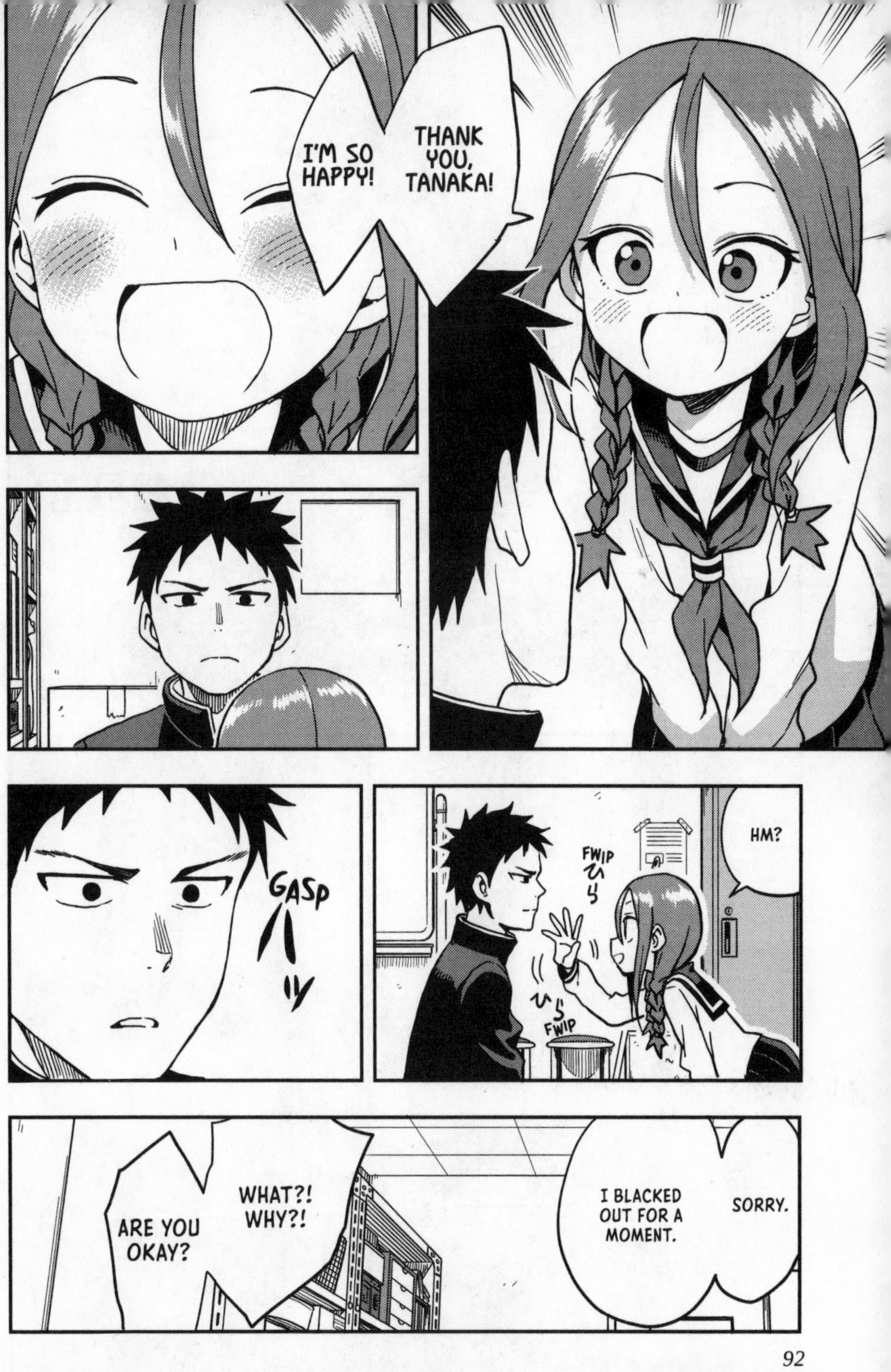
THANK YOU, TANAKA!
I'M SO HAPPY!
HM?
FWIP ひら
ひら FWIP
GASP
SORRY.
I BLACKED OUT FOR A MOMENT.
WHAT?! WHY?!
ARE YOU OKAY?

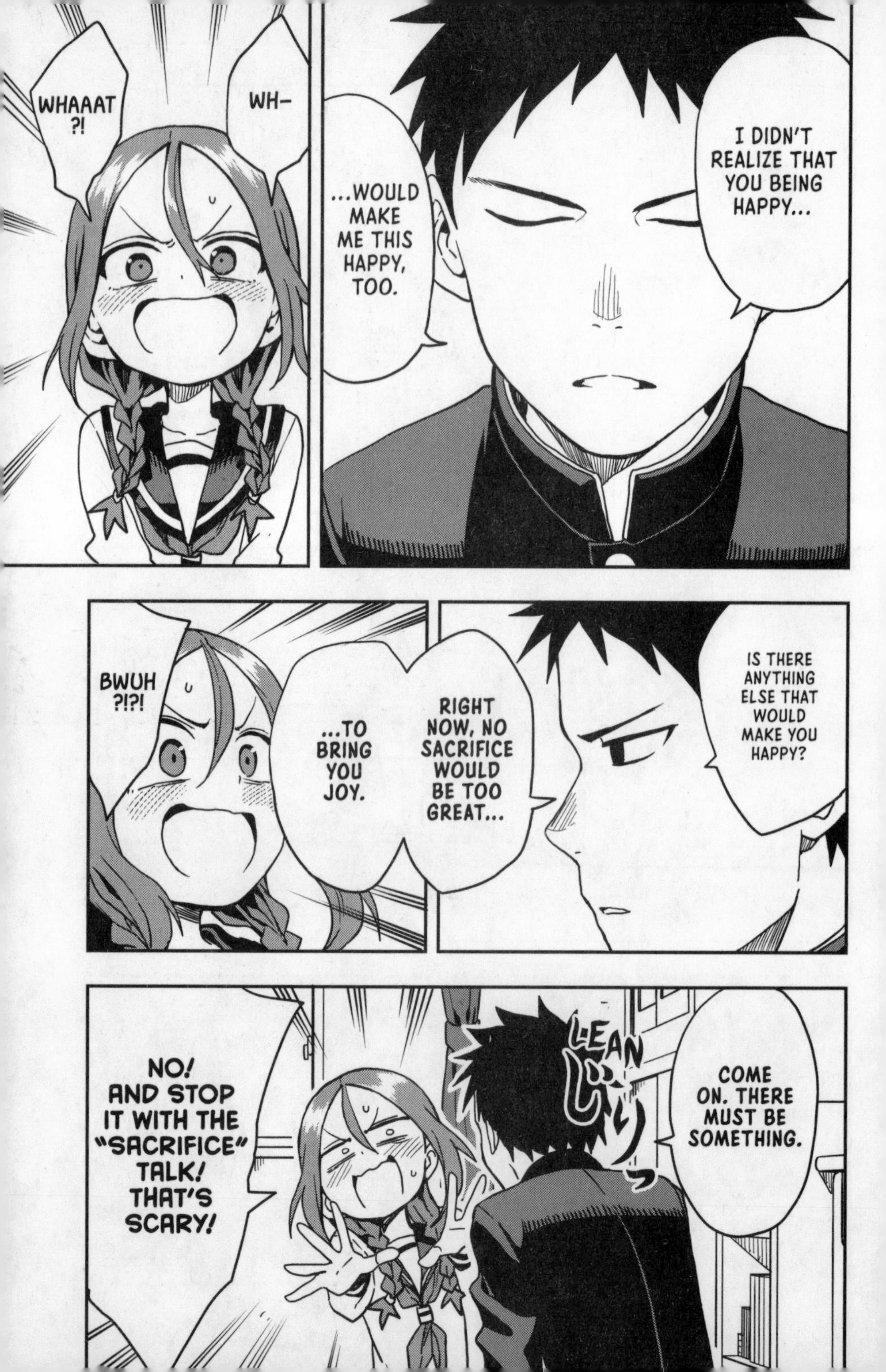
I DIDN'T REALIZE THAT YOU BEING HAPPY...
...WOULD MAKE ME THIS HAPPY, TOO.
WH-
WHAAAT ?!
IS THERE ANYTHING ELSE THAT WOULD MAKE YOU HAPPY?
RIGHT NOW, NO SACRIFICE WOULD BE TOO GREAT...
...TO BRING YOU JOY.
BWUH ?!?!
LEAN
COME ON. THERE MUST BE SOMETHING.
NO! AND STOP IT WITH THE "SACRIFICE" TALK! THAT'S SCARY!

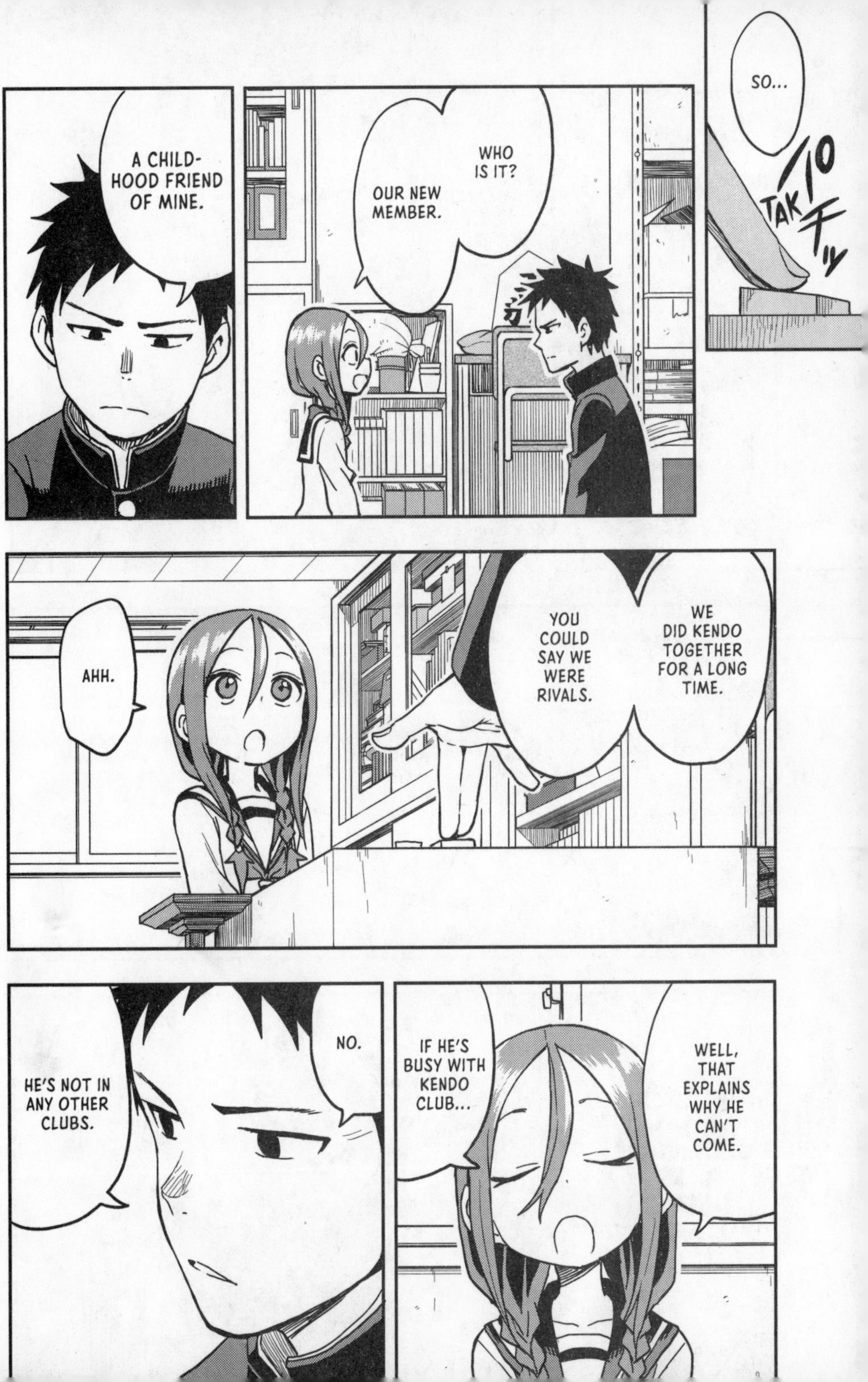
SO...
TAK
チッ
WHO IS IT?
OUR NEW MEMBER.
A CHILD-HOOD FRIEND OF MINE.
WE DID KENDO TOGETHER FOR A LONG TIME.
YOU COULD SAY WE WERE RIVALS.
AHH.
WELL, THAT EXPLAINS WHY HE CAN'T COME.
IF HE'S BUSY WITH KENDO CLUB...
NO.
HE'S NOT IN ANY OTHER CLUBS.

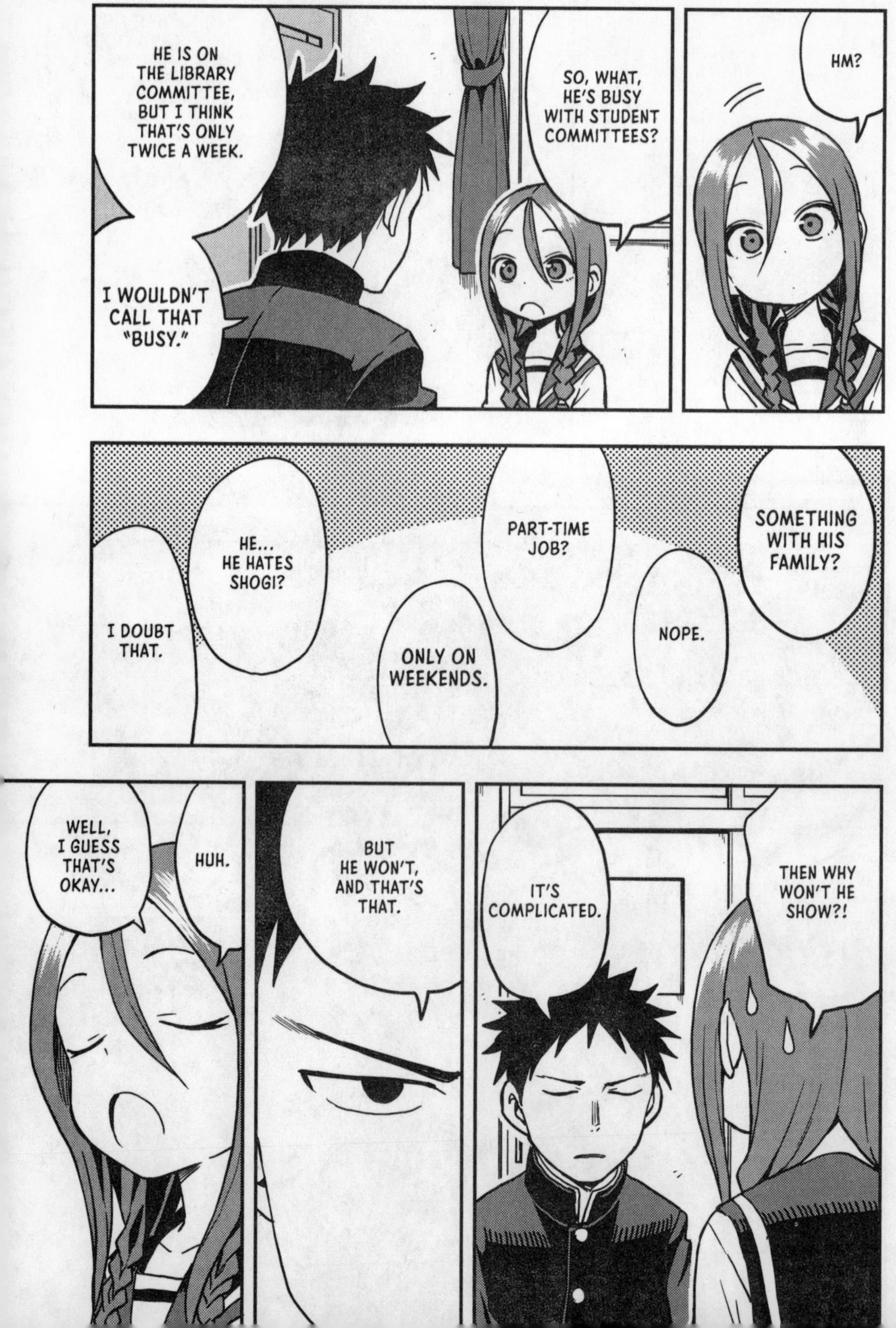
HM?
SO, WHAT, HE'S BUSY WITH STUDENT COMMITTEES?
HE IS ON THE LIBRARY COMMITTEE, BUT I THINK THAT'S ONLY TWICE A WEEK.
I WOULDN'T CALL THAT "BUSY."
SOMETHING WITH HIS FAMILY?
NOPE.
PART-TIME JOB?
ONLY ON WEEKENDS.
HE... HE HATES SHOGI?
I DOUBT THAT.
THEN WHY WON'T HE SHOW?!
IT'S COMPLICATED.
BUT HE WON'T, AND THAT'S THAT.
HUH.
WELL, I GUESS THAT'S OKAY...

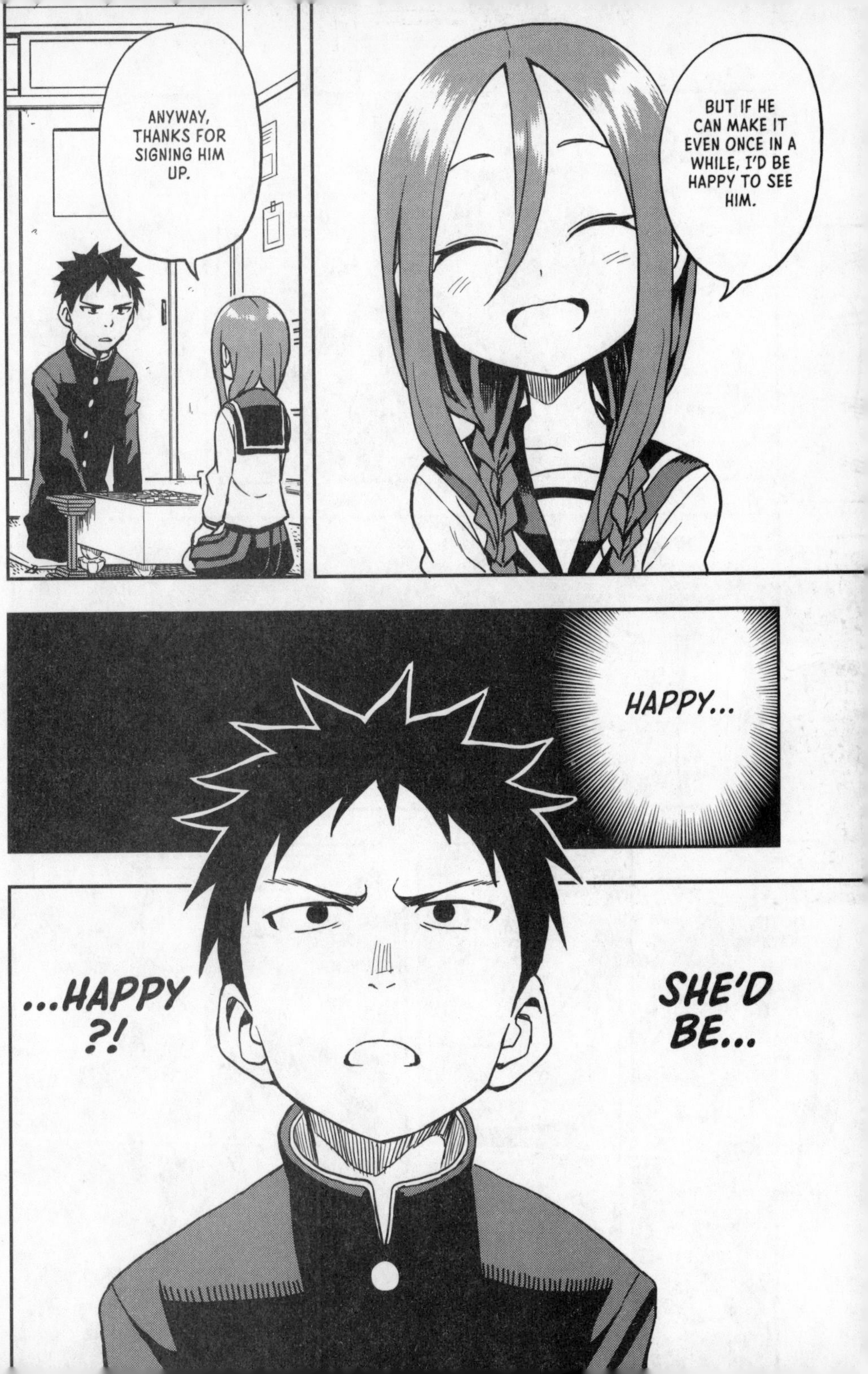
BUT IF HE CAN MAKE IT EVEN ONCE IN A WHILE, I'D BE HAPPY TO SEE HIM.
ANYWAY, THANKS FOR SIGNING HIM UP.
HAPPY...
SHE'D BE...
...HAPPY ?!

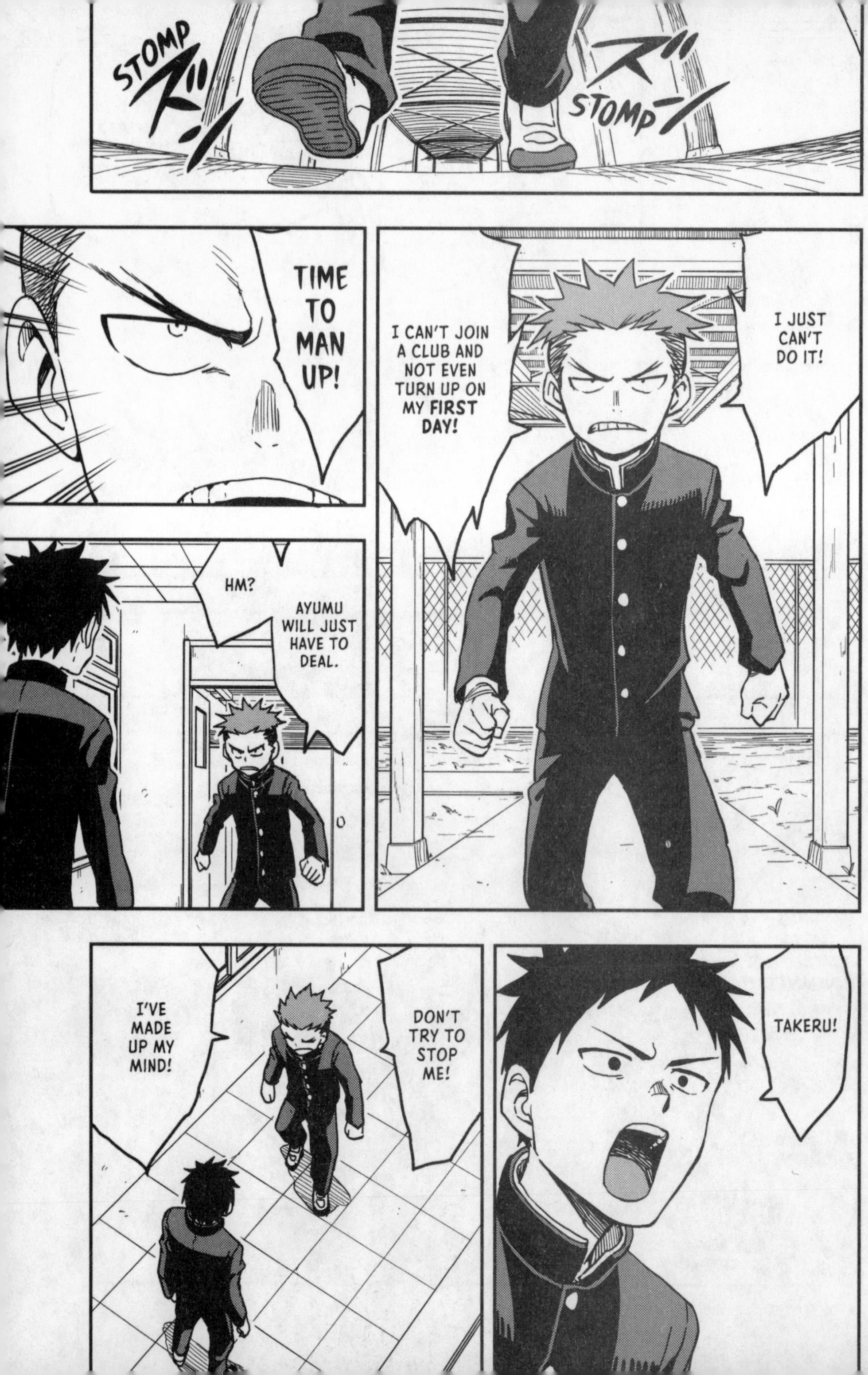
STOMP
STOMP
I JUST CAN'T DO IT!
I CAN'T JOIN A CLUB AND NOT EVEN TURN UP ON MY FIRST DAY!
TIME TO MAN UP!
HM?
AYUMU WILL JUST HAVE TO DEAL.
TAKERU!
DON'T TRY TO STOP ME!
I'VE MADE UP MY MIND!

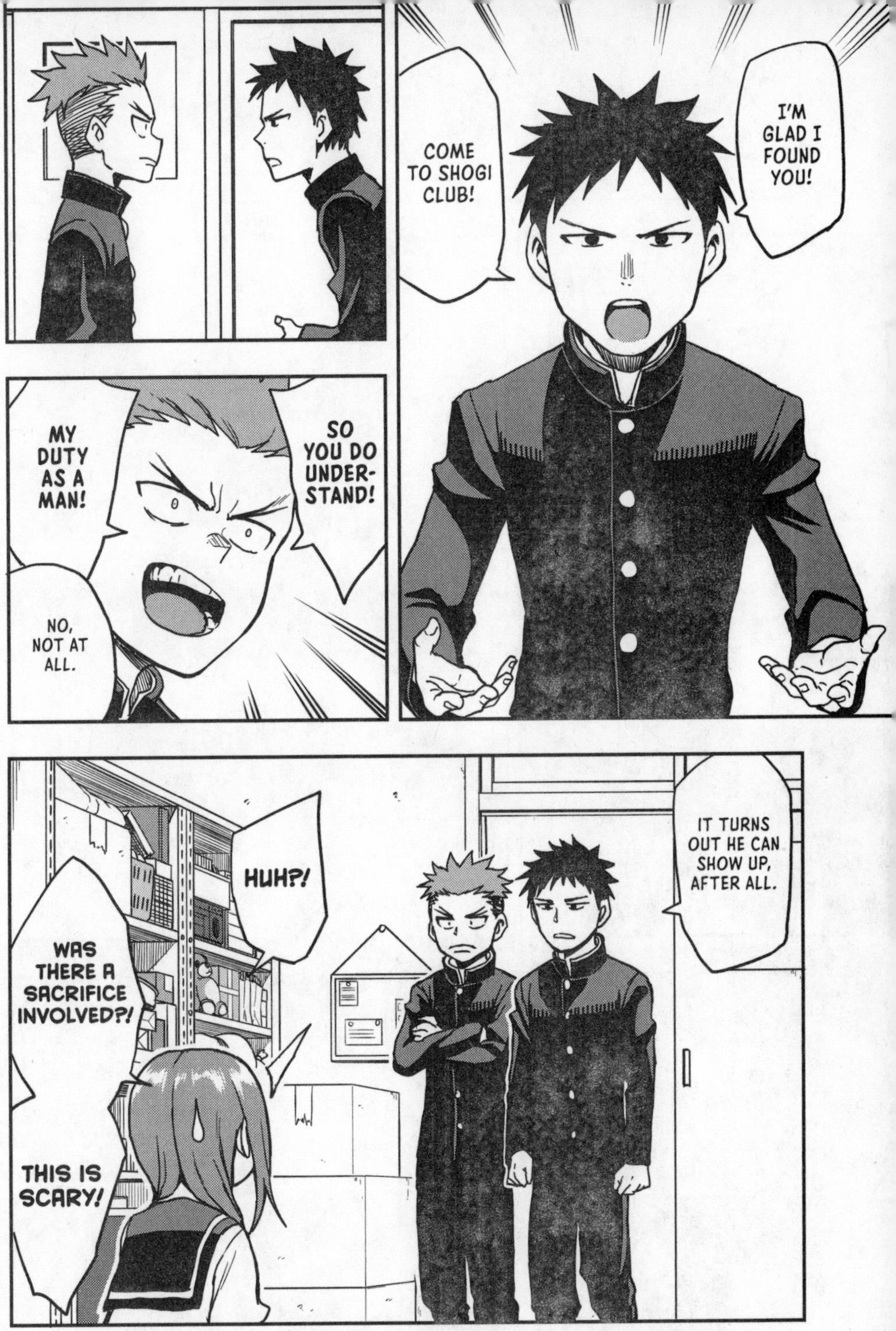
I'M GLAD I FOUND YOU!
COME TO SHOGI CLUB!
SO YOU DO UNDERSTAND!
MY DUTY AS A MAN!
NO, NOT AT ALL.
IT TURNS OUT HE CAN SHOW UP, AFTER ALL.
HUH?!
WAS THERE A SACRIFICE INVOLVED?!
THIS IS SCARY!

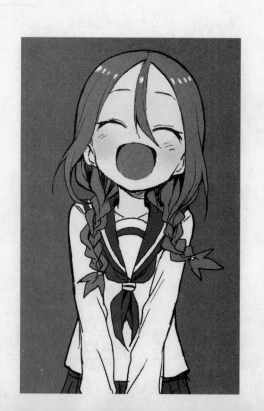

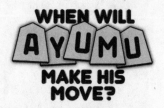

WHEN WILL
AYUMU
MAKE HIS
MOVE?

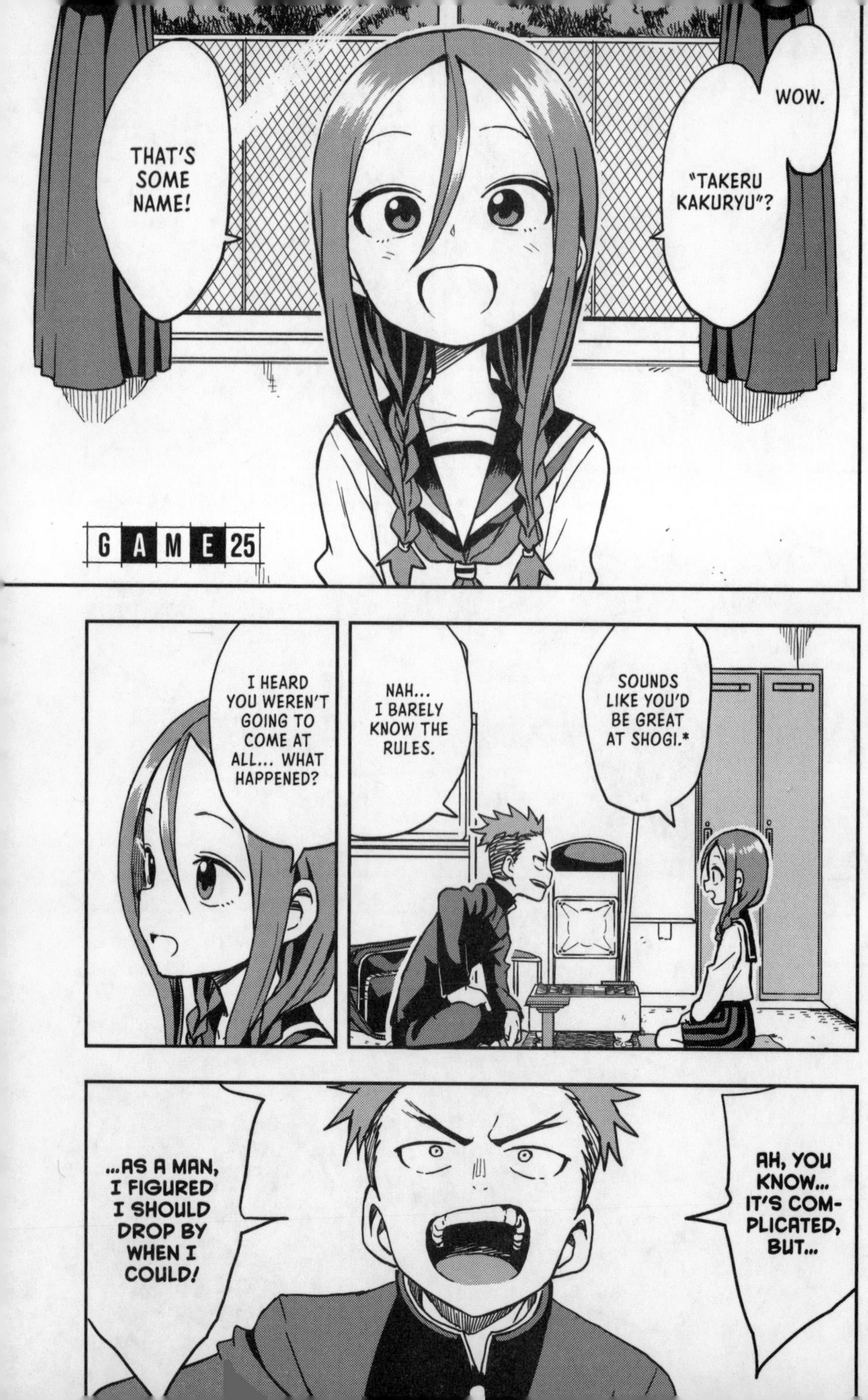
WOW.
"TAKERU KAKURYU"?
THAT'S SOME NAME!
GAME 25
SOUNDS LIKE YOU'D BE GREAT AT SHOGI.*
NAH... I BARELY KNOW THE RULES.
I HEARD YOU WEREN'T GOING TO COME AT ALL... WHAT HAPPENED?
AH, YOU KNOW... IT'S COMPLICATED, BUT...
...AS A MAN, I FIGURED I SHOULD DROP BY WHEN I COULD!

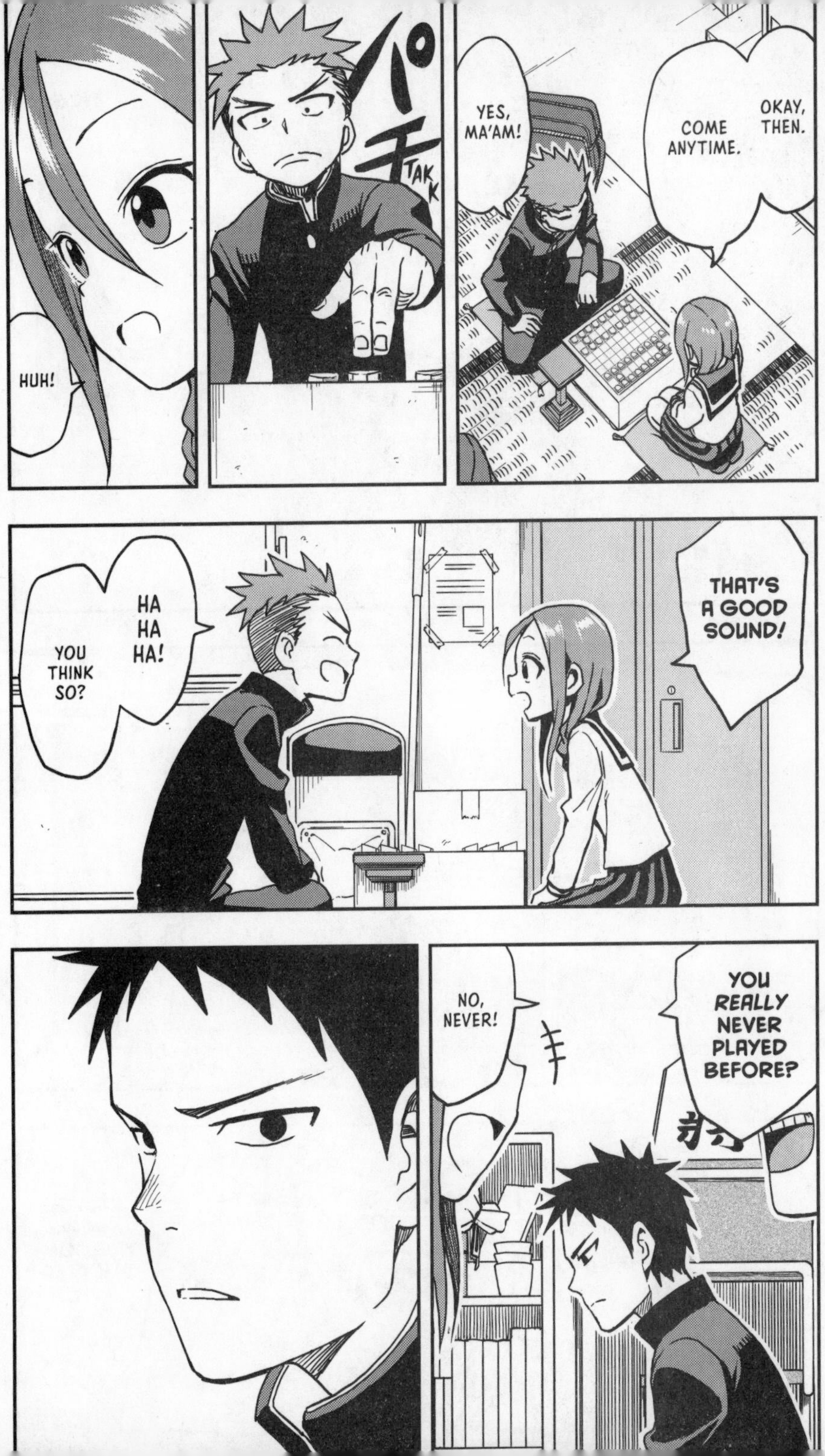
OKAY, THEN.
COME ANYTIME.
YES, MA'AM!
パチ
TAKK
HUH!
THAT'S A GOOD SOUND!
HA HA HA!
YOU THINK SO?
YOU REALLY NEVER PLAYED BEFORE?
NO, NEVER!

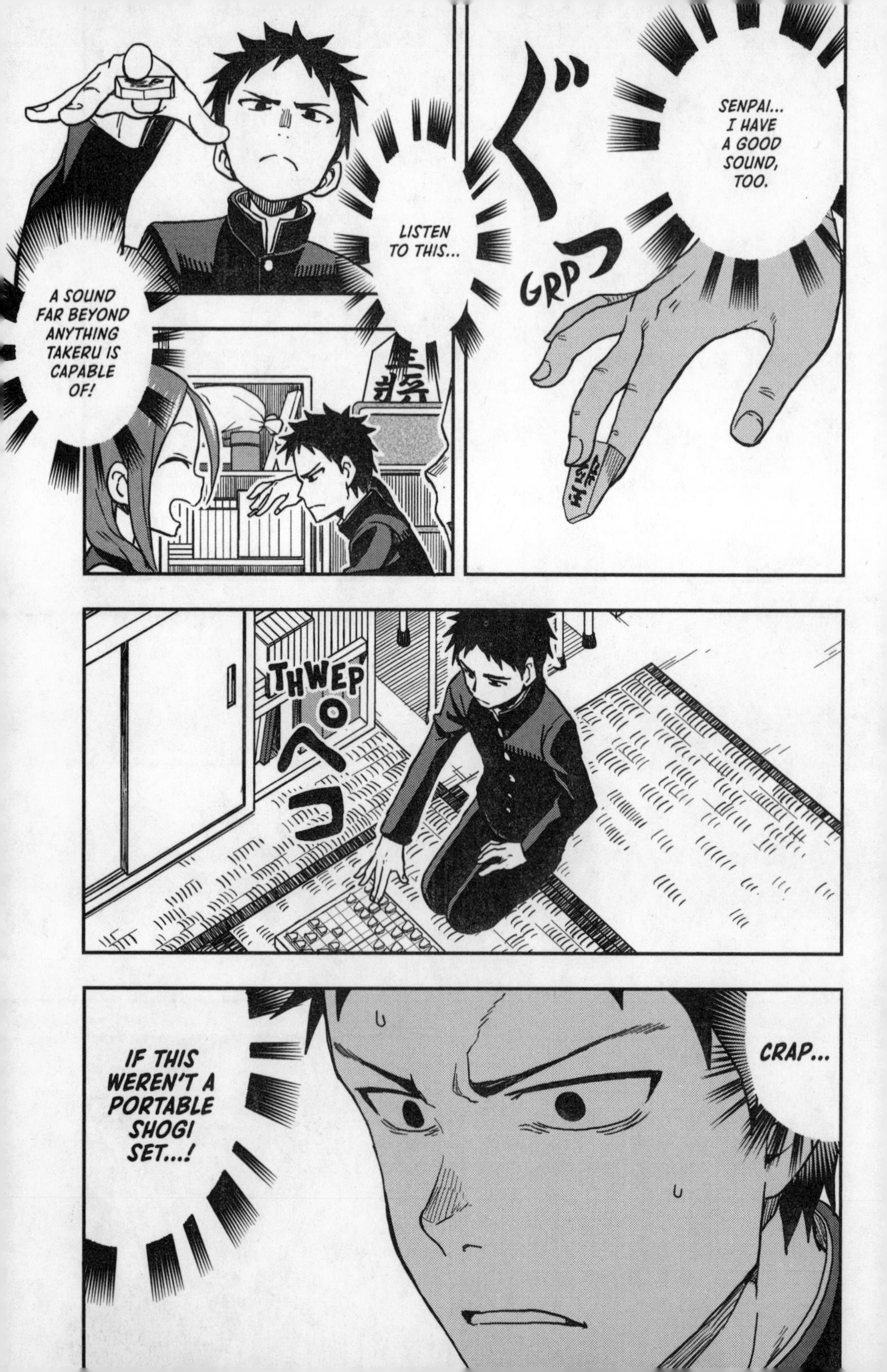
SENPAI... I HAVE A GOOD SOUND, TOO.
GRP
LISTEN TO THIS...
A SOUND FAR BEYOND ANYTHING TAKERU IS CAPABLE OF!
THWEP
CRAP...
IF THIS WEREN'T A PORTABLE SHOGI SET...!

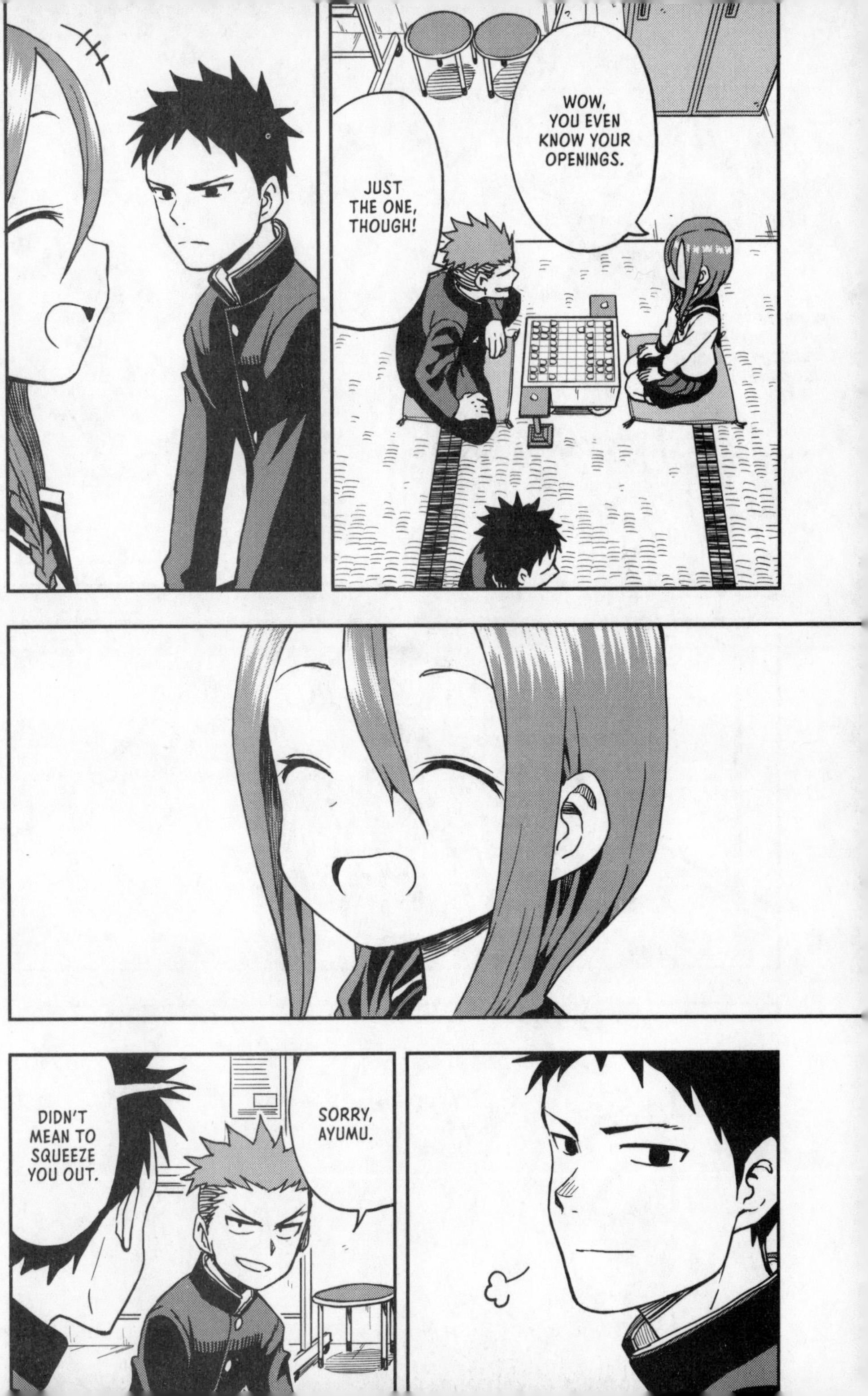
WOW, YOU EVEN KNOW YOUR OPENINGS.
JUST THE ONE, THOUGH!
SORRY, AYUMU.
DIDN'T MEAN TO SQUEEZE YOU OUT.

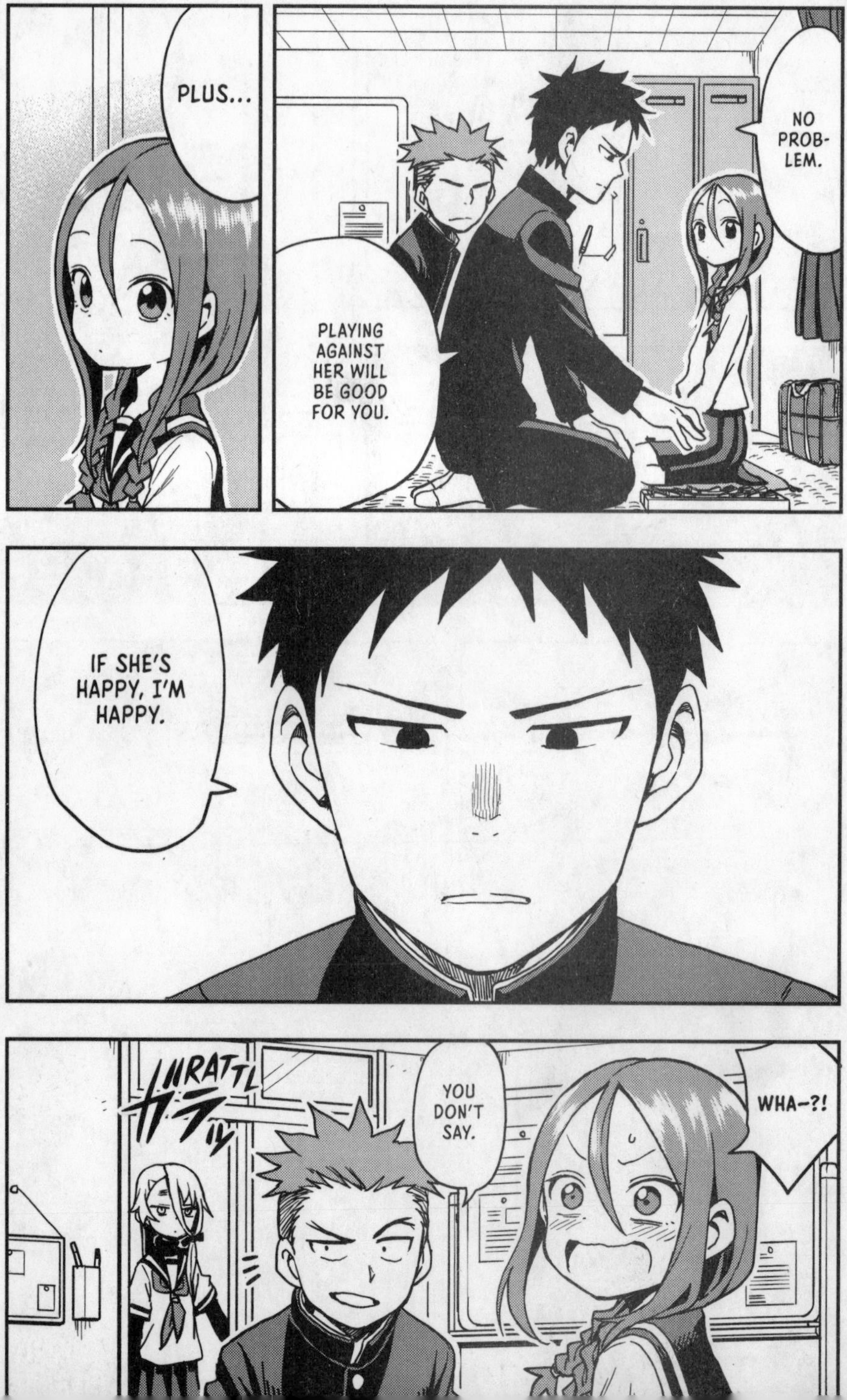
NO PROB-LEM.
PLAYING AGAINST HER WILL BE GOOD FOR YOU.
PLUS...
IF SHE'S HAPPY, I'M HAPPY.
WHA-?!
YOU DON'T SAY.
RATTL

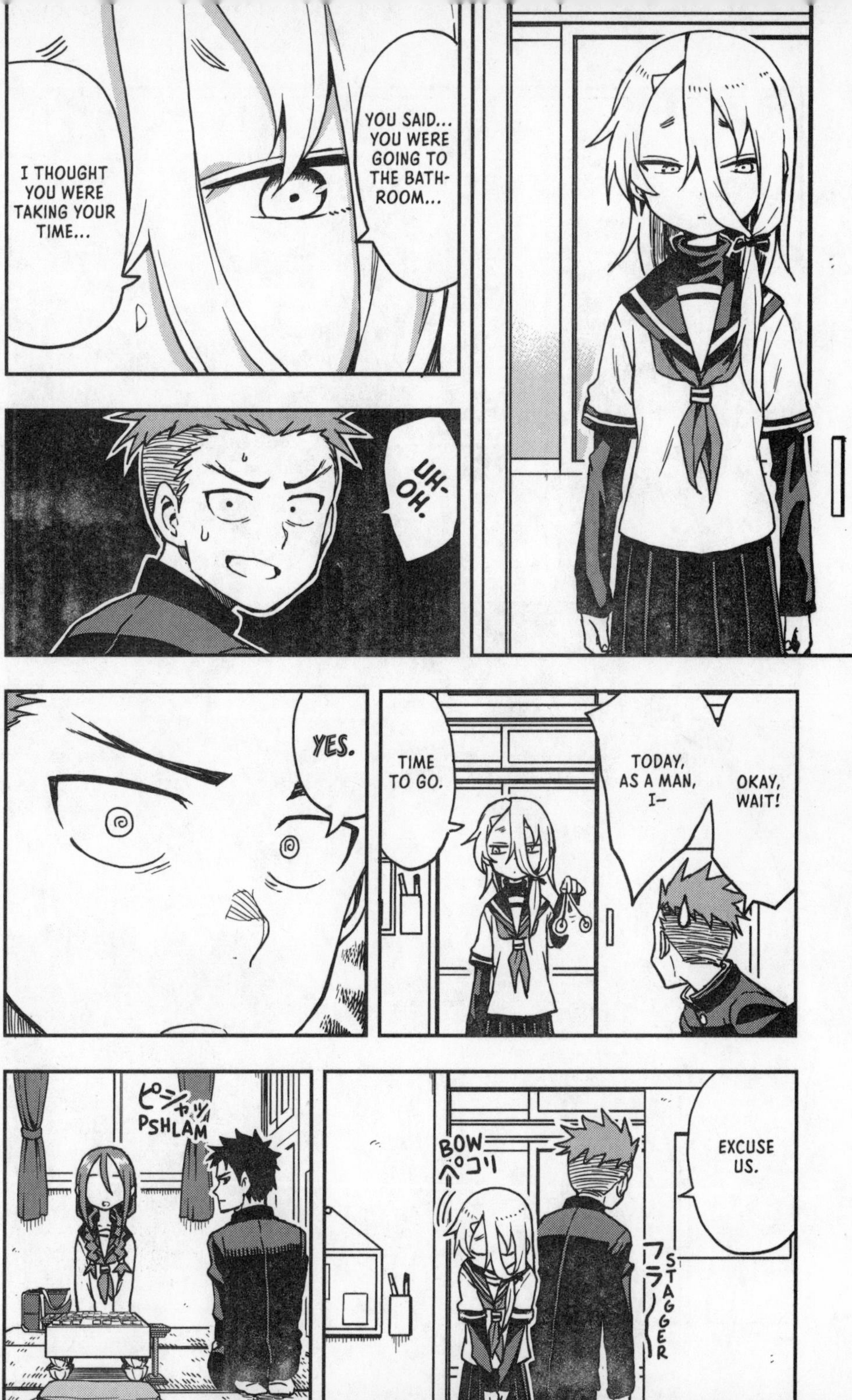
YOU SAID... YOU WERE GOING TO THE BATH-ROOM...
I THOUGHT YOU WERE TAKING YOUR TIME...
UH-OH.
OKAY, WAIT!
TODAY, AS A MAN, I–
TIME TO GO.
YES.
EXCUSE US.
BOW
ぺこり
フラー
STAGGER
ピシャッ
PSHLAM

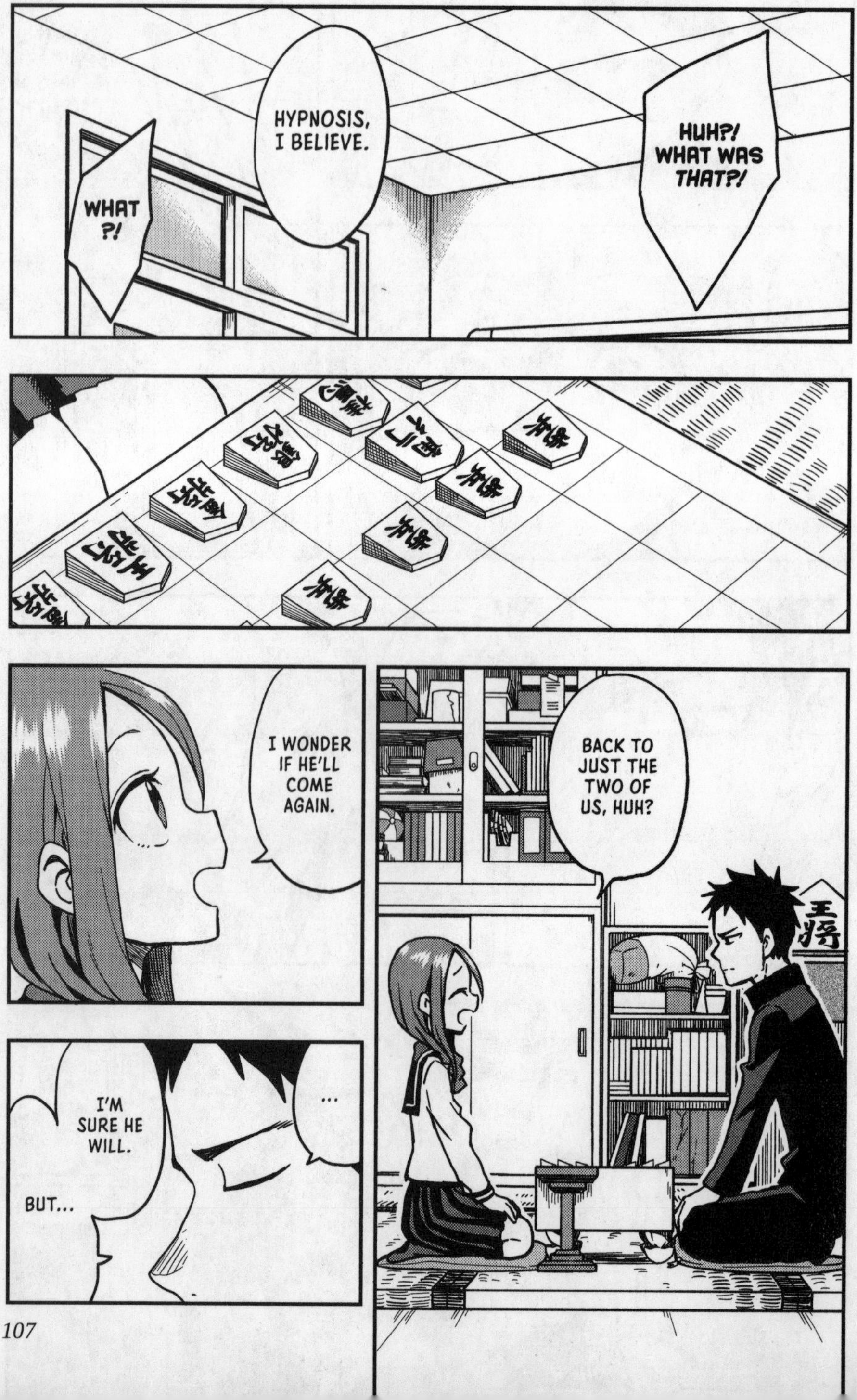
HUH?! WHAT WAS THAT?!
HYPNOSIS, I BELIEVE.
WHAT ?!
BACK TO JUST THE TWO OF US, HUH?
王将
I WONDER IF HE'LL COME AGAIN.
...
I'M SURE HE WILL.
BUT...

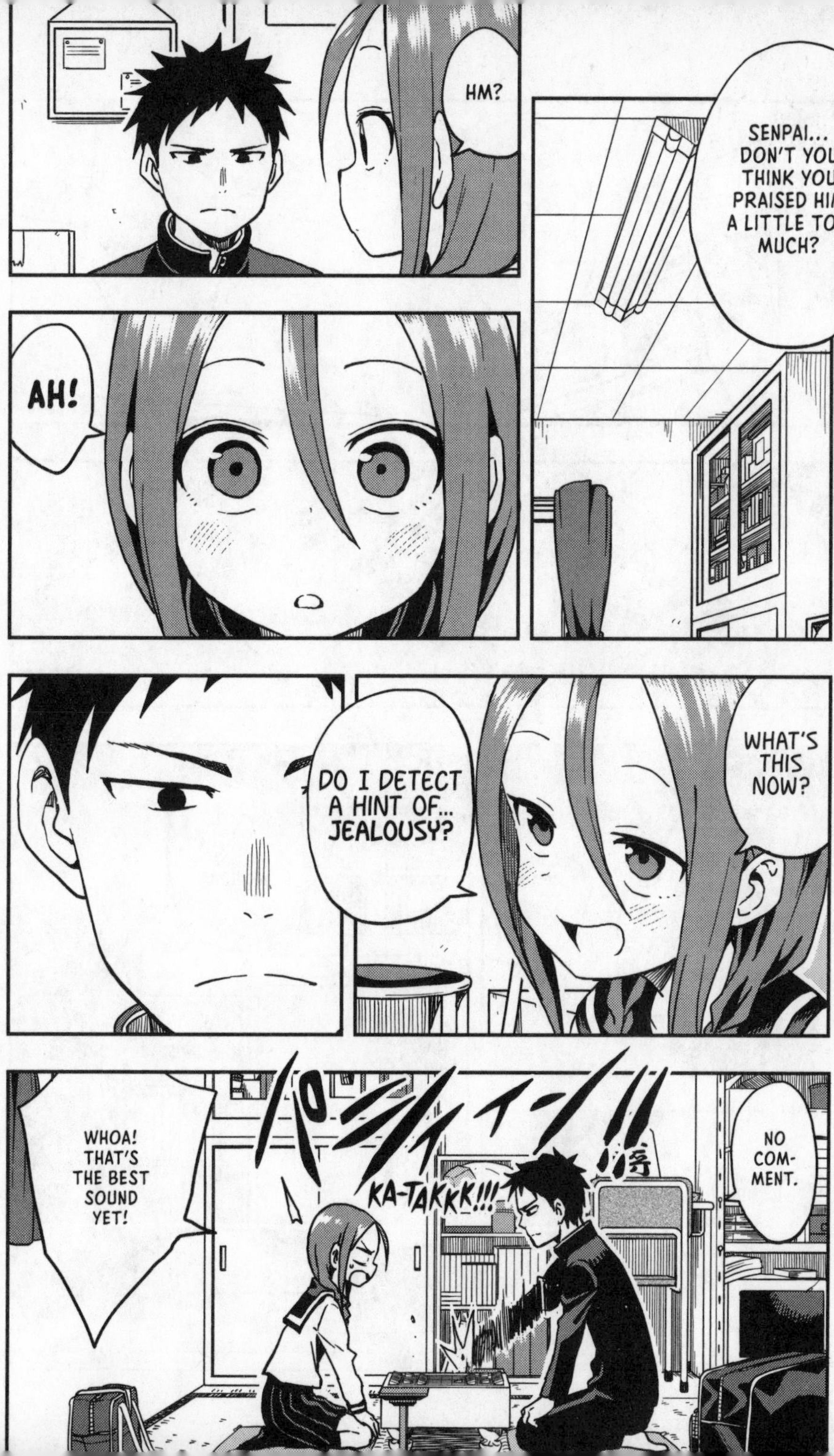
SENPAI... DON'T YOU THINK YOU PRAISED HIM A LITTLE TOO MUCH?
HM?
AH!
WHAT'S THIS NOW?
DO I DETECT A HINT OF... JEALOUSY?
NO COM-MENT.
KA-TAKKK!!!
WHOA! THAT'S THE BEST SOUND YET!

▲ BLACK (SENTE): TAKERU KAKURYU △ WHITE (GOTE): URUSHI YAOTOME
(DIAGRAM SHOWS BOARD AFTER MOVE 17, ▲ S-3H)

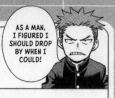

AS A MAN,
I FIGURED I
SHOULD DROP
BY WHEN I
COULD!

◁ URUSHI: P

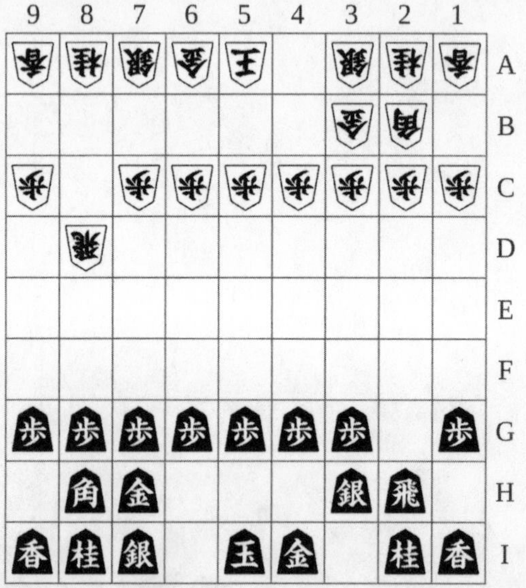

▲ TAKERU: P

	9	8	7	6	5	4	3	2	1	
A	香	桂	銀	金	王		金	桂	香	A
B							角	飛		B
C	歩		歩	歩	歩	歩	歩	歩	歩	C
D		銀								D
E										E
F										F
G	歩	歩	歩	歩	歩	歩	歩		歩	G
H		角	金				銀	飛		H
I	香	桂	銀		玉	金		桂	香	I

▲ P-2F	△ P-8D
▲ P-2E	△ P-8E
▲ G-7H	△ G-3B
▲ P-2D	△ P×2D
▲ R×2D	△ P×2C
▲ R-2H	△ P-8F
▲ P×8F	△ P×8F
▲ P×8G	△ R-8D
▲ S-3H	

(RECORD ENDS AT MOVE 17)

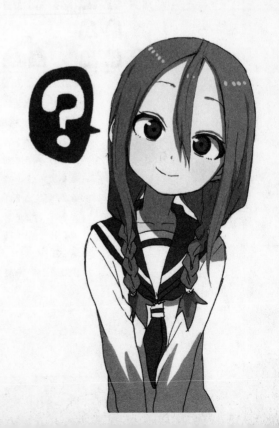

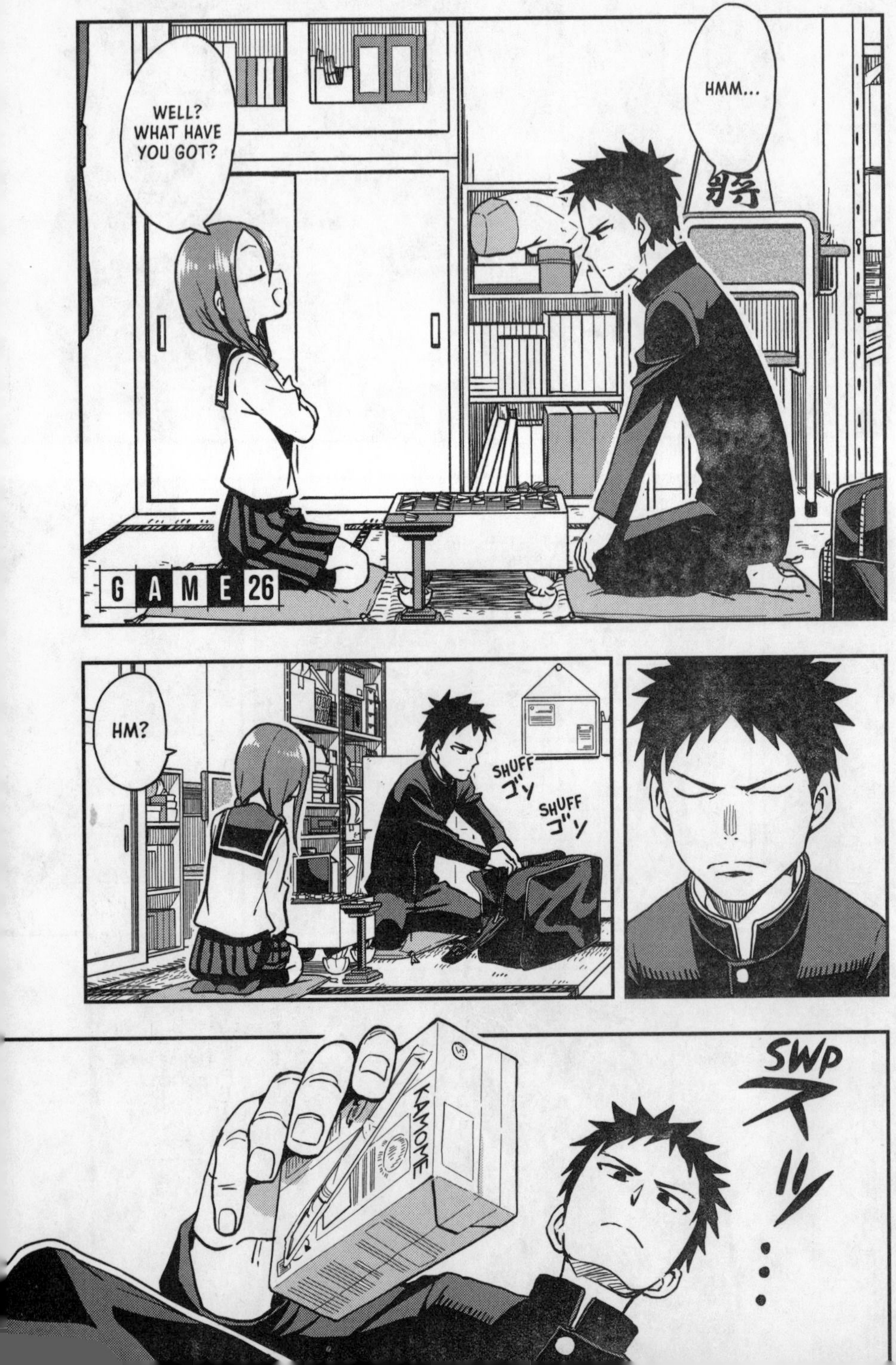
HMM...
WELL? WHAT HAVE YOU GOT?
GAME 26
SHUFF
ゴソ
SHUFF
ゴソ
HM?
SWP
スッ
KAMOME
...

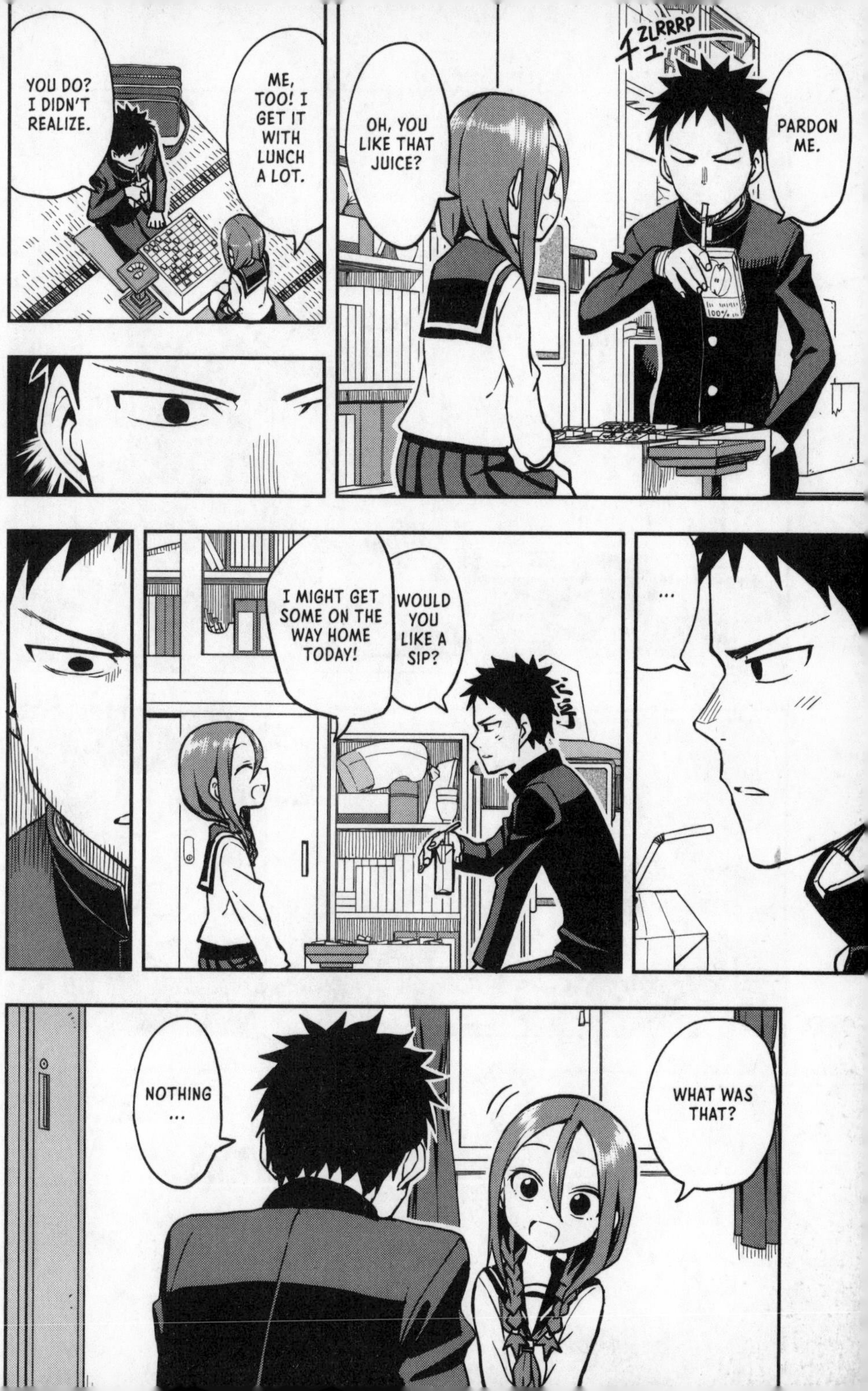
チュ ZLRRRP
PARDON ME.
OH, YOU LIKE THAT JUICE?
ME, TOO! I GET IT WITH LUNCH A LOT.
YOU DO? I DIDN'T REALIZE.
...
WOULD YOU LIKE A SIP?
I MIGHT GET SOME ON THE WAY HOME TODAY!
WHAT WAS THAT?
NOTHING ...

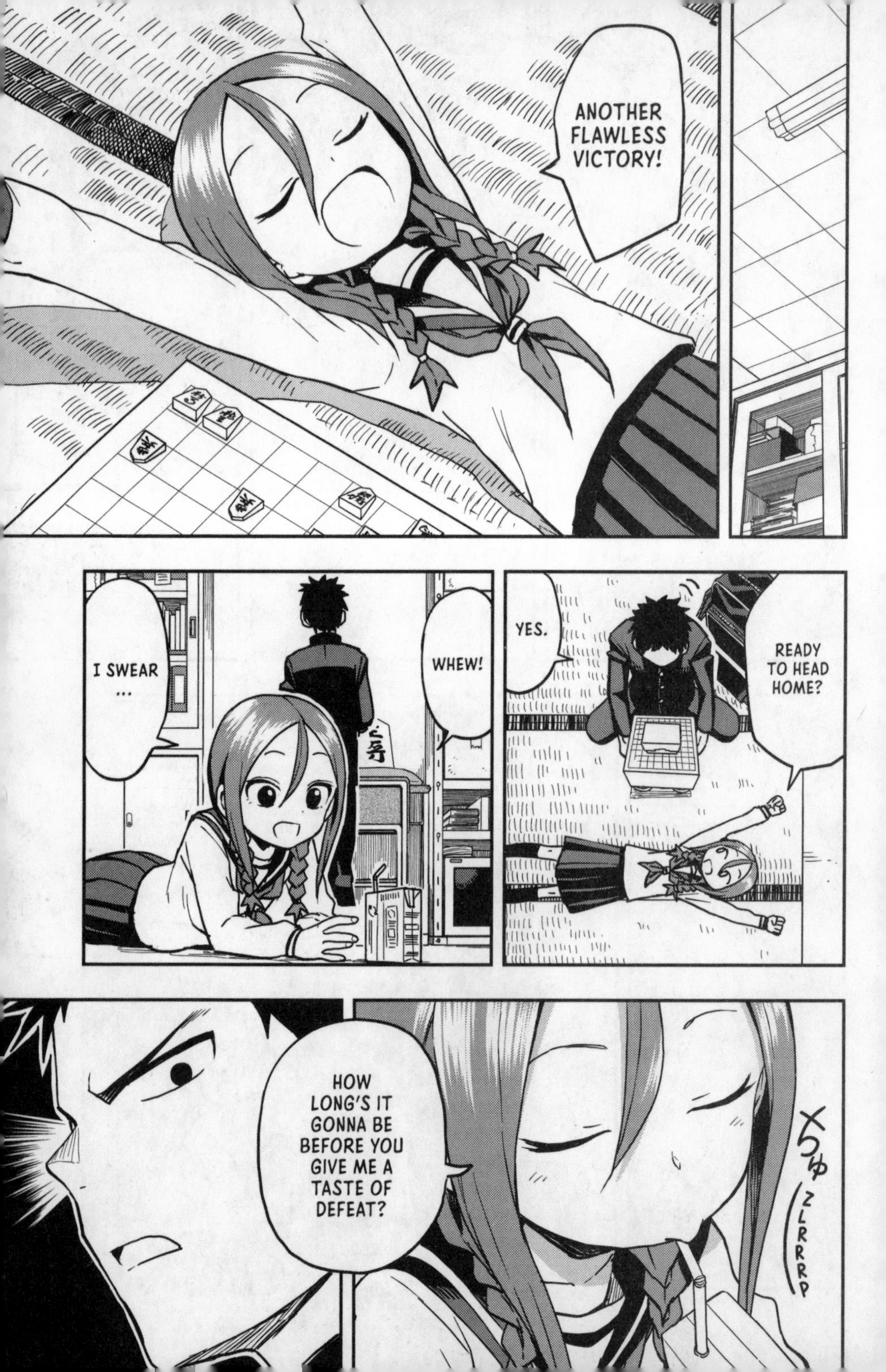
ANOTHER FLAWLESS VICTORY!
READY TO HEAD HOME?
YES.
WHEW!
I SWEAR ...
ZLRRRP
HOW LONG'S IT GONNA BE BEFORE YOU GIVE ME A TASTE OF DEFEAT?

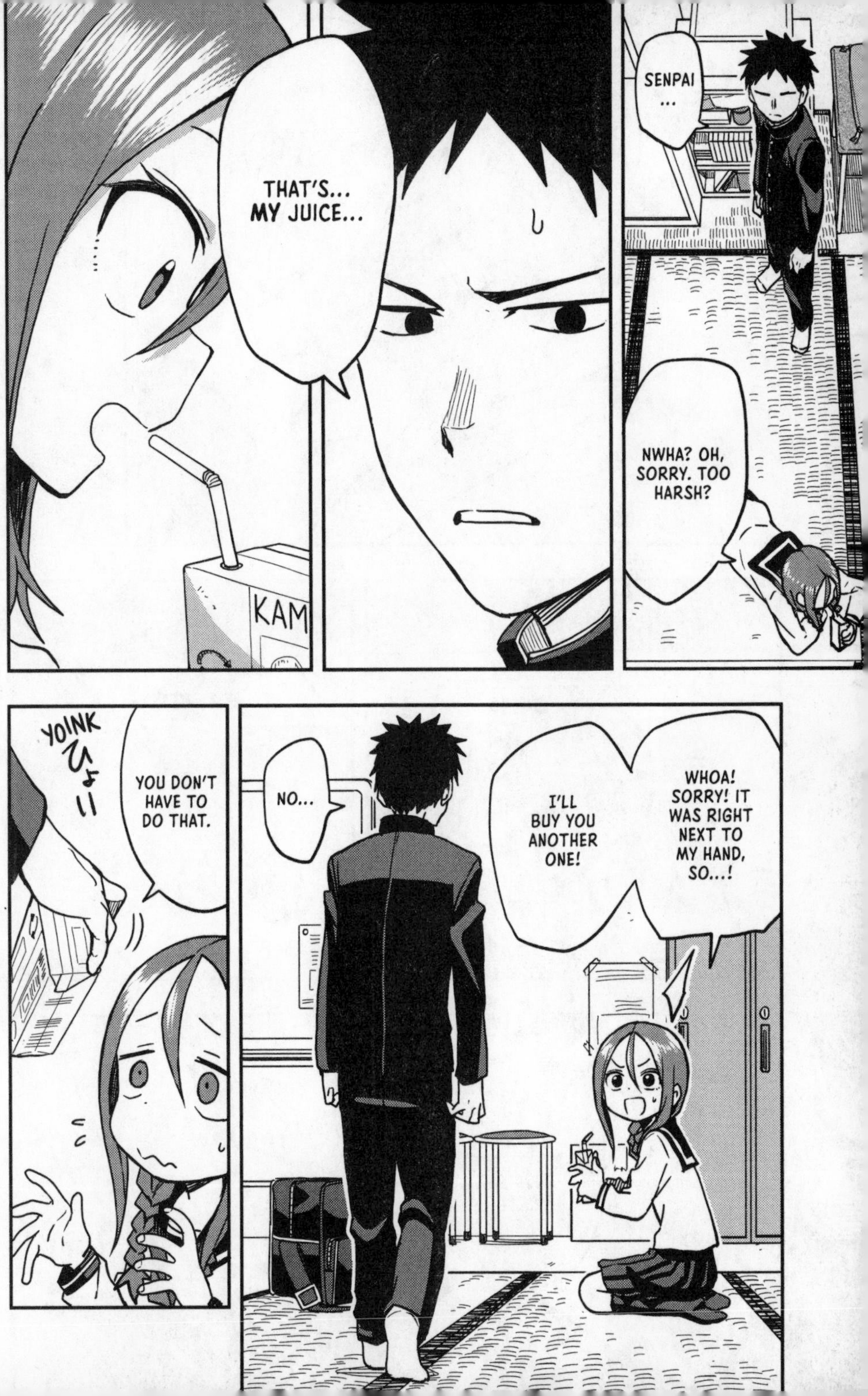
SENPAI ...
NWHA? OH, SORRY. TOO HARSH?
THAT'S... MY JUICE...
KAM
WHOA! SORRY! IT WAS RIGHT NEXT TO MY HAND, SO...!
I'LL BUY YOU ANOTHER ONE!
NO...
YOINK
ひょい
YOU DON'T HAVE TO DO THAT.

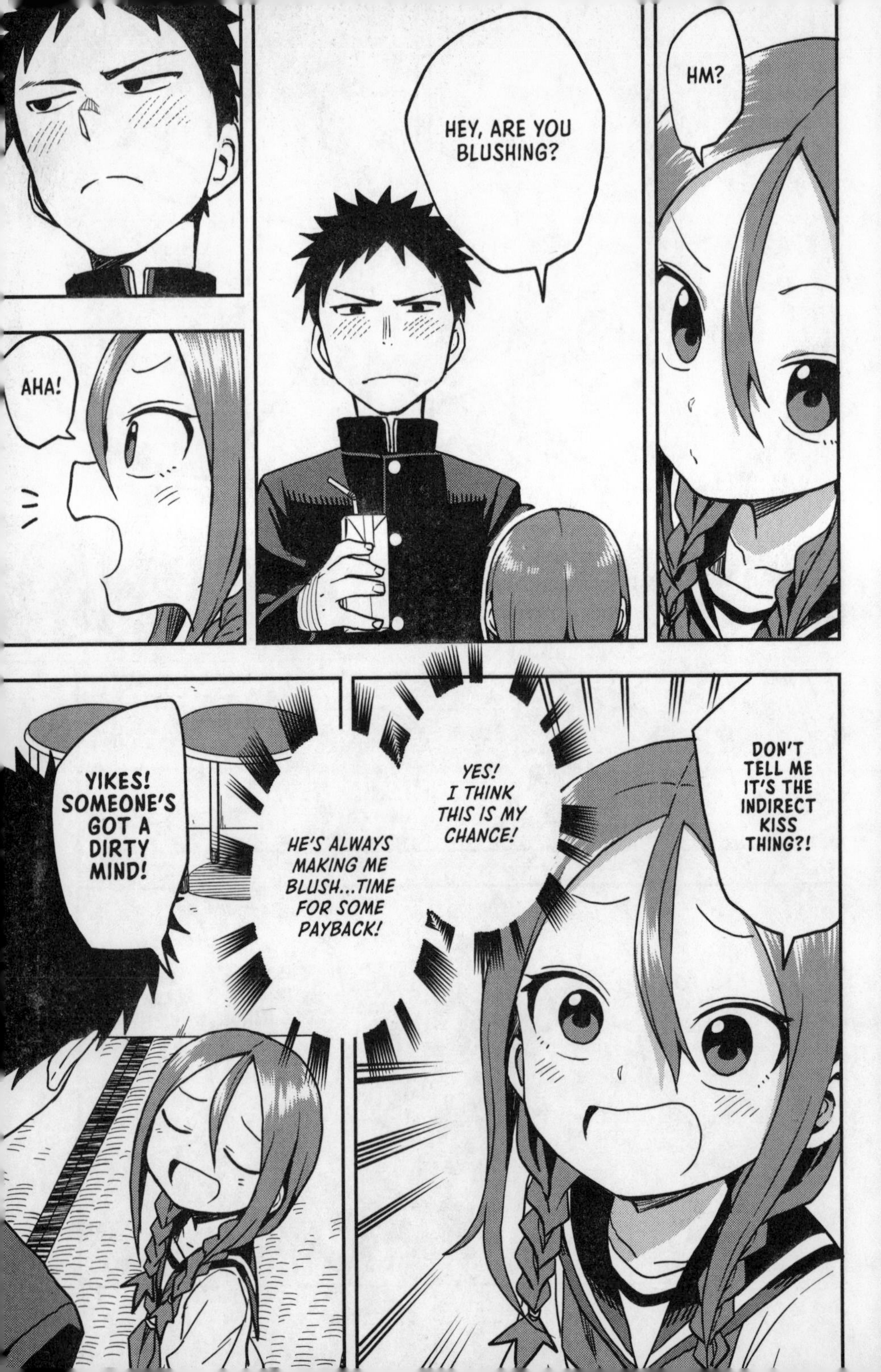
HM?
HEY, ARE YOU BLUSHING?
AHA!
DON'T TELL ME IT'S THE INDIRECT KISS THING?!
YES! I THINK THIS IS MY CHANCE!
HE'S ALWAYS MAKING ME BLUSH...TIME FOR SOME PAYBACK!
YIKES! SOMEONE'S GOT A DIRTY MIND!

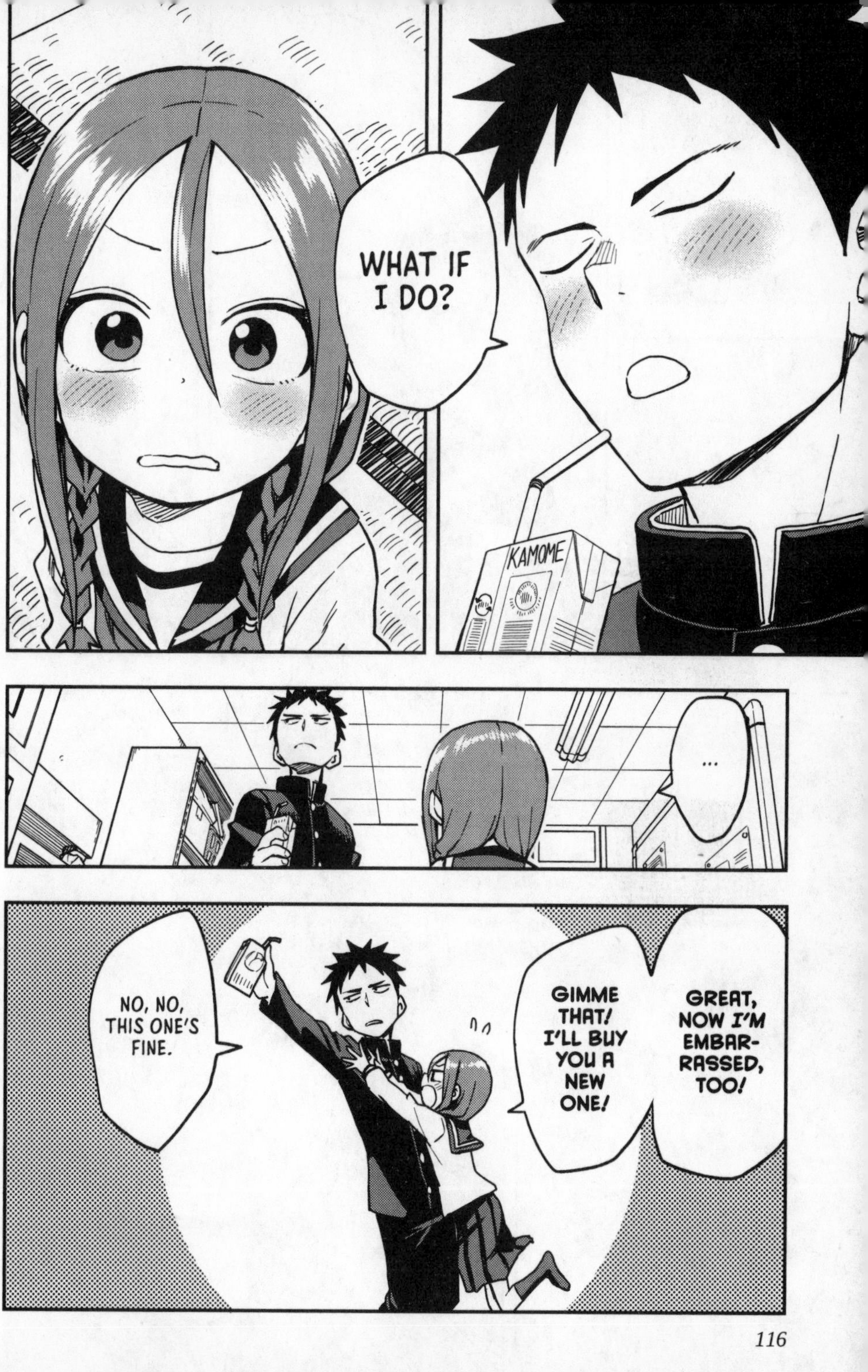
WHAT IF I DO?
KAMOME
...
GREAT, NOW I'M EMBAR-RASSED, TOO!
GIMME THAT! I'LL BUY YOU A NEW ONE!
NO, NO, THIS ONE'S FINE.

▲ **BLACK (SENTE): AYUMU TANAKA** △ **WHITE (GOTE): URUSHI YAOTOME**
[DIAGRAM SHOWS BOARD AFTER MOVE 92, △ +N-2F]

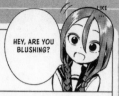

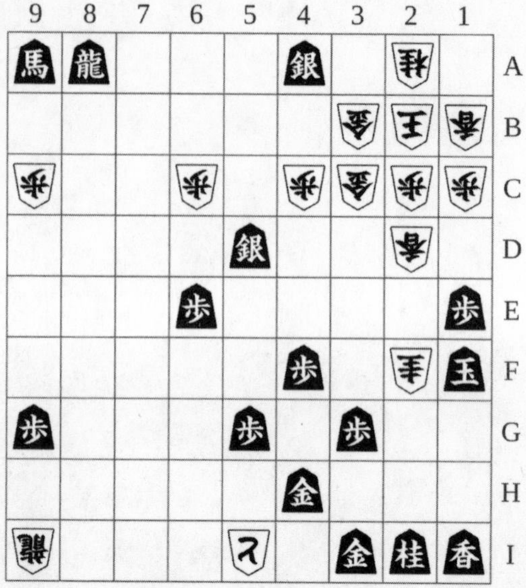

HEY, ARE YOU BLUSHING?

LIKE

▽URUSHI: N

◄AYUMU: B, S, N, L, P×5

	▲ P-7F	△ P-3D		▲ S-5F	△ P-7E		▲ B×9A+	△ +R×9I
	▲ P-6F	△ P-8D		▲ P×7E	△ S×7E		▲ +R×8A	△ P-5I+
	▲ R-6H	△ P-8E		▲ R-7H	△ R-7B		▲ G-3I	△ N×3E
	▲ B-7G	△ S-6B		▲ B-8H	△ P×7F		▲ G4G-4H	△ L×2D
	▲ G6I-5H	△ K-4B		▲ S-4E	△ R-8B		▲ N×3D	△ B-3C
	▲ K-4H	△ P-5D		▲ S×3D	△ B-4B		▲ N×2B+	△ K×2B
	▲ S-7H	△ K-3B		▲ P-6E	△ G-3B		▲ L×3D	△ G5A-4B
	▲ K-3H	△ P-7D		▲ S-4E	△ P-8F		▲ L×3C+	△ G4BX3C
	▲ S-6G	△ S-7C		▲ P×8F	△ S×8F		▲ S×4A	△ N×2G+
	▲ K-2H	△ S-8D		▲ R×7F	△ S-8G=		▲ S×2G	△ L×2G+
	▲ R-8H	△ B-3C		▲ R-7A+	△ R-8E		▲ K×2G	△ N×3E
	▲ S-3H	△ K-2B		▲ B-6F	△ S-7F+		▲ K-2H	△ L×2D
	▲ P-1F	△ L-1B		▲ +R×7F	△ R×8I+		▲ K-1G	△ N-2G+
	▲ P-1E	△ K-1A		▲ +R-7B	△ G-5A		▲ K-1F	△ +N-2F
	▲ P-4F	△ S-2B		▲ S×5D	△ +R-6I		[WHITE WINS AT MOVE 92]	
	▲ G-4G	△ G6A-5B		▲ B-5E	△ P×5H			

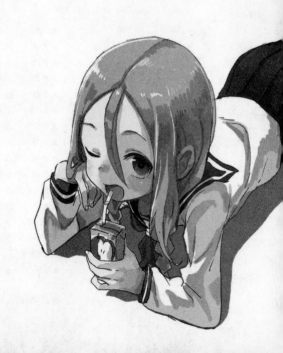

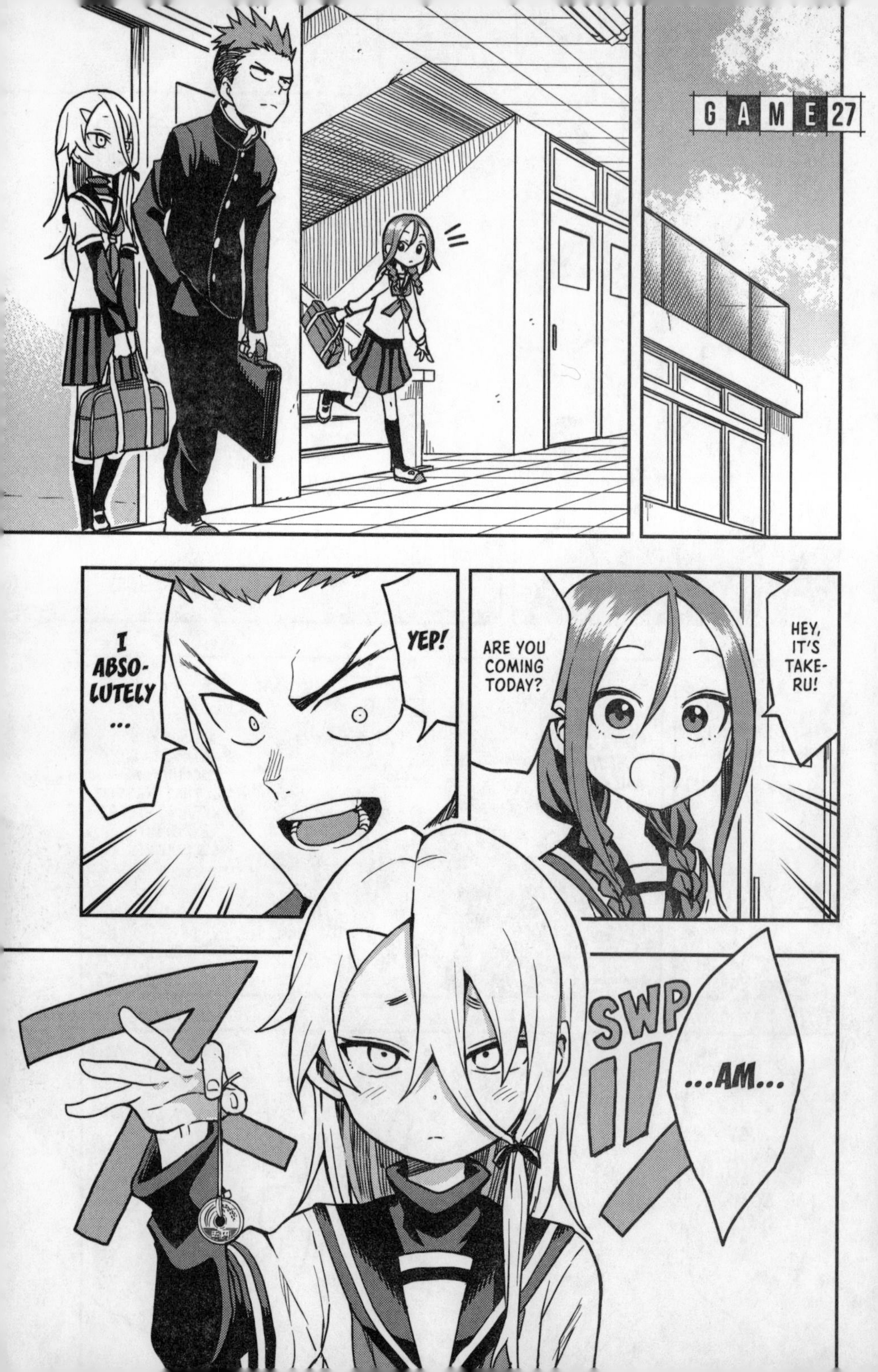
GAME 27
HEY, IT'S TAKE-RU!
ARE YOU COMING TODAY?
YEP!
I ABSO-LUTELY...
SWP
...AM...

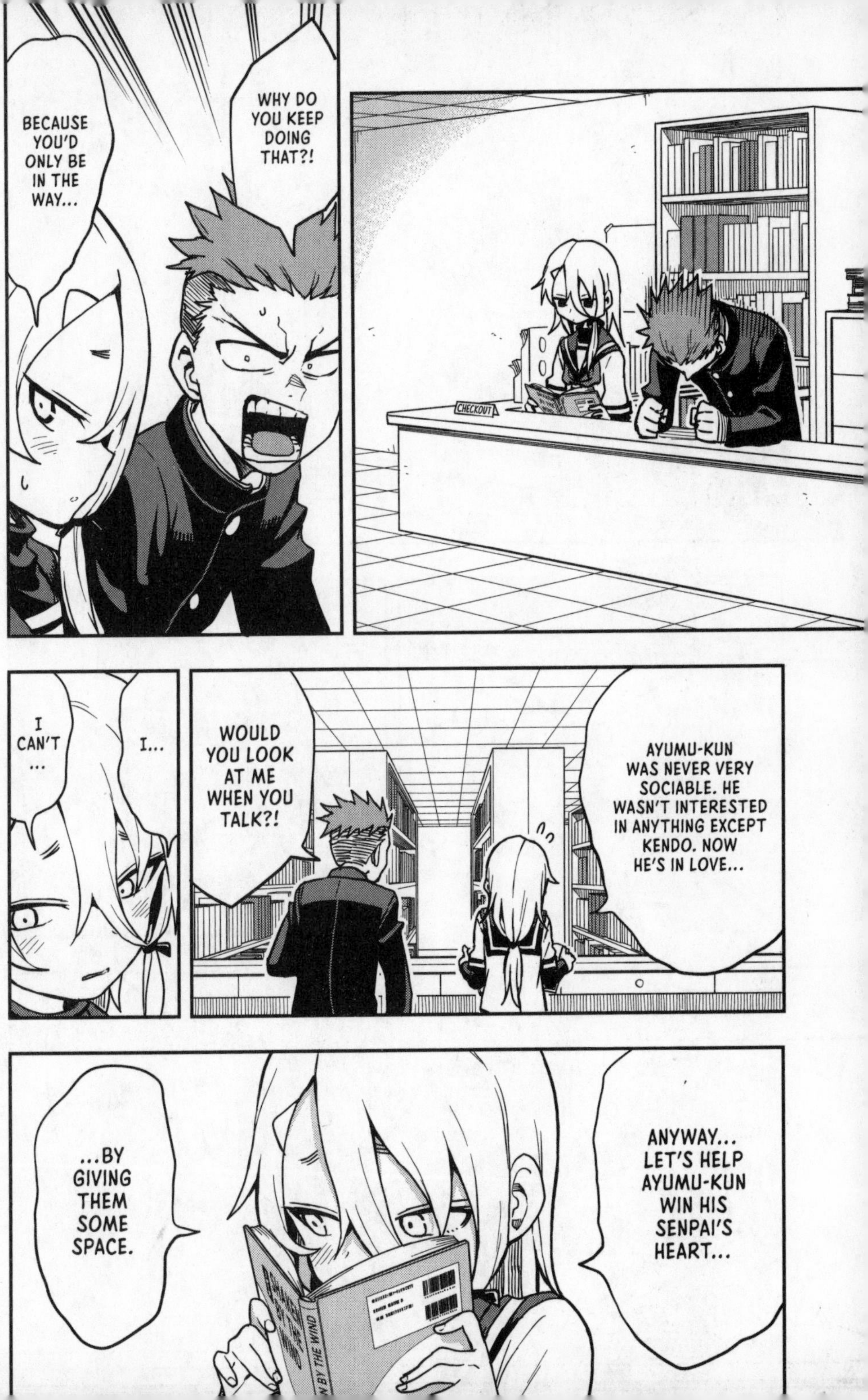
CHECKOUT
WHY DO YOU KEEP DOING THAT?!
BECAUSE YOU'D ONLY BE IN THE WAY...
AYUMU-KUN WAS NEVER VERY SOCIABLE. HE WASN'T INTERESTED IN ANYTHING EXCEPT KENDO. NOW HE'S IN LOVE...
WOULD YOU LOOK AT ME WHEN YOU TALK?!
I...
I CAN'T ...
ANYWAY... LET'S HELP AYUMU-KUN WIN HIS SENPAI'S HEART...
...BY GIVING THEM SOME SPACE.

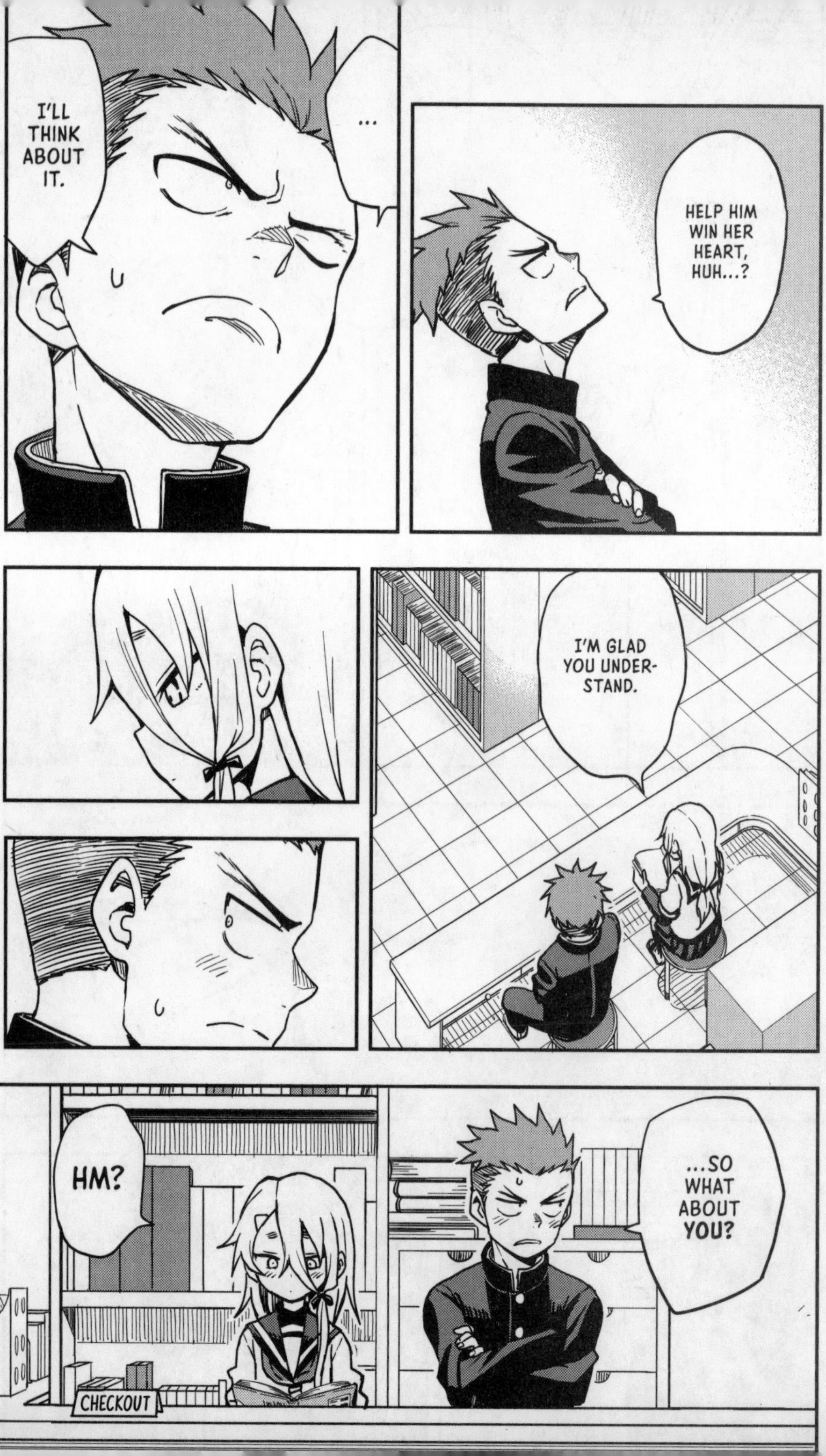
HELP HIM WIN HER HEART, HUH...?
...
I'LL THINK ABOUT IT.
I'M GLAD YOU UNDERSTAND.
...SO WHAT ABOUT YOU?
HM?
CHECKOUT

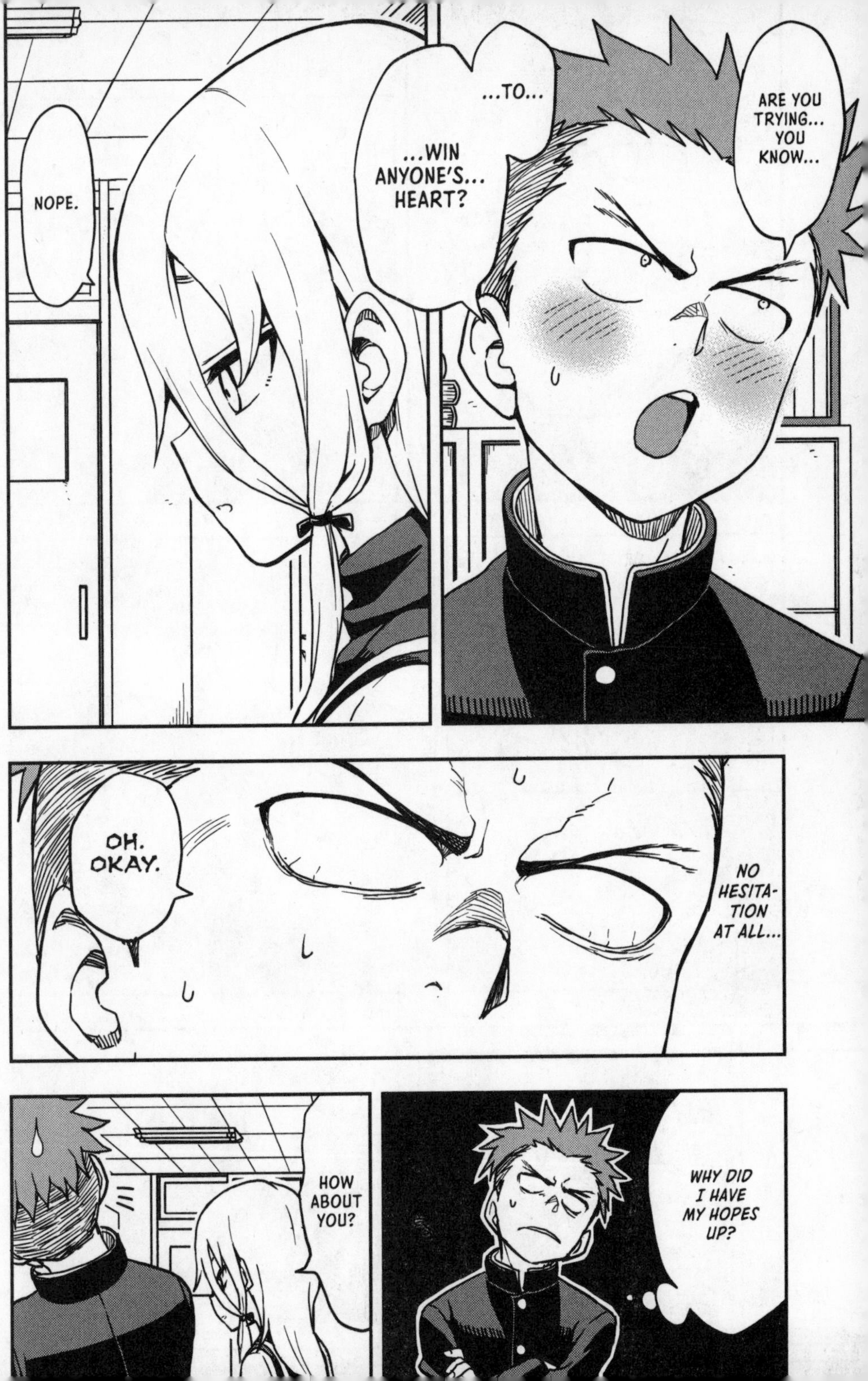
ARE YOU TRYING... YOU KNOW...
...TO...
...WIN ANYONE'S... HEART?
NOPE.
NO HESITA-TION AT ALL...
OH. OKAY.
WHY DID I HAVE MY HOPES UP?
HOW ABOUT YOU?

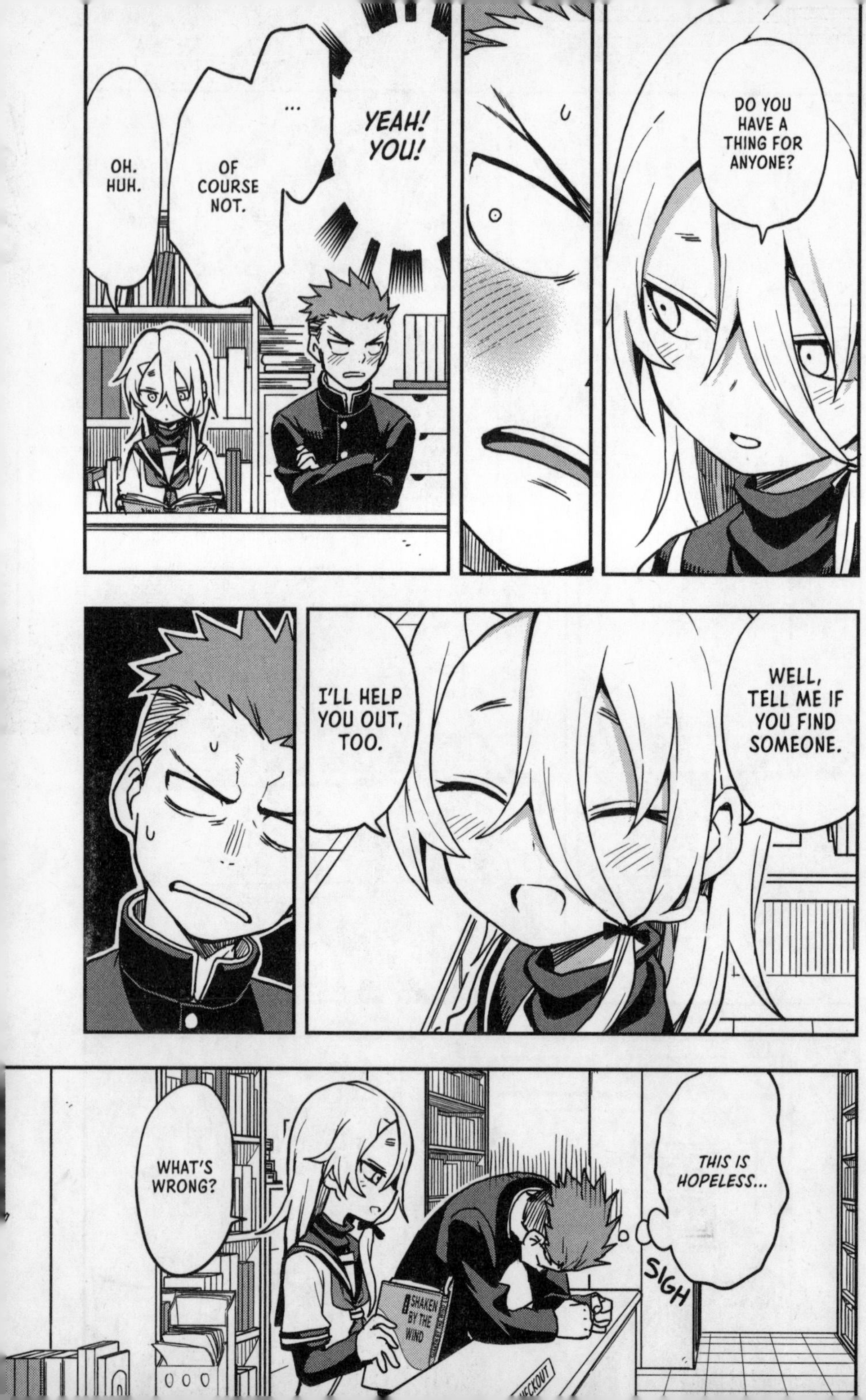
DO YOU HAVE A THING FOR ANYONE?
YEAH! YOU!
...
OF COURSE NOT.
OH. HUH.
WELL, TELL ME IF YOU FIND SOMEONE.
I'LL HELP YOU OUT, TOO.
THIS IS HOPELESS...
SIGH
WHAT'S WRONG?
SHAKEN BY THE WIND

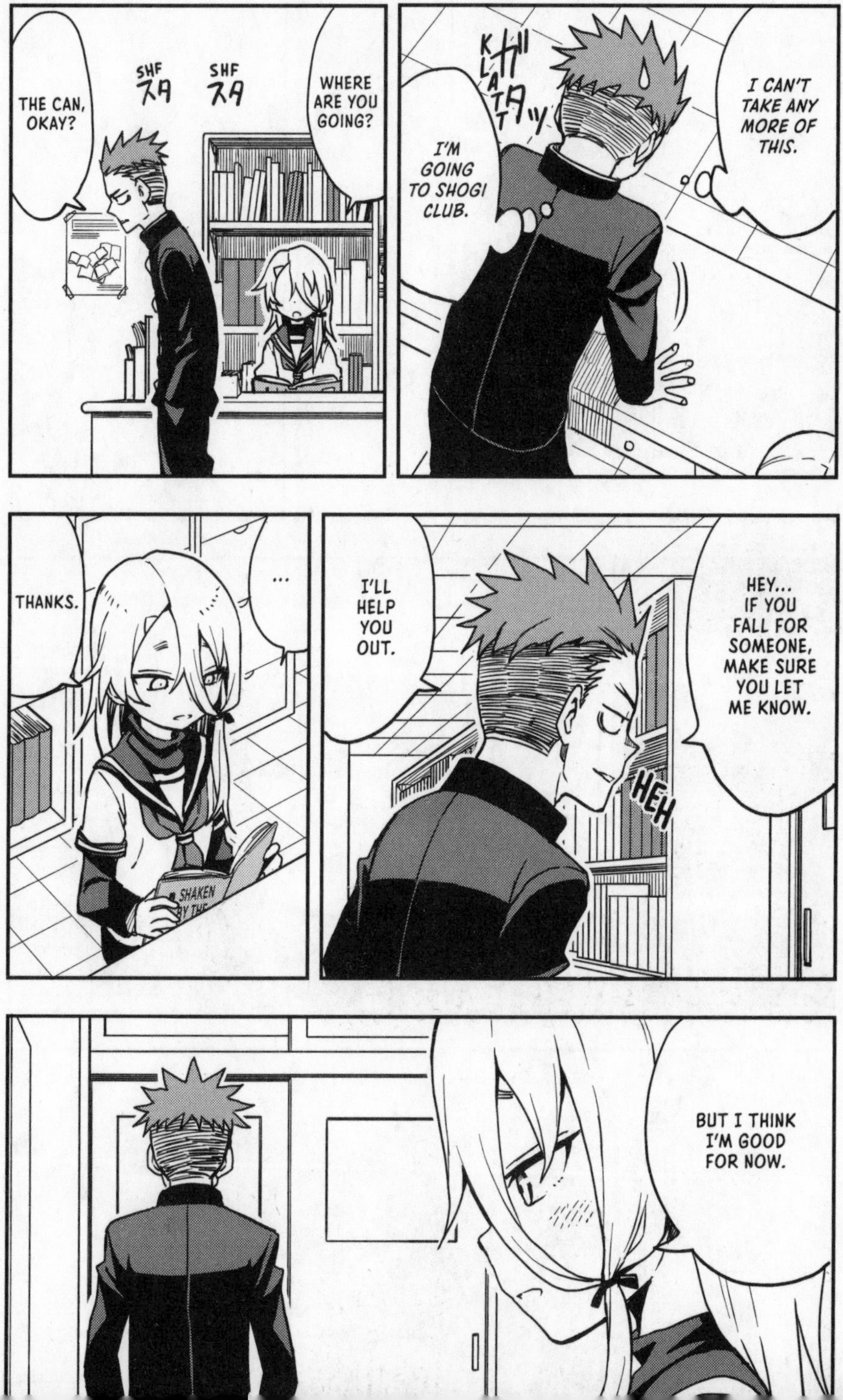
I CAN'T TAKE ANY MORE OF THIS.
KLATT
ガタッ
I'M GOING TO SHOGI CLUB.
WHERE ARE YOU GOING?
SHF
スタ
SHF
スタ
THE CAN, OKAY?
HEY... IF YOU FALL FOR SOMEONE, MAKE SURE YOU LET ME KNOW.
I'LL HELP YOU OUT.
HEH
...
THANKS.
SHAKEN BY THE
BUT I THINK I'M GOOD FOR NOW.

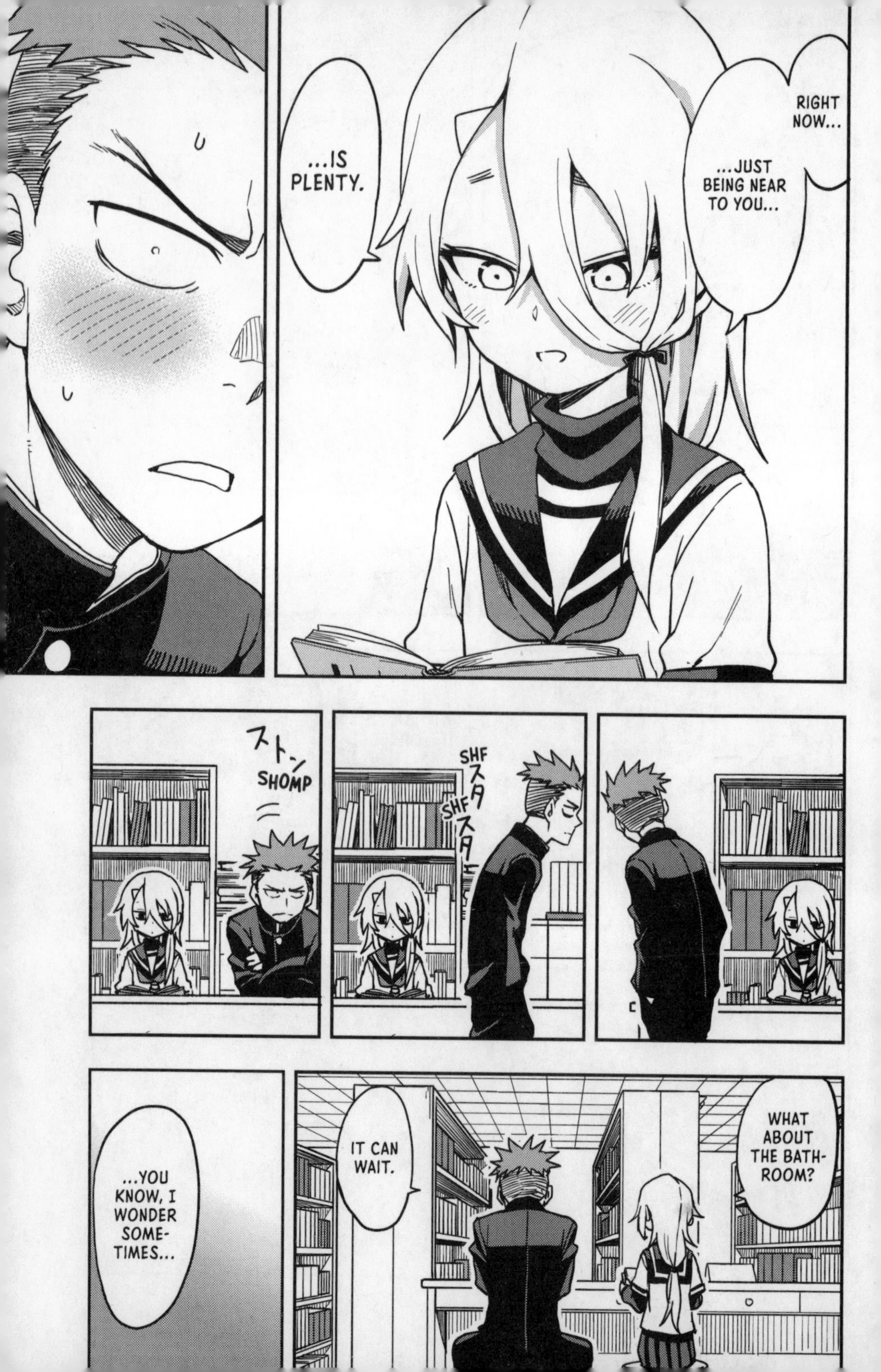
RIGHT NOW...
...JUST BEING NEAR TO YOU...
...IS PLENTY.
SHF
スタ
SHF
スタ
ストン
SHOMP
WHAT ABOUT THE BATH-ROOM?
IT CAN WAIT.
...YOU KNOW, I WONDER SOME-TIMES...

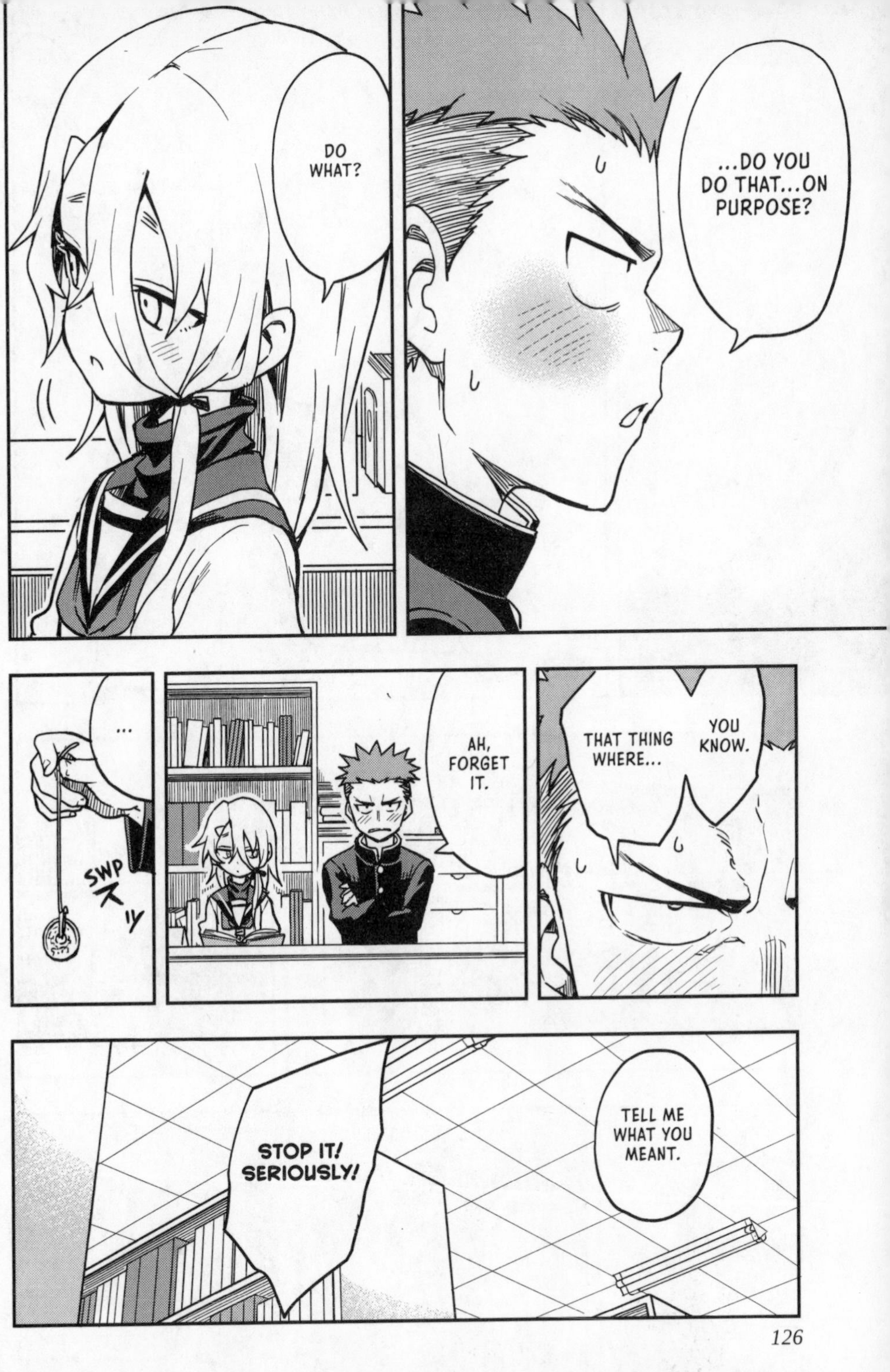
...DO YOU DO THAT...ON PURPOSE?
DO WHAT?
YOU KNOW.
THAT THING WHERE...
AH, FORGET IT.
...
SWP
スッ
TELL ME WHAT YOU MEANT.
STOP IT! SERIOUSLY!

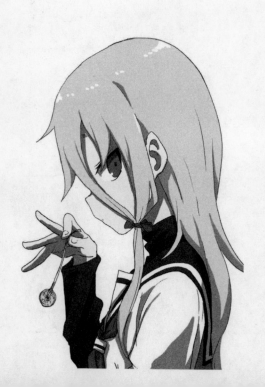

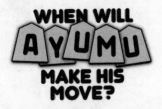
WHEN WILL AYUMU MAKE HIS MOVE?

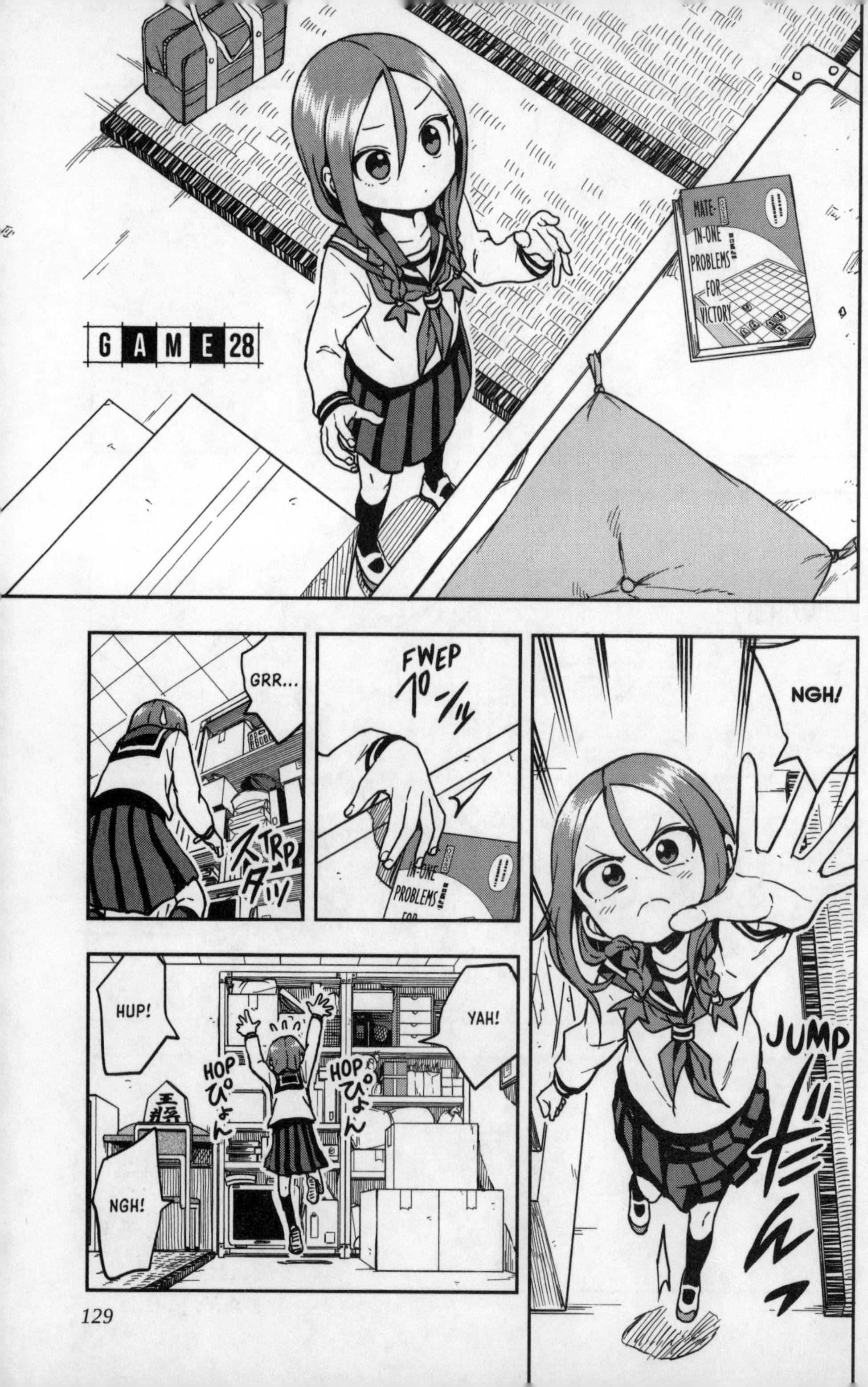
GAME 28
MATE-IN-ONE PROBLEMS FOR VICTORY
NGH!
JUMP
FWEP
IN-ONE PROBLEMS
GRR...
TRP
YAH!
HOP ぴょん
HUP!
HOP ぴょん
NGH!

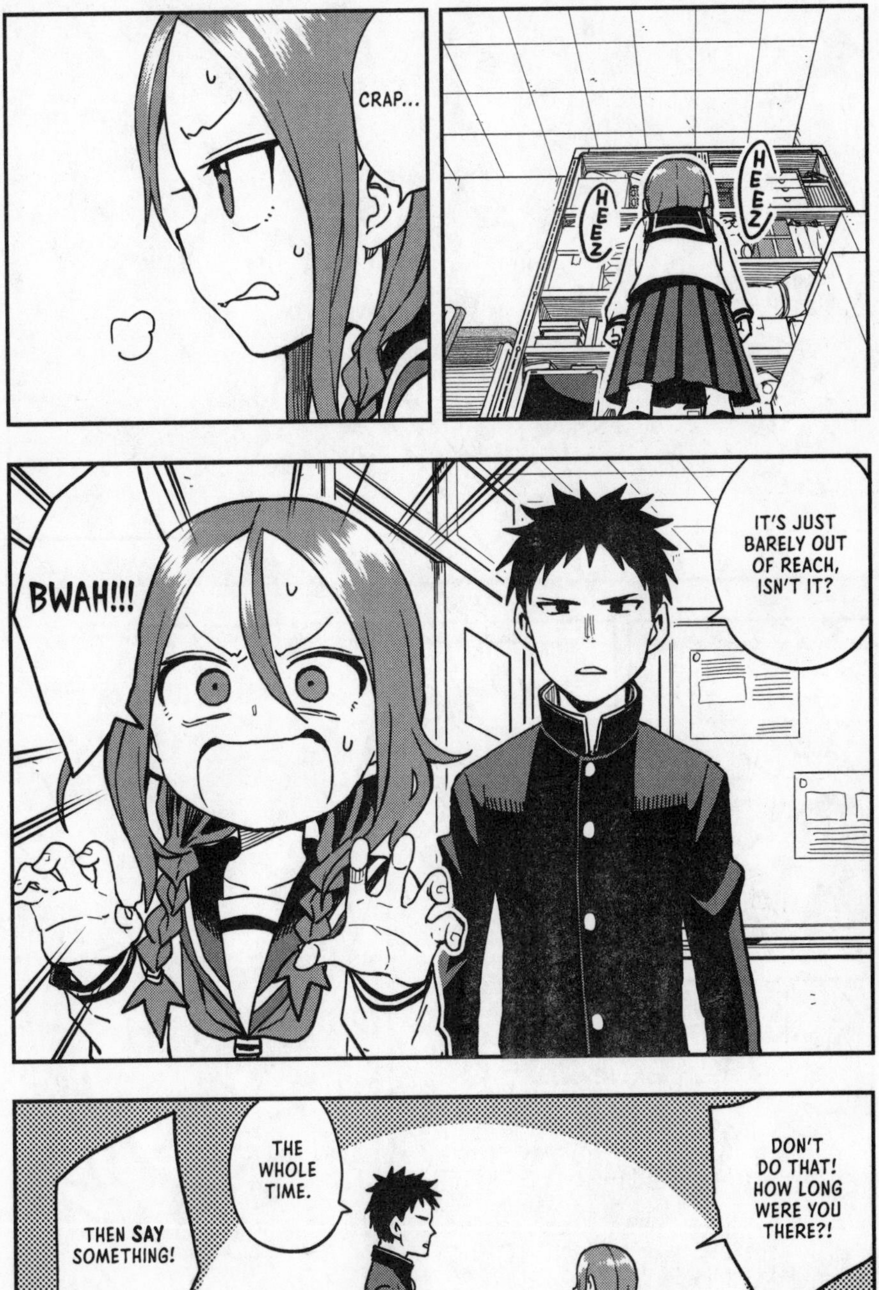
HEEZ
HEEZ
CRAP...
IT'S JUST BARELY OUT OF REACH, ISN'T IT?
BWAH!!!
DON'T DO THAT! HOW LONG WERE YOU THERE?!
THE WHOLE TIME.
THEN SAY SOMETHING!

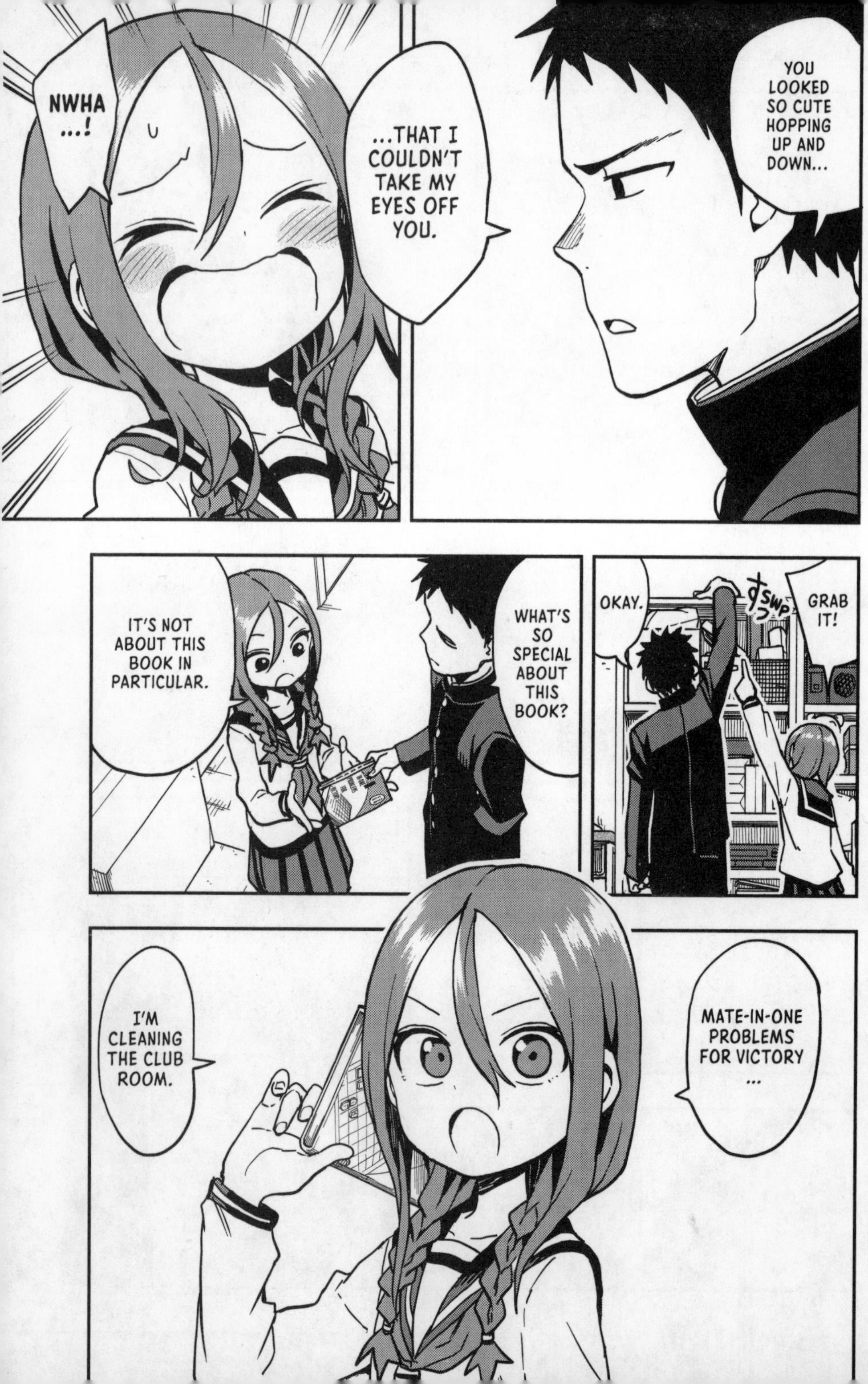
YOU LOOKED SO CUTE HOPPING UP AND DOWN...
...THAT I COULDN'T TAKE MY EYES OFF YOU.
NWHA ...!
GRAB IT!
SWP
OKAY.
WHAT'S SO SPECIAL ABOUT THIS BOOK?
IT'S NOT ABOUT THIS BOOK IN PARTICULAR.
MATE-IN-ONE PROBLEMS FOR VICTORY ...
I'M CLEANING THE CLUB ROOM.

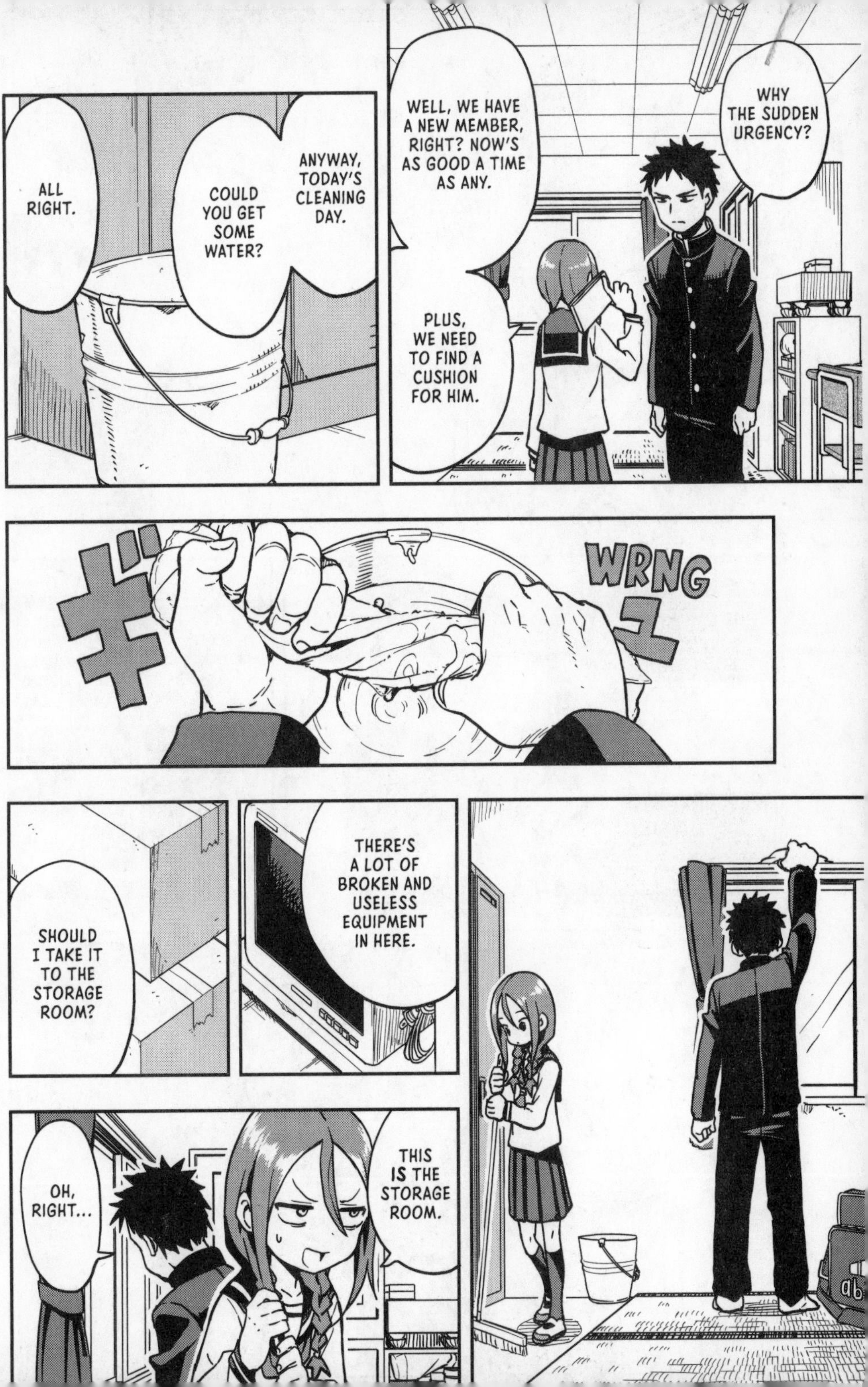
WHY THE SUDDEN URGENCY?
WELL, WE HAVE A NEW MEMBER, RIGHT? NOW'S AS GOOD A TIME AS ANY.
PLUS, WE NEED TO FIND A CUSHION FOR HIM.
ANYWAY, TODAY'S CLEANING DAY.
COULD YOU GET SOME WATER?
ALL RIGHT.
WRNG
THERE'S A LOT OF BROKEN AND USELESS EQUIPMENT IN HERE.
SHOULD I TAKE IT TO THE STORAGE ROOM?
THIS **IS** THE STORAGE ROOM.
OH, RIGHT...

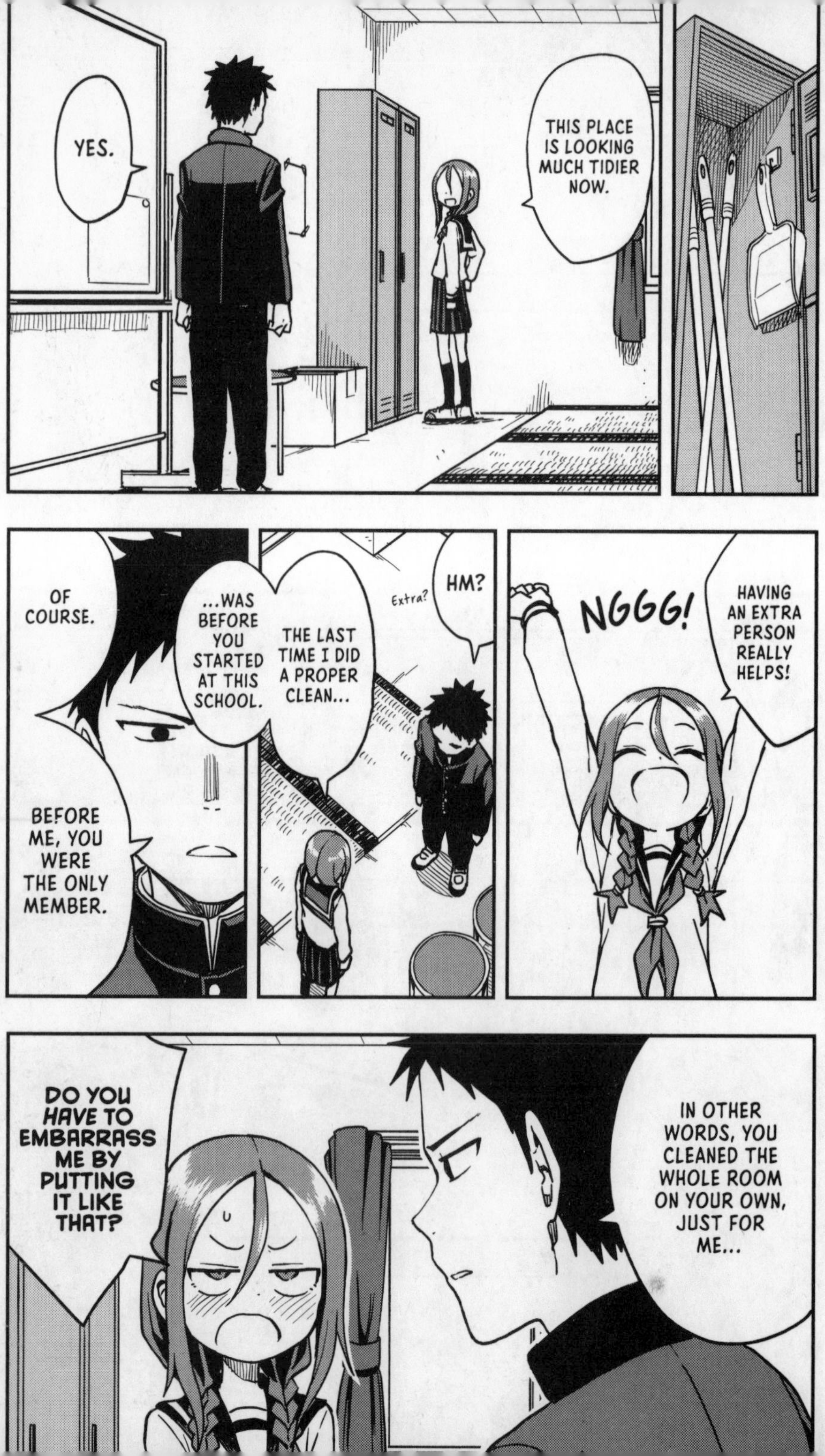
THIS PLACE IS LOOKING MUCH TIDIER NOW.
YES.
HAVING AN EXTRA PERSON REALLY HELPS!
NGGG!
HM?
Extra?
THE LAST TIME I DID A PROPER CLEAN...
...WAS BEFORE YOU STARTED AT THIS SCHOOL.
OF COURSE.
BEFORE ME, YOU WERE THE ONLY MEMBER.
IN OTHER WORDS, YOU CLEANED THE WHOLE ROOM ON YOUR OWN, JUST FOR ME...
DO YOU *HAVE* TO EMBARRASS ME BY PUTTING IT LIKE THAT?

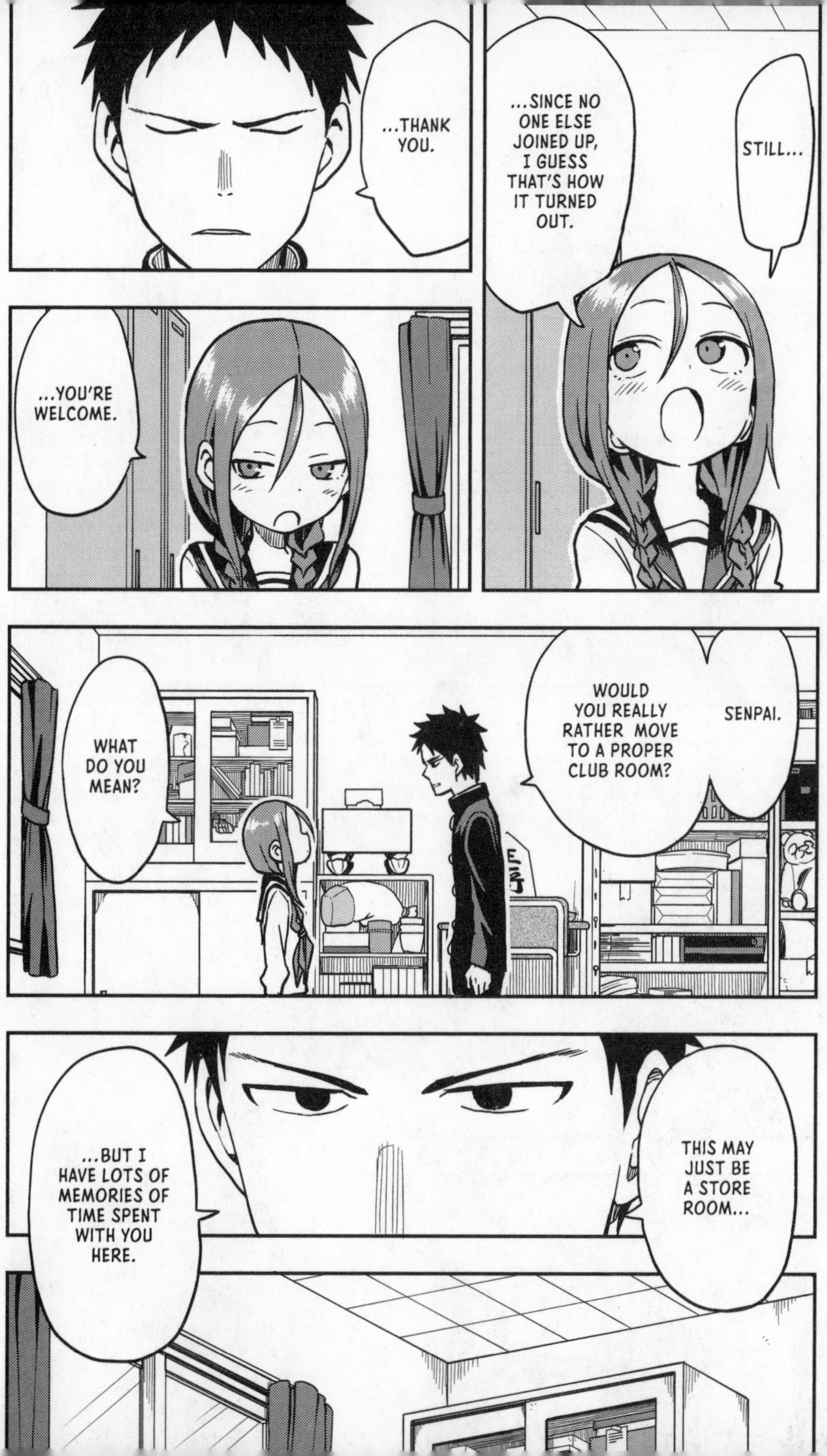
STILL...
...SINCE NO ONE ELSE JOINED UP, I GUESS THAT'S HOW IT TURNED OUT.
...THANK YOU.
...YOU'RE WELCOME.
SENPAI.
WOULD YOU REALLY RATHER MOVE TO A PROPER CLUB ROOM?
WHAT DO YOU MEAN?
THIS MAY JUST BE A STORE ROOM...
...BUT I HAVE LOTS OF MEMORIES OF TIME SPENT WITH YOU HERE.

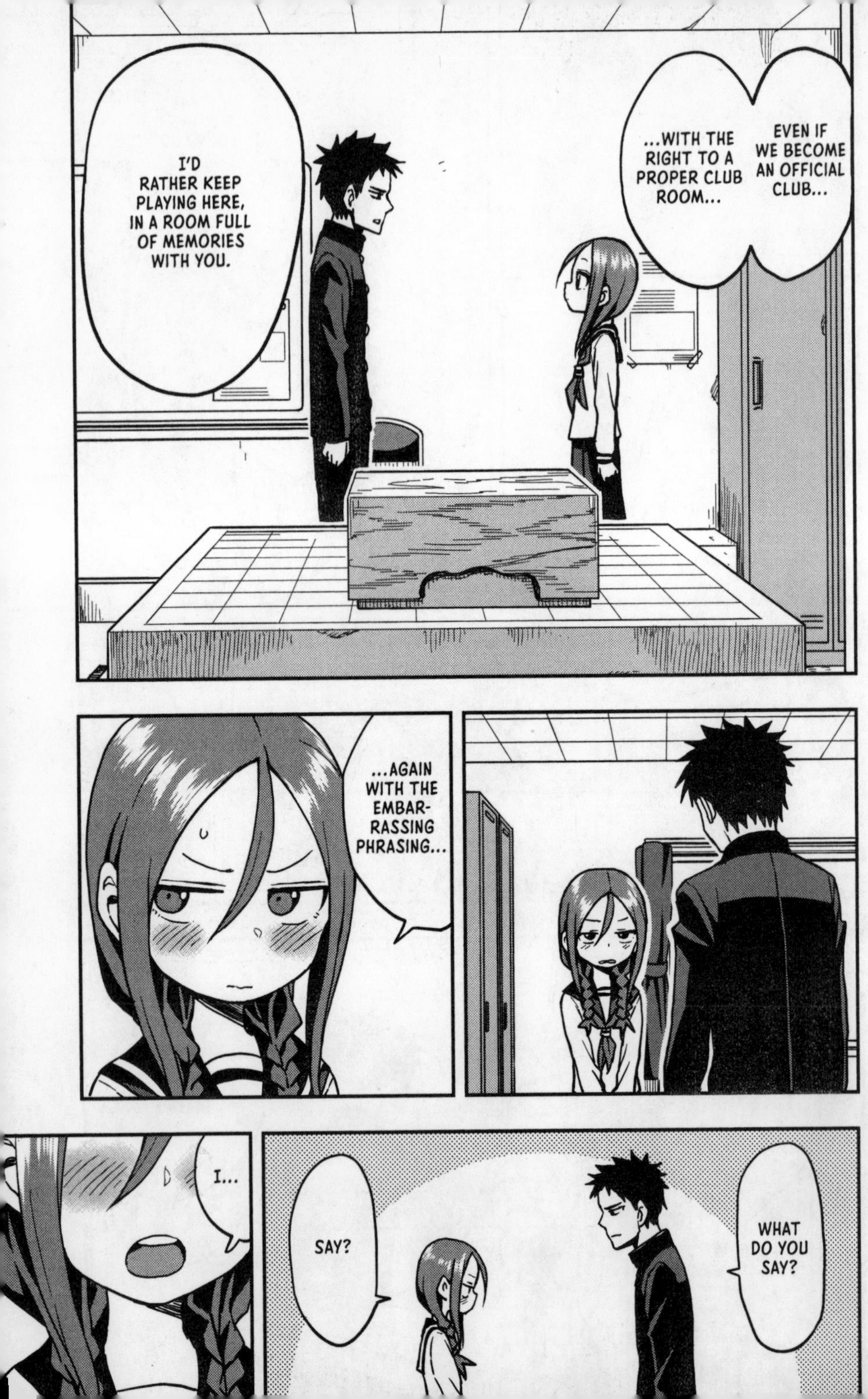
EVEN IF WE BECOME AN OFFICIAL CLUB...
...WITH THE RIGHT TO A PROPER CLUB ROOM...
I'D RATHER KEEP PLAYING HERE, IN A ROOM FULL OF MEMORIES WITH YOU.
...AGAIN WITH THE EMBAR-RASSING PHRASING...
WHAT DO YOU SAY?
SAY?
I...

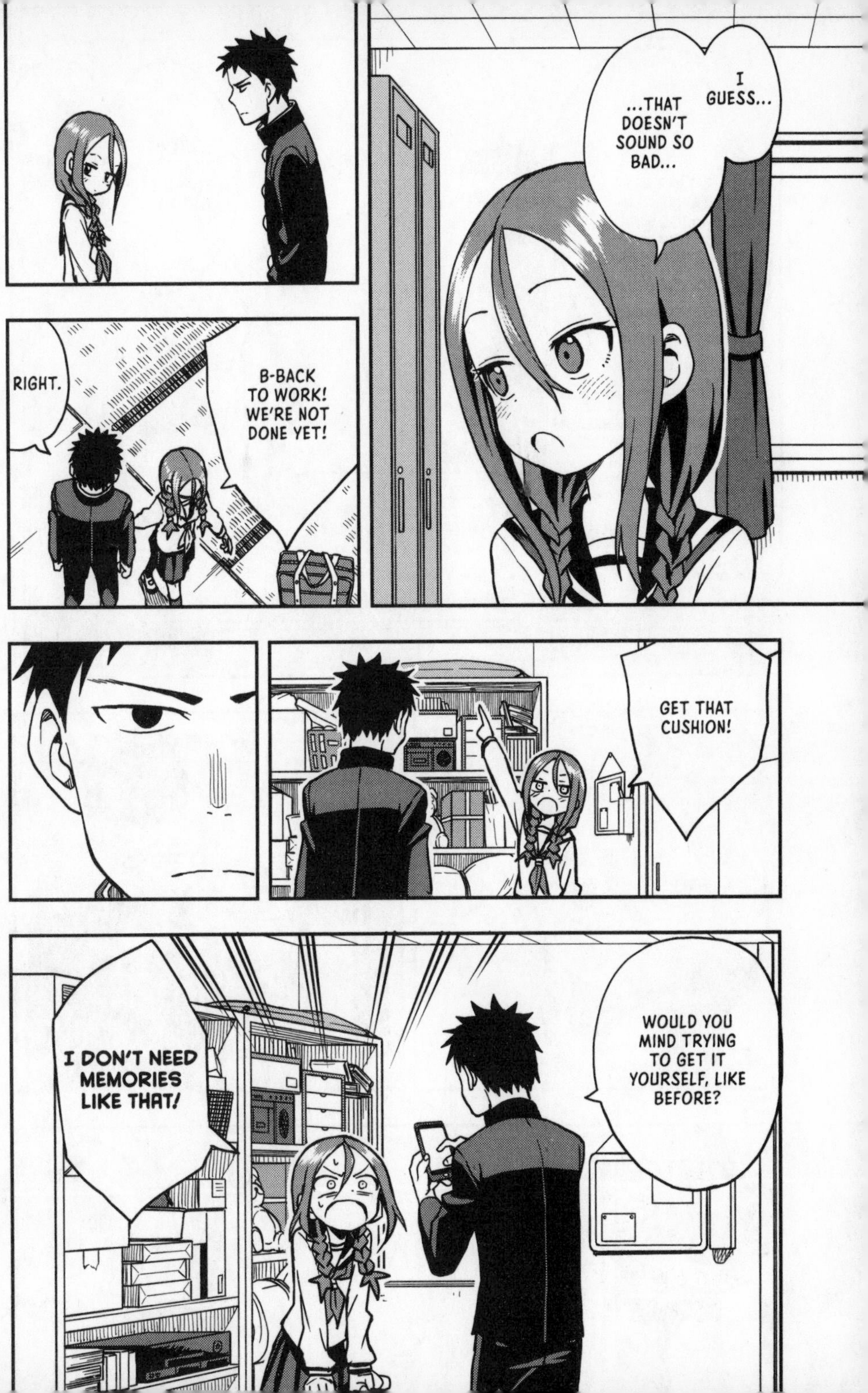
I GUESS... ...THAT DOESN'T SOUND SO BAD...
B-BACK TO WORK! WE'RE NOT DONE YET!
RIGHT.
GET THAT CUSHION!
WOULD YOU MIND TRYING TO GET IT YOURSELF, LIKE BEFORE?
I DON'T NEED MEMORIES LIKE THAT!

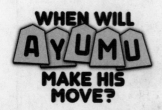

WHEN WILL
AYUMU
MAKE HIS
MOVE?

BONUS GAME

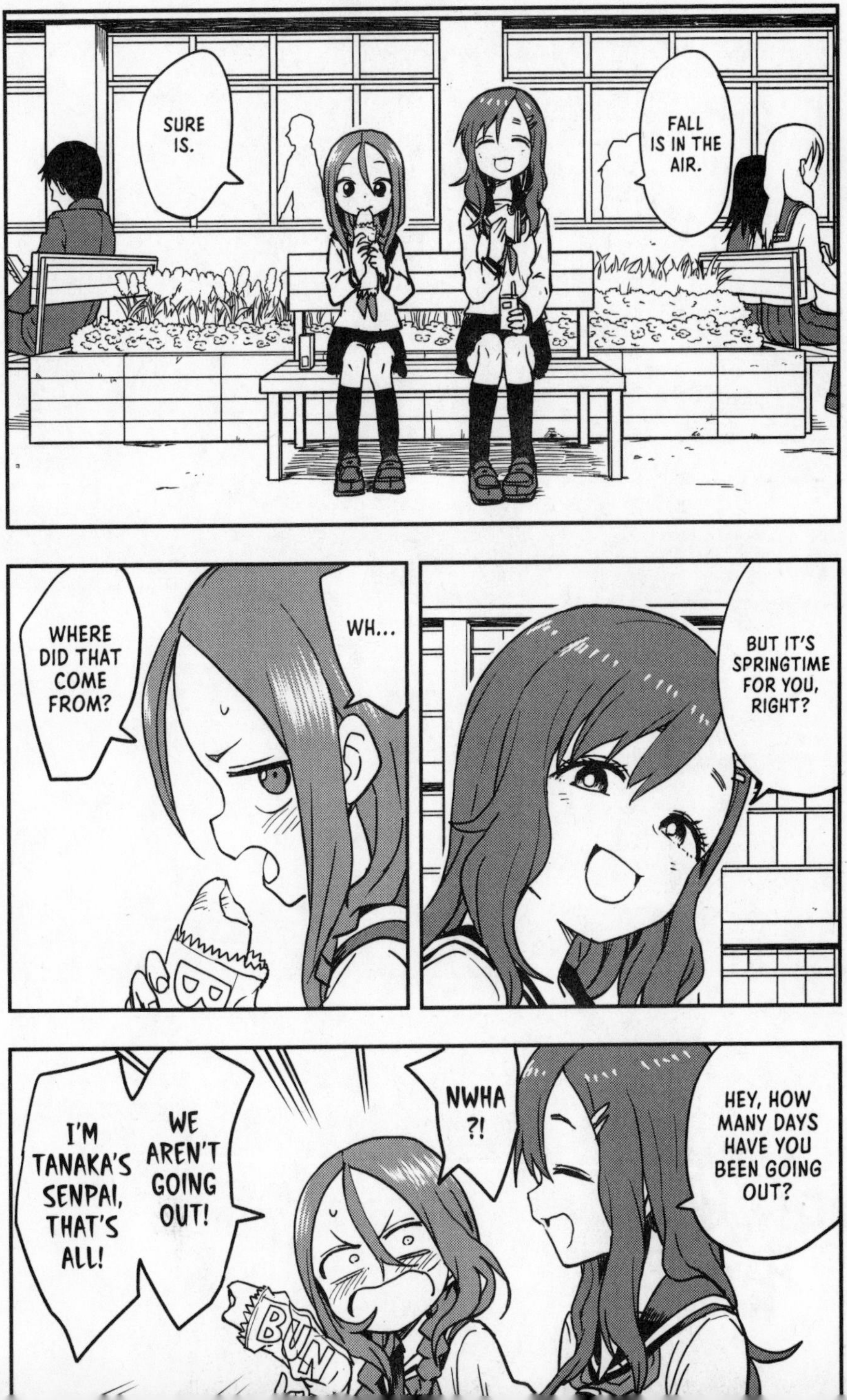
FALL IS IN THE AIR.
SURE IS.
BUT IT'S SPRINGTIME FOR YOU, RIGHT?
WH...
WHERE DID THAT COME FROM?
HEY, HOW MANY DAYS HAVE YOU BEEN GOING OUT?
NWHA?!
WE AREN'T GOING OUT!
I'M TANAKA'S SENPAI, THAT'S ALL!
BUN

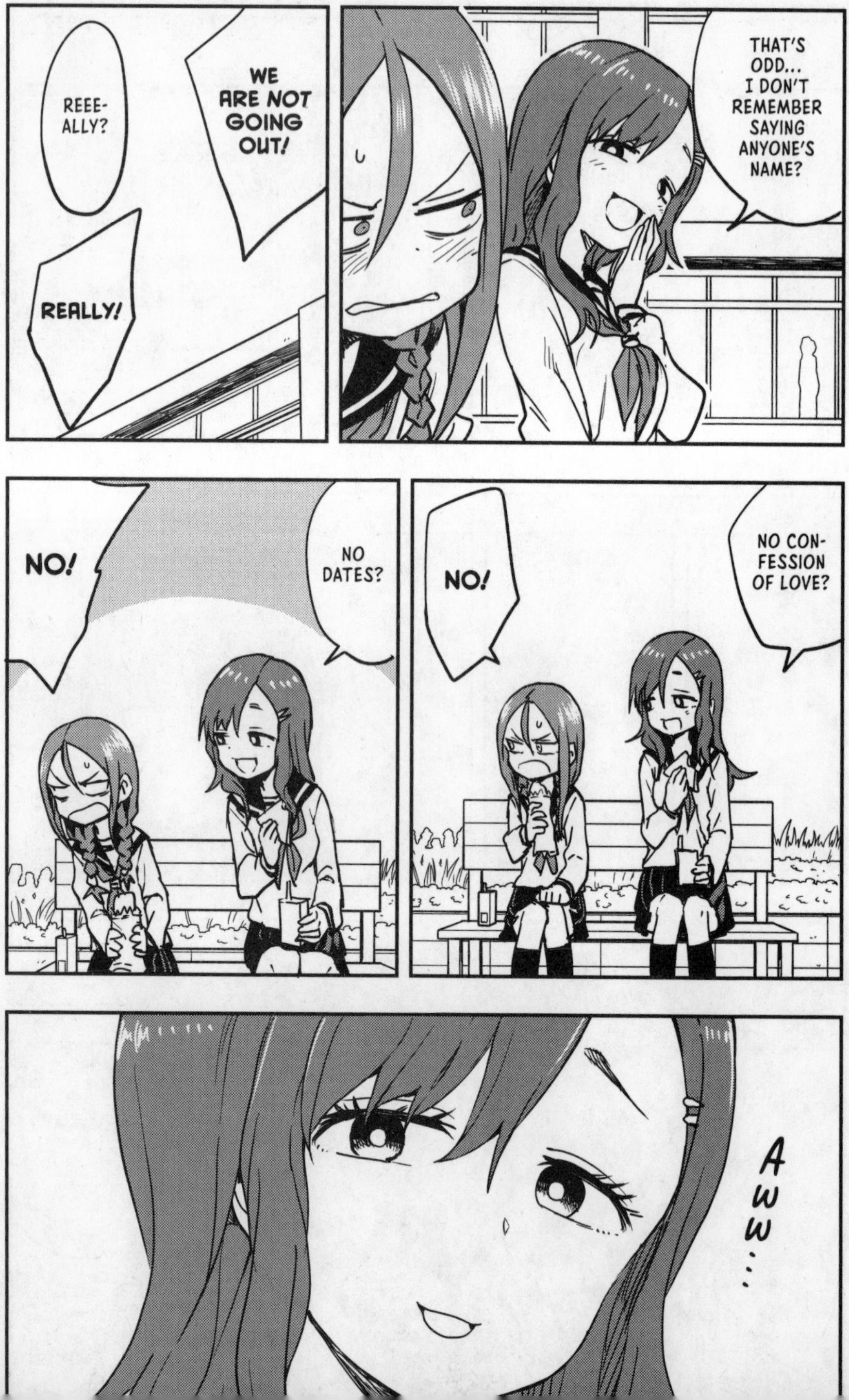
THAT'S ODD... I DON'T REMEMBER SAYING ANYONE'S NAME?
WE ARE NOT GOING OUT!
REEE-ALLY?
REALLY!
NO CON-FESSION OF LOVE?
NO!
NO DATES?
NO!
AWW...

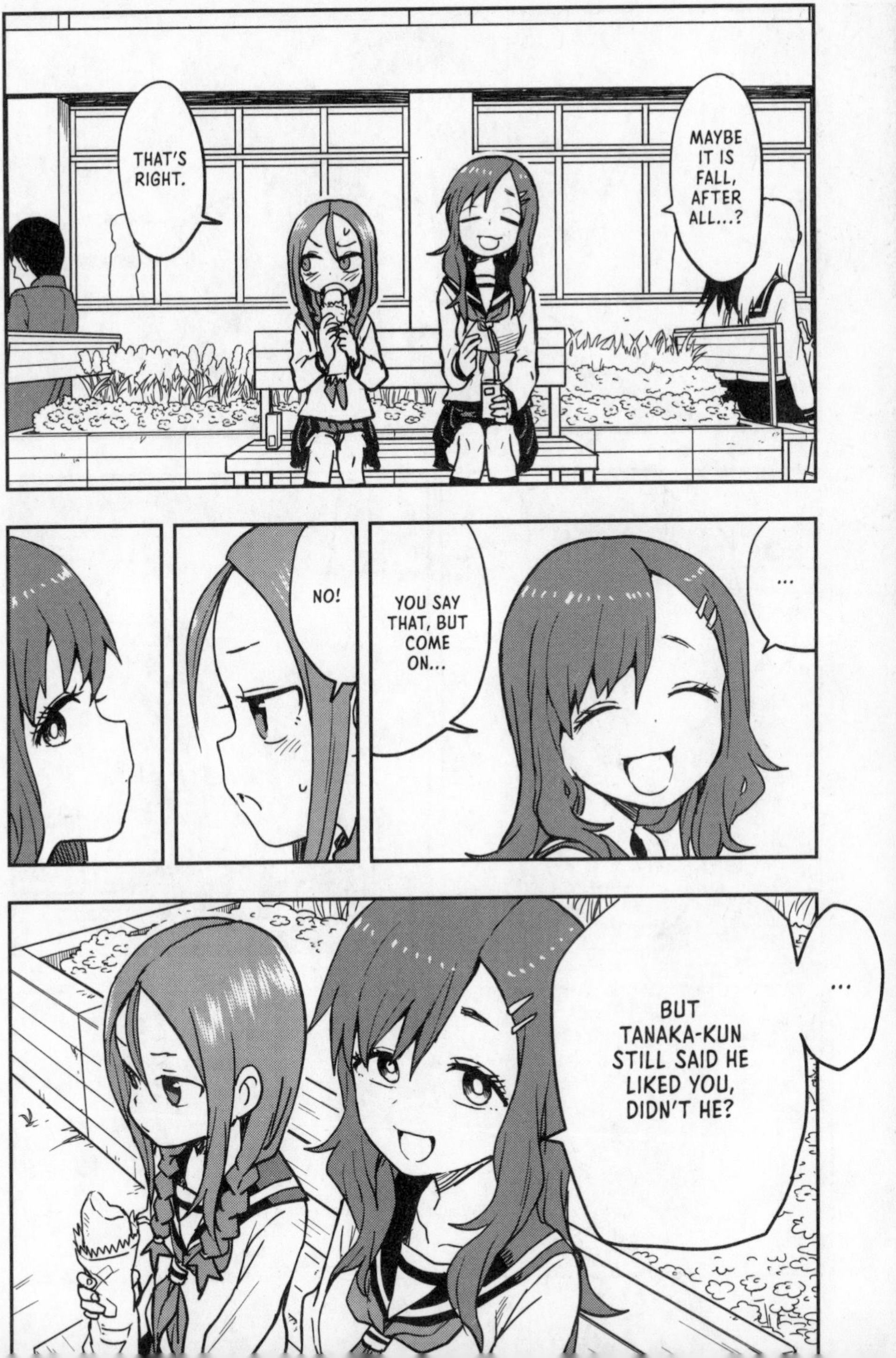
MAYBE IT IS FALL, AFTER ALL...?
THAT'S RIGHT.
...
YOU SAY THAT, BUT COME ON...
NO!
...
BUT TANAKA-KUN STILL SAID HE LIKED YOU, DIDN'T HE?

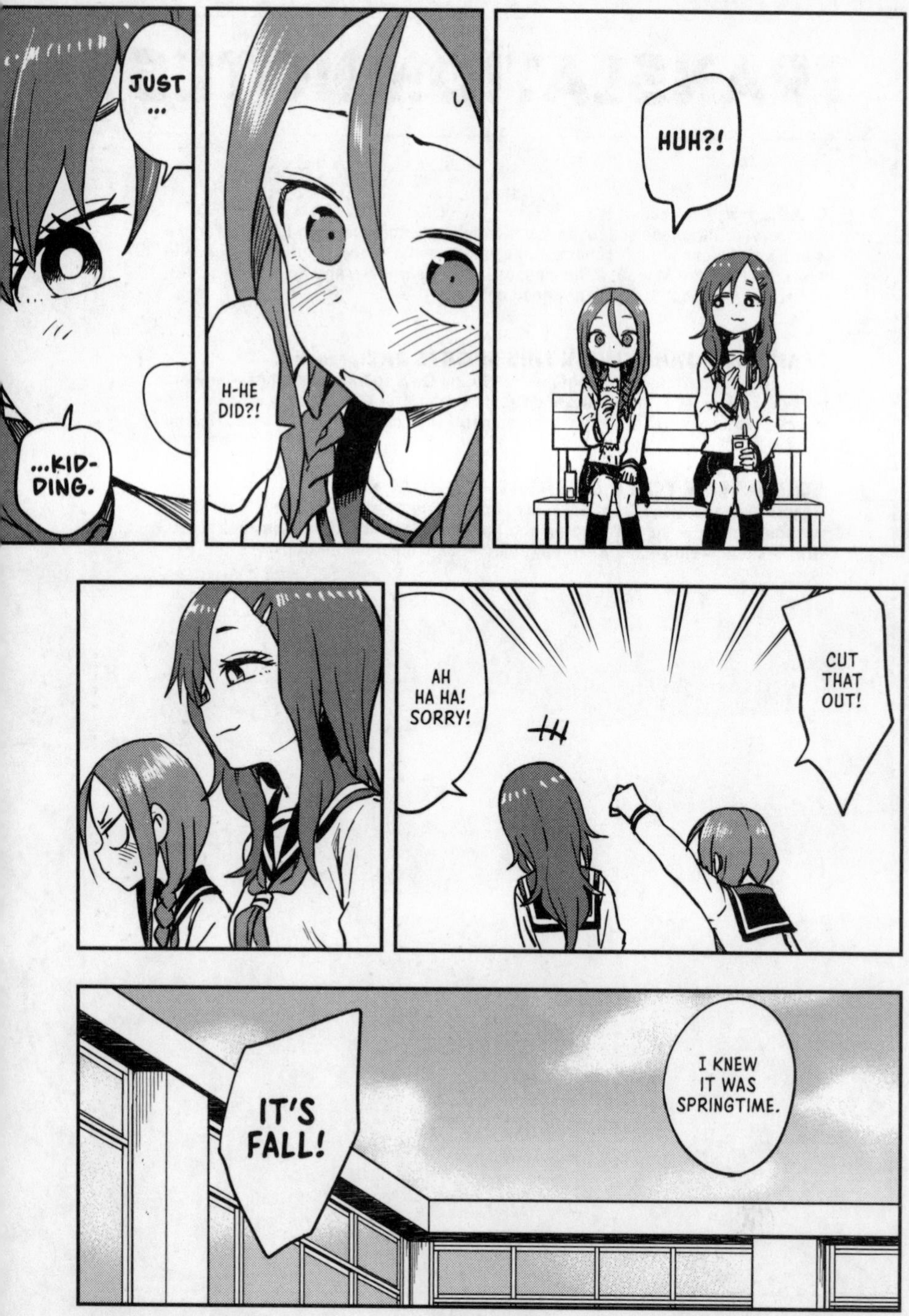
HUH?!
H-HE DID?!
JUST ...
...KID-DING.
CUT THAT OUT!
AH HA HA! SORRY!
I KNEW IT WAS SPRINGTIME.
IT'S FALL!

THE END

TRANSLATION NOTES

CLASS 1-3, PAGE 40
Each level of Japanese schooling starts counting year levels from 1 again. Tanaka is in his first year of high school, equivalent to tenth grade (sophomore year) in the U.S. There are at least three classes in that year level, and he is in class 1-3. (Urushi is in class 2-3, one year ahead of him.)

TEAM 3 IS GONNA CRUSH THIS SPORTS DAY!, PAGE 40
The whole school competes together on Sports Day, so each team has members from every year level. At Tanaka and Urushi's school, teams are evidently decided by which class you're in. "Team 3" presumably includes class 1-3, class 2-3, and class 3-3.

SOUNDS LIKE YOU'D BE GREAT AT SHOGI, PAGE 101
"Takeru" means "Roar" or "Run rampant," while "Kaku" and "Ryu" are both symbols for shogi pieces—the bishop (kakugyo) and the promoted rook (*ryuo*, dragon king). Meanwhile, "*Kakuryu*" together also means "Ceratops"!

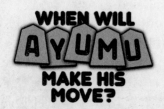

WHEN WILL AYUMU MAKE HIS MOVE?

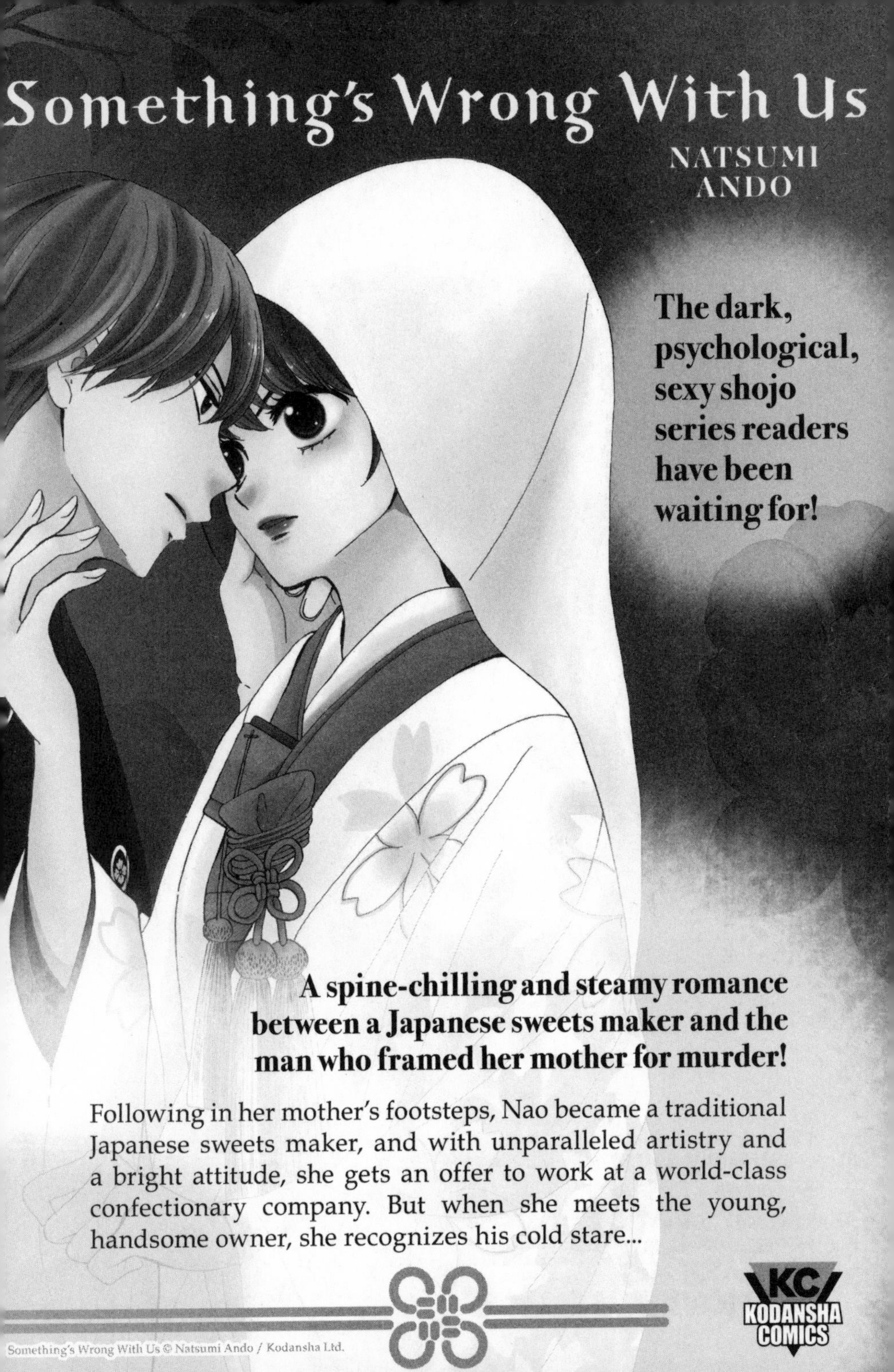
Something's Wrong With Us
NATSUMI ANDO
The dark, psychological, sexy shojo series readers have been waiting for!
A spine-chilling and steamy romance between a Japanese sweets maker and the man who framed her mother for murder!
Following in her mother's footsteps, Nao became a traditional Japanese sweets maker, and with unparalleled artistry and a bright attitude, she gets an offer to work at a world-class confectionary company. But when she meets the young, handsome owner, she recognizes his cold stare...
KC KODANSHA COMICS

PERFECT WORLD

Rie Aruga

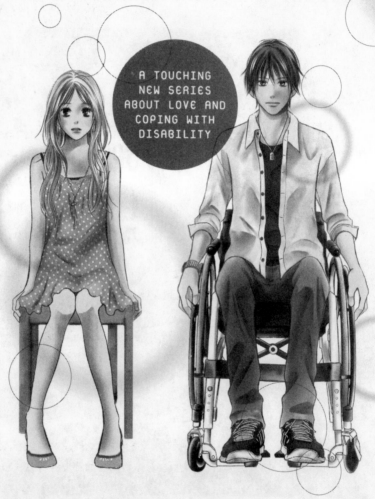

A TOUCHING NEW SERIES ABOUT LOVE AND COPING WITH DISABILITY

An office party reunites Tsugumi with her high school crush Itsuki. He's realized his dream of becoming an architect, but along the way, he experienced a spinal injury that put him in a wheelchair. Now Tsugumi's rekindled feelings will butt up against prejudices she never considered — and Itsuki will have to decide if he's ready to let someone into his heart...

KC KODANSHA COMICS

Young characters and steampunk setting, like *Howl's Moving Castle* and *Battle Angel Alita*

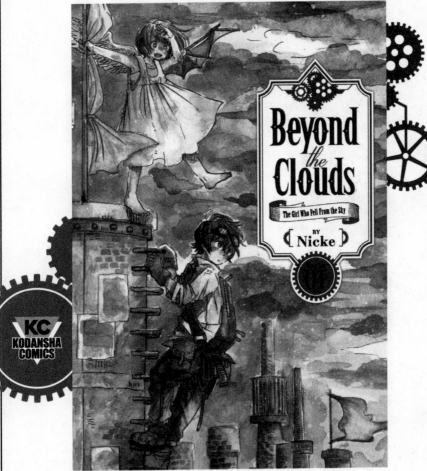

Beyond the Clouds © 2018 Nicke / Ki-oon

A boy with a talent for machines and a mysterious girl whose wings he's fixed will take you beyond the clouds! In the tradition of the high-flying, resonant adventure stories of Studio Ghibli comes a gorgeous tale about the longing of young hearts for adventure and friendship!

The boys are back, in 400-page hardcovers that are as pretty and badass as they are!

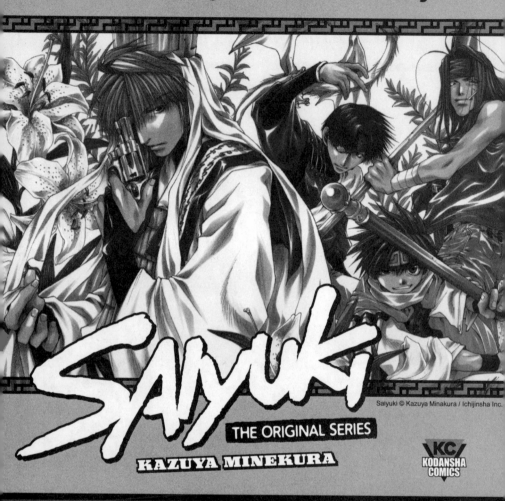

Saiyuki © Kazuya Minakura / Ichijinsha Inc.

SAIYUKI

THE ORIGINAL SERIES

KAZUYA MINEKURA

"AN EDGY COMIC LOOK AT AN ANCIENT CHINESE TALE." —YALSA

Genjo Sanzo is a Buddhist priest in the city of Togenkyo, which is being ravaged by yokai spirits that have fallen out of balance with the natural order. His superiors send him on a journey far to the west to discover why this is happening and how to stop it. His companions are three yokai with human souls. But this is no day trip — the four will encounter many discoveries and horrors on the way.

FEATURES NEW TRANSLATION, COLOR PAGES, AND BEAUTIFUL WRAPAROUND COVER ART!

A SMART, NEW ROMANTIC COMEDY FOR FANS OF *SHORTCAKE CAKE* AND *TERRACE HOUSE!*

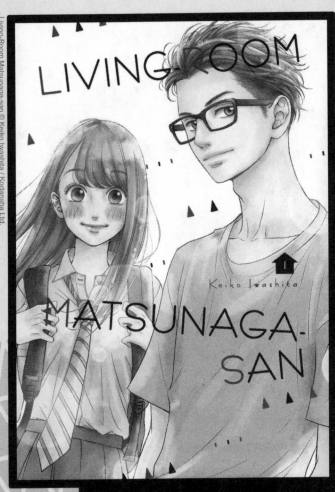

A romance manga starring high school girl Meeko, who learns to live on her own in a boarding house whose living room is home to the odd (but handsome) Matsunaga-san. She begins to adjust to her new life away from her parents, but Meeko soon learns that no matter how far away from home she is, she's still a young girl at heart — especially when she finds herself falling for Matsunaga-san.

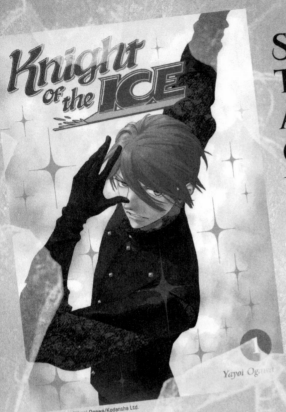

Knight of the Ice ©Yayoi Ogawa/Kodansha Ltd.

SKATING THRILLS AND ICY CHILLS WITH THIS NEW TINGLY ROMANCE SERIES!

A rom-com on ice, perfect for fans of *Princess Jellyfish* and *Wotakoi*. Kokoro is the talk of the figure-skating world, winning trophies and hearts. But little do they know... he's actually a huge nerd! From the beloved creator of *You're My Pet* (*Tramps Like Us*).

Chitose is a serious young woman, working for the health magazine *SASSO*. Or at least, she would be, if she wasn't constantly getting distracted by her childhood friend, international figure skating star Kokoro Kijinami! In the public eye and on the ice, Kokoro is a gallant, flawless knight, but behind his glittery costumes and breathtaking spins lies a secret: He's actually a hopelessly romantic otaku, who can only land his quad jumps when Chitose is on hand to recite a spell from his favorite magical girl anime!

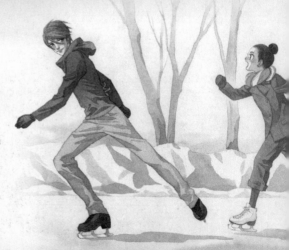

KC/
KODANSHA
COMICS

A Kodansha Trade Paperback Original

Published in the United States by
Kodansha USA Publishing, LLC, New York.

Publication rights for this English edition arranged through
Kodansha Ltd., Tokyo.

First published in Japan in 2019 by Kodansha Ltd., Tokyo
as *Sore demo Ayumu ha yosetekuru*, volume 2.

ISBN 978-1-64651-350-5

Printed in the United States of America.

1st Printing

Translation: Max Greenway
Lettering: Phil Christie
Editing: Nathaniel Gallant
Kodansha USA Publishing edition cover design by Phil Balsman

Publisher: Kiichiro Sugawara

Director of Publishing Services: Ben Applegate
Associate Director of Operations: Stephen Pakula
Publishing Services Managing Editors: Alanna Ruse, Madison Salters
Production Managers: Emi Lotto, Angela Zurlo

KODANSHA.US

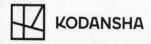

KODANSHA